Real Estate Action:
55 Actions Takers Share Their Secrets

D0943316

REAL ESTATE ACTION: 55 ACTION TAKERS SHARE THEIR SECRETS

Ozzie Jurock

JUROCK PUBLISHING LTD.

Canadian Cataloguing in Publication
Data:

Jurock, Ozzie, 1944 –
Ozzie Jurock: Real Estate Action: 55
Action Takers Share Their Secrets
  ISBN 978-0-9684642-3-6

JUROCK PUBLISHING LTD.
• 253-970 Burrard St.
  Vancouver, BC V6Z 2R4
  Canada

Typeset, printed and bound in Canada.

YOU can't get fit watching other people exercise

YOU can't hear a song on AM 980 if you are tuned into FM 920

YOU can't create passive income by wishing for it

YOU have to take action ... the right kind of action

This book is dedicated to the
ACTION TAKERS
of the world...

"Do, or do not. There is no 'try'."

YODA, "THE EMPIRE STRIKES BACK"

TABLE OF CONTENTS

BEST ADVICE – Thinking 'out of the box'

BEST ADVICE – From real estate professionals

BEST ADVICE – Keeping what you have

BEST ADVICE – Buying and selling in the USA

Foreword

By Michael Campbell

Host of "MoneyTalks Radio"

It's funny how a thing starts. Once Andrew Carnegie threw out the off hand remark that, "ninety percent of all millionaires become so through owning real estate," the land rush was on.

Personally I love the real estate frenzy. It's fun, as in Donald Trump's hair. It's entertaining, as in Tom Vu's infomercials. It's titillating, as in all the celebrity foreclosures. And people really can make a lot of money investing wisely in real estate. They can also get hooped, as in subprimed into financial ruin but contrary to popular opinion that had a lot more to do with how much debt people took on to finance their homes rather than the real estate itself.

History makes it pretty clear that other than wars, crime waves or the odd location unlucky enough to be frequented by a natural disaster, excess leverage is really the only way to loose in real estate long term. Unfortunately the most popular method in all the get rich quick real estate schemes is to borrow other people's money to purchase real estate. It can work but in their efforts to sell you their books or courses they forget to tell you that all bets are off during periods of declining real estate prices.

In fact, there have been many purveyors of questionable "get rich quick" real estate schemes sold by real estate investment gurus - often with the highest profile - and virtually all of the customers who followed their advice blindly found out the hard way about one of the most basic fundamentals of business: do you have a plan for "what if?" What if the markets decline for a few years? What if my cash flow drops by 20%? What if interest rates go up a couple of points or more? What if I get stiffed by my tenant? What if there is a major recession? What if my expenses suddenly exceed my revenues?

What the darlings of late night tv and the authors of the get rich quick real estate books fail to point out is that their "extra special, secret strategies" only work in bull markets but then again virtually any method works in a bull market. By definition, real estate prices rise in bull markets so by simply being in the game you will make money. It doesn't take a genius to appreciate that the more properties you own the more you will make in a rising market.

It's never been tough to make money in real estate during good times but employing strategies that protect your investment and cash flow in bad times is where savvy investors show their stuff. And that's where this book comes in.

While many decry the subprime real estate meltdown in 2008 as a one of a kind phenomena history tells a different story. Real estate cycles are nothing new. One only has to the look at the aftermath of the California real estate boom of 1880s, the years after the Florida land boom of the 1920s or the Savings and Loan disaster of the late 80s and early 90s to see dramatic declines in real estate prices. You don't even have to go that far back. In the twelve month period ending in January, 1991 US home prices fell an average of 12.9%. The point being that employing a strategy that does not take into account the possibility of falling prices for a period of time can be dangerous to your financial health.

It's also important to note that after each period of decline real estate prices did eventually exceed their previous highs. The longest recovery period took place after the Great Depression but that was in large part because governments reacted to the economic contraction by reducing the money supply and raising interest rates. That is in direct contrast to the reaction of governments to the latest crisis where across the world interest rates were dramatically cut and central banks took unprecedented measures to increase the availability of credit.

This approach has laid the groundwork for the overall recovery of real estate and indeed in many areas sales volumes have improved and prices have stabilized or increased. But here's the point. This time, for this cycle, let's do it right, which is where this book comes in.

As the old saying goes, "those who can do, those who can't teach." In this book - well known real estate expert and best selling author, Ozzie Jurock brought together 55 real estate professionals and some newbies who "can" and continue to "do". It draws on their experience and expertise in order to bring to you an insider's view on essential real estate subjects ranging from making the right purchase for first time buyers to what are the keys to being a successful investor.

Most of us have no idea when it comes to questions like what do I look for in checking out a home's plumbing or electrical fittings? What specifically will a home inspection do for me and are they worth the money? When I sell where do I get the best bang for the buck in terms of last minute touch-ups?

What are the essential tax considerations for real estate investors? How can I get a deal through foreclosures and auctions? Is there something to that "no money down" promise of the infomercials? What do the pros know about real estate investing that I don't know?

Whether you are a buyer or a seller, a novice or a professional, this book offers you great insight and value that could end up saving or making you tens of thousands of dollars.

INTRODUCTION

by Ozzie Jurock

From personal experience – investing in real estate can be one of the most exhilarating adventures of life. Throughout my career, I have worked as a real estate salesperson, a branch manager, and eventually as president of Royal LePage (Residential). I write a newsletter to thousands of subscribers, author books and am the only Canadian in Donald Trump's *The Best Real Estate Advice I Ever Received* with my own chapter.

As a private investor, I have sold, bought, owned, and managed properties too numerous to count. Based on these experiences I have developed a few theories about what sells and what doesn't, what to buy and what not to, and how to keep out of trouble.

Also, over the years I have met other successful investors, some that started with absolutely nothing and amassed a fortune through planning for capital gain. Others chose the 'passive income' route and created several thousand dollars a month in cash flow. I noted the very different approaches of individual investors and quickly learned that there are some professionals – the unsung heroes – in every real estate transaction without which we simply could not be making that perfect buy. What I learned and what I know, I know well, but I don't know everything. For instance I have learned that we make the most money on the day that we buy. But that 'perfect buy' does not come only through negotiation….other experts are involved.

What I have tried to do in this book is to gather the best information from some of the brightest people that I know in real estate. They share their experiences, their know-how, the ACTIONS they took and their best advice.

Here are some 55 ACTION TAKERS from all around the real estate transaction that contribute to that 'best buy' and to read their perspectives an anything and everything to do with a real estate transaction.

This book not only features sage advice from some seasoned investors, but also stories from the 'newbie', the first deal, the first sweet profit. As well, there are a number of 'tools of the real estate investor trade' from people that actually **do** them…the rent-to-own ACTION TAKER, the lease option millionaire, the recreational secrets.

We start off first by looking at ourselves. Do you understand yourself and your investment objectives? That is why I recommend taking a good, hard look at yourself from a variety of perspectives financial, intellectual, and temperamental. Are you a shark, an investor or a flipper? How involved do you want to be with your properties? What is your tolerance for risk? Are you trying to build a portfolio of income producing properties, or are you simply looking to buy a second home for its rental income? Then we discuss – very importantly…what real estate cycle we are in and how to assess that.

Our next section deals with the **basics of the purchase**. From home inspector and appraiser to plumber, from electrician to landscaper to home stager.

Then we look at **understanding the purchase** and our ACTION TAKERS discuss the pre-sale process, small town and recreational buying. We also have a few ACTION TAKERS on **buying in the United States**.

We also look at what to do **after you have bought**. The vital aspect of proper property management, the verifying of tenants and aspects of improving your home.

Selling for profit is easier if **we understand the sale**…if we stage the home properly; add landscaping and know how to zero in on our target market.

Interested in **understanding development and the larger deal?** Well, our ACTION TAKERS talk about green buildings, building marketing teams with Mojo and doing your due diligence at city hall.

For every transaction that has been tried and true there are a few that you may never have heard of. Our ACTION TAKERS **think 'out of the box'**. How about trading your work for your down payment? Or renting – to own, using other people's money and buying that foreclosure? Or even the importance of good Feng Shui (YES!)

There are of course hundreds of **Real estate professionals**, but what do the good ones do? How do we find them? And what advice do they give us when buying or selling.

Finally **keeping what we have**…is of the utmost importance and our ACTION TAKER accountant and bookkeeper help 'lift the fog'.

Now, don't get me wrong. I'm not suggesting that this book alone will tell you everything you need to know about investing in real estate. But in this book you get to read from people that are dealing with the intangibles daily.

Of course, in the end the only way you'll really learn everything is to **get out there and do it.** Become an ACTION TAKER yourself. If you want to experience writing offers, get out there and write some. If you want to understand how to research and do due diligence, start at the bottom and learn as you go. However, no matter what you will be doing – as you grow into your future best as a real estate investor – this book is designed to help you along the way. Learn from the ACTION TAKERS.

People have lived before us; they have learned things that it may take a newcomer ten years to learn. And after all, the real secret is not only to learn from our own mistakes but to learn from the mistakes of others.

I believe, that whatever your real estate journey will look like, this book can make that journey a little less rocky (and hopefully full of a lot of trial but very little error).

So what does it all amount to in the end? Well, I want this book to make you aware of how vast in scope the real estate investment game truly is. The key to being a successful player is to educate yourself, and I hope this book will be a well guided step in that process. But don't just read it once and then put it on the shelf. Keep it close at hand, so you can refer to it time and again. I truly believe you'll get something new with each new reading.

Remember that we assembled ACTION TAKERS at every level of the transaction. There is gold in 'them thar' real estate advice hills. Reading their advice will bring to light things you've over-looked and remind you of things you've forgotten.

But most of all, I want this book to teach you that this game isn't difficult to play. You don't need to be rich, brilliant, or even lucky to be successful at it. All it takes is hard work, patience, re-sourcefulness, and self awareness. And as our ACTION TAKERS show, these are qualities anyone can master.

Whether it's buying or selling your own house, condo, or co-op, or whether you're in or entering the real estate business, I think you'll learn a lot from *REAL ESTATE ACTION – 55 Action Takers share their secrets*.

BEST ADVICE:
Understanding yourself
and the general market

1

Ralph Case

President of the Real Estate Action Group, an
organization with monthly membership designed to
help members take action in Real Estate investing

BEST ADVICE: *Make a plan for your Real Estate passive income machine, follow the plan and revise as you move forward, be patient.*

Have you ever noticed that most people like the idea of financial freedom but many don't take the time to sit down and make a plan to achieve it? To plan for it we need to define it and just about everyone has a different picture of what it means to be financially free. To me, financially free is being able to do what I want for the rest of my life without having to work for income. The important thing is to define the minimum you need and the time frame of when you want to have it. The next step is to come up with a plan to achieve your goal. And then you will create a **real estate passive income machine**

I was lucky enough to grow up in a family where my parents owned a rental property and was able to observe firsthand what an amazing investment a piece of Real Estate can be. For this reason I decided in my early 20s that my plan for financial freedom would be through rental properties. Because I was starting out with virtually no money (I had a good job but little down payment), I decided to start with a small house as a personal residence (with a government insured 90% loan!) and then small houses and condos as investments.

Owning your personal residence is the first step unless you are living rent free. The reason for this is that you will be using your hard earned cash to pay down debt with your mortgage payment instead of wasting it paying rent. (You have to pay rent anyway so you might as well pay a mortgage instead.) If you are living rent free then save an amount every month equal to what you would be paying in rent. Put this money in a savings account for future down payments on investments. A free and clear personal residence with no mortgage is the cornerstone for any passive income plan. My recommendation is to find a house with a secondary suite that you can rent out as a mortgage helper.

The next step is to accumulate cash flow properties. Condos and houses make excellent investments for the following reasons:

1) **Ease of management.** It is usually simple to find someone to do the property management at a reasonable cost.
2) **Cash flow.** Lower priced condos and houses have good income relative to the purchase price.
3) **Appreciation potential.** Unlike GICs you get the benefit of long term appreciation in value on top of the monthly cash flow.

I recently did a comparison and found that $100,000 invested and compounded annually at 5% in a GIC becomes $162,889 over 10 years. If this $100,000 is invested as a 20% down payment on $500,000 worth of Real Estate which appreciates at 3% per year, at the end of 10 years it's worth $671,958. With a $400,000 mortgage at 5% interest the balance owing would be $247,216 after 10 years with bi-weekly payments and 20 year amortization. This leaves

$424,742 of equity ($671,958 minus the mortgage balance). Plus you get the ongoing cash flow! Quite a substantial difference!

With zero growth in value the Real Estate equity would be $252,784. ($500,000 minus the mortgage balance) This is almost $90,000 more than the GIC amount and the Real Estate investment had cash flow for 10 years as well!

What is a good plan for financial freedom? Buy small condos and houses and pay them off so that you have long term cash flow and your assets keep pace with inflation. How do you get started? Buy your personal residence first. Try and find one with a secondary suite that helps pay the mortgage. Make sure the property you buy is structurally sound. Get it inspected by a professional. If you are buying a condo also check the Strata meeting minutes for the last 3 years.

The next step is to buy a property where the rent pays the mortgage and expenses in a location that has long term economic viability. Hopefully you can find a property where you can raise the rent and reduce expenses to provide positive cash flow. **(Passive income!)**

How many should you buy? I suggest you start with a plan to buy 5 properties and then you can always increase your goal as you go. As a rule of thumb a free and clear property should give you a 5 – 10% net cash flow. Buying 5 properties worth $100,000 each should give you between $25,000 and $50,000 per year once they are mortgage free. What time frame should you plan for purchasing them? Start with 5 years. That would represent one $100,000 property per year on average. You can buy one or two higher priced properties if you have the down payment but stick to the plan of a fixed dollar amount worth of Real Estate within 5 years. If you repeat this every 5 years the sky is the limit as to how big your passive income machine can be. All it takes is a plan to achieve it, the discipline to stick with it, and the courage to begin!

Do:

- Buy cash flow condos and houses.
- Seek advice from and hang out with experienced Real Estate investors.
- Be a Contrarian (buy when people are crying, sell when people are yelling).
- Buy with a business perspective and negotiate hard.
- Buy for the long term but flip if you can reallocate the profit to a better property.

Don't:

- Procrastinate (start today!).
- Buy without seeing the property yourself.
- Manage your properties yourself.
- Forget your long term goal.
- Overextend yourself with debt.

2

Ozzie Jurock

Best Advice: *Above all – know who you are*

The best real estate advice I ever received was from my first branch manager in 1968: "For the individual, there is no such thing as a good market or a bad market, only whether or not he or she has a good or a bad deal."

People always want to know whether it is a good market or a bad market. For forty years I have listened to talk about bubbles, hot markets, seller's markets, and buyer's markets. But you know what? No matter what the market, ownership of the average home outperforms any other investment.

KNOW WHO YOU ARE

To be successful in real estate, you need to find the good deals, have the guts to act, and know who you are. Are you a Shark, a Flipper, or an Investor?

Do you want to

- make the quick deal, quick profit?
- build a long-term portfolio?
- create long-term passive income?

The *Shark* is a grave dancer. He benefits from the misery of others. The Shark will always be able to find someone, whether in good times or bad, who needs to sell quickly and cheaply because of an illness, a death, a divorce, a job transfer, a business reversal, the loss of a job, bankruptcy, or because someone got too greedy, too sleepy, or too stupid. Bad times simply make the soup a little thicker, but such sellers are always there. If you want to deal in foreclosures, auctions, and tough deals, you have to sit in court. Evaluate. Learn about how to buy cheaply and wisely.

The *Flipper* works on the other side of the scale. For him, the good times with a rising market and rapidly rising inflation give him the most opportunities. But even in a flat market with no inflation, he can find deals; he just has to work a little harder and wait a little longer for them.

There is a tendency in a rising, inflationary market to jump on the conveyor belt at any price because of the 'bigger fool theory"-a bigger fool will come along and buy your property and give you a profit. This is fine as long as you are not the last fool in line.

Yes, you can be both a Shark and a Flipper. The Shark and the Flipper need to have the ability to recognize the signs, interpret them correctly, and then act without hesitation. But remember that the Shark and the Flipper don't deal in averages. They deal in exceptions!

If you want to be a Shark or a Flipper, you have to ask yourself where you draw the line between morals and business because the Shark prospers from someone else's misery and the Flipper takes advantage of someone else's ignorance to deprive him of potential profit. Everyone has to decide on the morals of the situation for himself or herself.

The Investor is primarily concerned with finding low-down-payment, cash-flowing property using personal rules (e.g., the 1 percent rule - the monthly rent payments of 1 percent of the purchase price will service a 100 percent financed property and cash flow). The Investor looks for safety and quality tenants to create a passive income stream sometime in the future. For instance, the Investor may buy five condominiums at, say, $80,000 each, with an $800 per month income and nothing down. After owning them for eighteen years, the investor will have an income of $4,000 per month forever ($4,000 will service $1 million).

The Shark and the Flipper can buy anywhere. They are in and out of the deal within three to six months. The Investor must buy where the ratio of rental income is in line with the price he pays. The investor looks for a good working environment such as a suburb or a smaller town. Investors generally outperform Sharks and Flippers over time.

The bad news? Whether you decide you are a Shark, a Flipper, or an Investor, you have to do some work! No guru, no Realtor, no "market" is going to find you the great deal. You must do it yourself. The market is irrelevant. Your commitment to learning and growing is everything.

Do:

- Understand that understanding your own objectives clearly is more important than anything else. Who are you? Flipper or investor?
- Remember that real estate markets-unlike stock markets-are local in nature. Gold sales last night in Hong Kong affect gold prices in New York today. Real estate market changes in Hong Kong don't mean beans in San Francisco. Understand your local market.
- Understand that 'location, location' for the average person is not nearly as important as knowing how long the cycles have run and what stage the local cycle is in.
- Understand that you make the most money on the day you buy. No matter what the market, you will always make the most money because of your due diligence, your astute assessment, and your guts to act.

Don't:

- Believe that it is only 'location, location, location'. Real estate is local and cyclical. You could have bought in the greatest location in New York, San Diego, and a thousand other places in the late '80s and lost your shirt. You could have bought anything in the same places from 2002-2006 and made a fortune.

• Forget, that in the end, the quality of your life is determined not by how much you understand and know, but by the actions you take.

3

John Murphy

Founder and President of 2020 Properties Inc
marketing properties in Canada, the United States
and Mexico

BEST ADVICE: *The best time to buy real estate is when a region is coming out of a recession or is in the early stages of strong, sustainable economic growth.*

Although just about everyone wants financial independence when they retire, there are few who reach retirement age with anything more than the equity in their homes, a government pension plan, old-age security and maybe a small pension benefit from a former career. That's because wanting and planning are two different things. Planning is a vital element of most any endeavour, including your strategy for financial independence.

Most people can live comfortably on $60,000 a year in today's dollars; however, in 25 years, assuming an inflation rate of 3% (while recent events may have us questioning a 3% inflation rate in the short term, I suspect that, unless the world population rate begins to decline, long-term inflation is inevitable), you'll need to earn or draw down almost $125,000 per year in order to enjoy the same lifestyle that $60,000 can afford today. To generate that kind of income when you retire, you'll need to have accumulated almost $1.8 million in capital and have it grow 7% each year. Even with government tax deferral plans taken into account, you would have to invest $1,100 every month at 10.5% growth over 25 years to accumulate that.

The good news is that, with the current decline in North American real estate prices, there is an opportunity to generate exponential returns buying undervalued real estate. Investing in a number of carefully-selected properties today will generate positive cash-flow and a passive income stream for you in the long run. For example, say you buy a $100,000 condominium – a bargain in today's market – with a down payment of $25,000. Assuming a conservative growth rate of 3% per year over 25 years, your condominium will be worth just over $209,000. And over this same period, your tenant has paid off your mortgage. The way to really build equity in real estate is through the combination of capital appreciation and mortgage reduction. After the mortgage is paid off, your tenant will continue to pay rent, thereby providing you, after expenses, with a monthly income stream. As property values increase over time, so do rents. Assume that, on your $100,000 property, a tenant pays $800 in rent monthly. At 3% growth over 25 years, the rent you receive has grown from $800 to $1,670. Assuming that ongoing operating expenses are 40%, you would still be left with more than $1,000 a month in income. Ownership of, say, six or seven such properties can translate into a high net worth and a large monthly income.

Deciding when to buy

While "location, location, location" is important, timing is vital. Real estate values go through cycles, creating opportunity for the patient and prepared investor. Having the right information and experience to know when in the cycle and in which market to buy in is key to successful investing. Ironically, when real estate prices are at their lowest point in a cycle, the general population becomes fearful of investing, having recently witnessed a falling market. At this same point, the experts are doing the opposite.

The best time to buy real estate is when a region is coming out of a recession or is in the early stages of strong, sustainable economic growth. At this point, property values are still low and affordable, yet are expected to rise as the regional economy improves.

Deciding where to buy

Most real estate investors begin with the assumption that it's safest to buy property close to where they live. But by expanding your scope beyond your neighbourhood to other communities, you avoid putting all your eggs in one basket. There are a number of factors that 20|20 Properties Inc., the professional real estate investment firm that I founded in 2000, looks for as signals – investment fundamentals, essentially – that a market may offer better than average potential for investors:

–A strong, diversified economy. If a region's economy is growing, or is strong, consumer confidence is usually high and income levels are often increasing.

–Population growth. Migration to cities or towns increases their population, thereby placing greater demand on both the housing and rental markets.

–Low unemployment. With low unemployment and a strong economy, more people are employed with higher income levels and are therefore more likely to buy housing.

–Infrastructure. Locations that plan ahead and contain significant infrastructure, such as health care, transportation and education, provide a higher quality of life and correspondingly higher real estate prices as the community grows.

–Demographics and desirability. We typically live where we work. But come retirement, many of us downsize and relocate to locations with more desirable climates and amenities. Locations that include infrastructure that allows boomers to "age in place" will continue to see rising demand.

Deciding what to buy

While single-family detached homes, duplexes and triplexes can be sound investments, they generally require more maintenance and "hands-on" management than condominiums and townhouses. In other words: more hassle. Demographics will ensure that the performance of real estate during the next 30 years will not mirror that of the last thirty. There will still be opportunities for significant gains, but the kinds of real estate that deliver returns is changing. In many cities, young people looking to buy their first home often choose condominiums over single-family homes because they are simply more affordable. As well, more and more retired folk are selling their large family homes and downsizing to condominiums.

Using other people's money

You can build significant wealth over time in real estate with an amount of money that is small in relation to the asset. Because real estate is a secure asset to borrow against, it can be leveraged, allowing for returns that aren't seen in many other investments. Leverage is the ability to purchase real estate with a down payment that is a fraction of the value of the whole asset, while borrowing the remainder in the form of a mortgage. What makes leverage such a powerful real estate investment tool is that your returns are magnified – you benefit from the growth in the entire value of the property, not just the amount of cash invested (your down payment). You can control a large investment with only a small amount of cash – the greater your leverage, the larger your profit potential. But leverage can be a double-edged sword: it can magnify the losses on a bad investment just as easily as the positive returns on a good investment.

Using the power of compounding

While the historical rate of growth varies from state to state, province to province, city to city and year to year, the value of a well-selected property in North America can be expected to appreciate over the long-term. Real estate in some cities has increased in value by as much as 30% annually during boom times. The long term average appreciation of well-selected real estate, when combined with leveraging, can produce rates of return that are almost impossible to duplicate with any other investment. Jane Bryant Quinn, a financial writer for *Newsweek* magazine, has said that the two most powerful forces in the world are gravity and compound growth. Compound growth is a familiar concept to many, yet often underutilized. Think of compound growth as the benefit of owning an investment that simply needs sufficient time to pass for it to grow substantially.

Using tax advantages

I have witnessed many smart, wealthy people make terrible investments motivated by tax advantages. Any investment decision should be based on the fundamentals. Any tax advice should come from a licensed professional, not a salesman. That said, tax advantages available to real estate investors can compound the effective rate of return on an investment. Astute investors understand the value of reducing or deferring taxes whenever possible. One of the most attractive tax advantages of owning real estate is the ability to shelter gains from taxation. Until you sell a property, or claim rental revenue as direct income, that gain is not taxable. Many of the expenses associated with owning and operating a property, such as mortgage interest, maintenance fees and property taxes are also tax-deductible.

One of the regrets most oft-voiced by the real estate investor is, "I wish I had started sooner." Don't let the analysis-paralysis paradigm preclude you from participating in the growth opportunity that is real estate investment.

Do:

- Make real estate investments a key part of your strategy for achieving financial independence during retirement.
- Understand where a specific market is in its real estate cycle before making investment decisions.
- Use other people's money responsibly. Leverage allows for returns that aren't available in many other types of investments.
- Before investing, consider the level of maintenance and "hands-on" management that will be required of you as owner.
- Build a team of specialized professionals to work with who can help identify factors that could impact your real estate investment.

4

David Peerless

President of Dexter Associates Realty
B.Comm, RI(BC), Chartered Arbitrator, Past Chair:
Real Estate Errors and Omissions Insurance
Corporation of B.C.
Director: Real Estate Board of Greater Vancouver

BEST ADVICE: *A price of a product is a function of the available supply to satisfy demand. If at any point in time the supply is less than demand, prices will rise and if greater than demand the price will fall.*

What I know about Real Estate I learned in Economics 101. My career in Real Estate has spanned thirty years and focused on the sale of residential properties and the management of Real Estate companies in the Vancouver, British Columbia market place. During that time I have had the opportunity to train and mentor many hundreds of Realtors during good markets, great markets and some much more challenging markets. Looking back I realize I learned the most valuable lessons about how Real Estate markets work from a first year business course; Economics 101.

Ironically, this was the first class of the day and after working late shifts at my job I frequently slept in this class. I did, however, pay attention to the principles of supply and demand. The instructor pressed home the idea that all markets are driven by the demand for a product and the price of that product is then a function of the available supply to satisfy that demand. If at any point in time the supply is less than demand, prices will rise and if greater than demand the price will fall. This revelation has been the backbone of how I have learned to identify market trends and in time has greatly helped my decision making in terms of buying and selling Real Estate and in the operations of Real Estate companies.

Real Estate markets or the factors that influence supply and demand can be identified in any market location and analyzed to determine trends or directions in prices. While I have never been able to control factors such as the rate of interest, the number of new homes being built, demographics of population movements or such things that affect supply and demand, by keeping track of some of these factors one can predict the future real estate cycles. A bold statement.

The supply side of the real estate cycle relies on such factors as how many new homes are being built in the area one is analyzing. Statistics are kept by the government both locally and regionally through building permit applications and approvals. This will indicate how much new supply is likely to be available in the near future. Builders and developers are encouraged by demand and favourable prices for their product and simply put will seek to build new housing when a reasonable profit is likely. The more profitable the market, the more the supply will increase and inevitably will lead to an over-supply as the balance in this real estate equation starts to tip in favour of buyers. At this stage in the cycle prices will flatten or drop as supply outstrips demand. Naturally as demand weakens and the profit potential drops, developers will pull back from the market and supply will drop re-balancing the equation and re-setting the cycle for new homes.

The largest part of the real estate supply in any market is that of used homes. This supply is largely influenced by factors of cost, prices, interest rates (affordability) and as well as the need for a change in housing as families grow or shrink. The overlying factor that controls these influences is that of confidence. If a buyer population feels confident in the economy, secure in their jobs and the future of real estate in their community, they will be inclined to spend money and increase their housing consumption, purchase property for investment or perhaps a second home for vacations. This confidence in a real estate market increases sales and reduces supply causing prices to rise. In time if the supply declines too much the market shifts to favour the seller and further pushes prices higher. Eventually as the prices start to affect affordability and the costs too high for the average buyer, sales will start to decline and supply increase. The real estate cycle continues. This process can be greatly affected by other factors that will influence the speed of change such as a change in interest rates, economic changes, population shifts among others.

Paying attention to these influences on supply will help spot trends in the real estate market and when combined with a sense of demand in a local economy, will give strong insight into where we are in the real estate cycle.

Demand in this context is the interest in acquiring real estate for personal use and investment. Like the supply side of the real estate equation demand is influenced by a number of factors such as the price of real estate, cost of borrowing, population growth and as before, the confidence in the market. In any local market if individuals feel that prices are affordable and borrowing for a purchase is reasonably priced the demand will rise and in doing so will put pressure on prices to rise. As this stage in the cycle takes hold demand is strong and large volumes of sales take place reducing supply and further affecting prices. In time, as affordability declines, demand slows and we move from a seller's market where demand exceeds supply to a balanced market where prices stabilize or perhaps start to decline into a buyer's market. Once again the real estate cycle moves on. Confidence in the economy will also affect demand. If a population feels insecure about real estate values, their job or about where the economy is going demand and prices will decline to a point where affordability is once again in balance between the existing supply and demand.

The normal ebbing and flowing of the real estate markets are generally local in nature with modest swings in values however they can be significantly affected by world events more likely to influence confidence. The principles of supply and demand are however reliable if carefully tracked. Trends follow similar patterns and in fact history does repeat itself. Every time I hear that this time the market and those factors that influence markets are different I realize that the effects are not. During the past thirty years there have been at least four distinct market cycles in the area I practice and in speaking with others active in real estate markets prior to my experience these cycles have behaved in a similar fashion for decades. One only needs to look at historical pricing data in a region over time to see these cycles in action.

I have learned over time to take comfort in the real estate market as a good place to invest, to have a business and to provide a home for my family. Time and patience have proven to be the greatest positive influences in owning real estate. Paying attention to those factors that consistently impact supply and demand will help you spot trends in any local real estate market.

It would seem Economics 101 had a lasting impression after all.

Do:

- Keep track of factors that influence supply and demand to predict future real estate cycles.
- Pay attention to influences and nurture your sense of demand in the local economy.
- Understand the power of confidence.
- Understand which part of the cycle you are in before you buy or sell.
- Understand that the ebb and flow of real estate markets is primarily local in nature.

BEST ADVICE:
Understanding the basics
(Getting ready)

5

Gary Blanes

Founder and owner of the award-winning
renovation and custom home building company,
G.W. Blanes Construction.

BEST ADVICE: *Before spending your hard-earned capital, hone your negotiating skills and educate yourself; know your buying strategies, market timing, demographics and tax considerations.*

I've received a lot of real estate advice over the years, but the best lessons I've learned were from mistakes – my own and other people's. "Success is a lousy teacher. It seduces smart people into thinking they can't lose," Bill Gates once said. Early failure made me work twice as hard and helped me become a motivated student of real estate investment.

I jumped blindly into the condo market in Calgary in 1981, when real estate prices were soaring and interest rates were climbing past 18%. My condo looked like a bargain, with a mortgage rate of 11%. But soon afterward property values dropped and my monthly payments were $200 higher than the $550 rent I was collecting. After a couple of years, I couldn't handle the financial drain anymore so I sold my "equity" to a friend for $1.

My university tuition at the time was about $2,500 annually, while my initial lesson in real estate investment cost close to $25,000. That may have been the best tuition I've ever paid. Business training guru Brian Tracy once said, "If you want to make money, lose some money and if you want to make a lot of money, lose a lot of money." That sums up my experience. From that initial loss, I learned all about doing due diligence, understanding market timing, and not following the pack.

Wanting to make up for lost time and lost cash, I decided to learn from the pros. I read Charles Givens' book *Wealth Without Risk* in 1990, and followed his advice on seeking a rent-to-own opportunity. My wife and I invested about $1,000 on classified advertising that read, "Professional couple looking for a home to lease with an option to purchase." After three months of careful searching, we finally found a great place and negotiated a fair market price, with an agreement that our lease payments would be applied against the purchase.

By the end of the period in which we could exercise our buy option, we had completed a lot of cosmetic renovations and the place looked outstanding. The house's market price had increased 40% above the price we had originally negotiated. And our lease payments had reduced that price even further. So it was no surprise when the owner had a sudden change of heart and didn't want to complete the deal. Fortunately, my wife Nina had insisted that we get everything drawn up by a lawyer who, in turn, registered our buy option on the property title – a move that ultimately saved us. We were able to close the deal, making a hefty profit with little risk.

Another important lesson I've learned comes straight from Ozzie Jurock himself, "You make the most money on the day you buy a property, not when you sell." I learned to invest time and patience in making offers and drawing up terms and conditions, because that ultimately determines future profitability. The asking price for a piece of real estate is arbitrary: deals are what you make of them. Think of how often you discovered the selling price of a property and said, "If I knew it would sell for that, I would have bought it myself." People will drive across town or stand in line all night to save $100 on the latest electronic gizmo, but they don't realize the benefit of bargaining over the price of real estate. When you consider that you can save a year's salary or more just by spending a little extra time negotiating, why wouldn't you?

In 1993, I read Sam Allman's book *Buy It By the Acre and Sell It By The Foot* and learned that smaller parcels of land can be worth almost as much as larger parcels. Allman taught me that buyers are often willing to pay the same amount for one acre as they are for five acres. For whatever reason, they conclude that they only really require the smaller parcel of land. This is why subdividing land can be so lucrative. I put this idea together with demographic information about baby boomers and their demand for recreational and retirement property, and started looking for land with subdivision potential. Nina and I eventually found 160 acres of lake view property in the Shuswap region of B.C. We purchased the land in 1994 and invested two years in the subdivision process, which included putting in wells and access roads. We hired a realtor to market the 20 acre lots, and sold them gradually over almost 10 years. The last lot sold in 2007 for roughly double the price we paid for the entire 160-acre property.

The market continued climbing while we sold the Shuswap lots and we couldn't help regretting leaving some money on the table, but we remembered the old adage, "No one ever went broke taking a profit." Warren Buffet has said that he got rich by selling too soon. There's nothing wrong with leaving a few crumbs on the table for the next guy.

The real estate strategy that works best for me is to think long term and run against the herd – the opposite of what I did in 1981. Real estate always cycles through ups and downs. If the cycle is down, the market will eventually climb, the key is predicting when. You're far more likely to find and negotiate bargain deals when everyone wants to sell, rather than following the herd into a buying frenzy near the peak of a cycle.

When I think of the tuition I paid in the real estate school of hard knocks, I am comfortable passing up risky or uncertain deals. What looks potentially lucrative could also be potentially disastrous. Before spending your hard-earned capital, hone your negotiating skills and educate yourself; know your buying strategies, market timing, demographics and tax considerations. It's important to weigh the costs against the potential reward of any venture and to avoid risking what you value the most. Family, health, and friends are worth far more than money.

Do:

- Pass up deals that sound too good to be true. Be very wary when people say, "You can't lose." You can.
- Ensure that your real estate deals are drawn up by a lawyer and registered on title.
- Think long term and run against the herd.
- Learn from reputable pros.
- Be willing to invest time, energy and research in a property before purchasing.

Don't:

- Try to time the market perfectly so you can sell at the peak. When you're selling in a rising market, don't be greedy.
- Be afraid to negotiate aggressively. Remember that asking prices are arbitrary.
- Get emotionally tied to investment property. Emotions can seriously cloud your judgment.
- Take risks you can't afford.
- Try to get rich quick. Real estate investing is a life-long process.

6

Gary Brisebois, RHI

Owner of AmeriSpec Inspection Services in the
Vancouver Lower Mainland and Registered Home
Inspector, Canadian Association of Home &
Property Inspectors

BEST ADVICE: *Not all home inspections are created equal — hire a qualified home inspector from a reputable company that carries Errors and Omissions Insurance.*

I started my home inspection business in the early '90s when "buyer beware" for purchasers was the norm. At that time less than one in ten homes sold in Canada was inspected prior to the sale. Today's numbers work out to about four home inspections for every ten houses sold and the take-up rate for home inspections is expanding.

Why do you require a home inspection? For most of us a home is one of the largest long-term investments we will make in our lives so it's wise to seek some protection before jumping in. For investors it's a good idea to get an inspection to avoid costly unforeseen repairs that can take a large bite out of profits. And completing a home inspection before you make the purchase offer may help you exert more control over the negotiation process and ultimately the purchase price.

So what is a home inspection? It's a thorough visual examination of the condition of the home and property by a qualified home inspector. The inspection includes both observation and when appropriate operation of the home's various systems, such as, plumbing, heating, and electrical systems. In addition, the inspection should cover all structural components such as the roof, attic, foundation, basement, walls, chimney, and doors. In total, **a professional home inspection should cover about 1,000 check-points on 400 or so items around the home.**

Typically the inspection takes about two to three hours during which the property is carefully examined. If you can attend the entire inspection or at the very least the walk-through with the inspector you will see first-hand the condition of the property's main components. A qualified inspector can also reassure you about findings which may seem distressing on paper but in reality may be fairly superficial. For example, the inspector may explain that an unsightly column needs only a coat of paint or a problem that caused a water mark has been corrected.

I've noticed that in hot real estate markets sellers are increasingly hiring a home inspector to determine the pre-sale condition of their property. In many cases problems in a house are relatively minor and can be repaired easily and inexpensively, such as chipped paint, doors or windows that stick, or a furnace filter that is dirty. These flaws are usually overlooked by sellers who may have lived in the home for some time but buyers tend to focus on these short-falls and use them for price negotiation. In this situation a professionally produced home inspection report can improve the speed, price, and likelihood of a sale for the seller.

Can a friend or family member who has a background in one of the trades such as carpentry or plumbing do a home inspection for you? Not in my opinion. I really don't think there's a substitute for the objective eye of a skilled and qualified home inspector who has been trained on what to look for and how to evaluate hundreds of key components throughout the property. Only a professional inspector has the benefit and experience of hundreds, if not thousands, of past home inspections to draw from.

There are limitations to a home inspection. An inspector can't see through the foundation, under the floors, through the walls, or inspect areas or items that are inaccessible. And the inspector generally doesn't move furniture or household effects. But a qualified inspector will be able to provide you with an accurate overall assessment of the home's condition.

You may want to hire a specialist in addition to a general home inspector. If you have concerns about cracks in the foundation, it could be a good idea to hire a structural engineer to thoroughly assess that component. Or if you're worried about the moisture soundness of the property, you may want to seek the expertise of a building envelope specialist. If you don't have these concerns and this type of potential defect is discovered during the inspection, a professional home inspector will always recommend follow-up with the appropriate specialist.

Hire a home inspection service that is also authorized to conduct home energy evaluations which recommend improvements for increasing the energy efficiency and comfort of a home. Sealing cracks around doors and windows, improving insulation in your home, and replacing old appliances with newer energy-efficient ones will reduce heating and electrical costs over the long term.

Do:

- Hire a qualified home inspector who is a member of a recognized professional home inspection association such as the Canadian Association of Home & Property Inspectors.
- Review your inspection agreement in advance even though your inspector should review it with you at the time of the inspection – you will be asked to sign the agreement.
- Attend the inspection for at least a walk-through of the property with the inspector.
- Ask questions of your inspector if you have concerns about anything in the home.
- Ensure the inspection company you hire carries Errors and Omissions liability insurance.

Don't:

- Agree to a verbal home inspection; it's unprofessional. A written inspection report documents the inspector's findings and also provides a useful resource for the ongoing maintenance of your property
- Expect a home inspection to detect every flaw. A home inspection is exhaustive covering about 1,000 check-points on 400 items in the home, but it can't assess areas and items that can't be seen such as those hidden through the walls and foundation
- Consider an inspection to be an appraisal. An appraisal is a formal process of estimating a property's value as it relates to a mortgage loan, mortgage insurance, estate purposes, divorce settlements, or the market value for resale
- Forget that home inspections help protect your investment

7

Jeff Fawcett

President Fawcett Insurance. Proud to be looking after our customers insurance needs since 1932.

Best Advice: *One of the most important elements of insurance is the relationship between consumer and broker.*

In 2005, I acquired a 77-year-old insurance agency in North Vancouver from my father, who had acquired it in 1969 and turned it into one of the most successful insurance businesses on the North Shore. He taught me that, although insurance agencies have to sell the "paper," the secret to success in the insurance business is what happens afterwards. Customer service is paramount, my dad would say. In 2000, when I was elected business person of the year by the North Vancouver Chamber of Commerce – a great honour – I realized just how well my father's advice had served me. He taught me the importance of offering the same level of service to all clients, never differentiating between the small and large clients. Over time, small clients grow into large clients.

Of course, everyone knows they need insurance. But there is much more to insurance than meets the eye. I'm not referring only to the fine print, although that needs careful consideration as well. Many insurance principles are found in the intangibles.

One of the most important elements of insurance is the relationship between consumer and broker. Take the time to interview the broker before you commit to doing business with them or their company. It's the broker's responsibility to help you get the best product at the best price, so ask about their experience; what programs they have available; and how their firm handles the claims process. At today's pace, a lot of business is done over the phone or computer. If you have a problem, however, it's nice to have a broker that will at the very least meet you in person.

Even if you are a smaller client, will the broker go to bat for you with the insurer? Will your broker answer the phone when your water pipes break at 6 a.m.? When I get that late night call, I not only guide the client through the mishap, but get in touch with a restoration company. In order to limit damage, a good insurance broker will have someone wet-vacuuming your basement within an hour. In fact, the faster a repair is completed, the better the broker has fulfilled his or her duty to mitigate damages. Some brokers don't like being involved in the claims process, but the good ones will walk you through it and help you deal with the local adjustor.

Unfortunately, many people do not receive adequate insurance coverage. Brokers must ensure you are insured properly and at a competitive price for the perils of your particular exposure.

There are of course a hundred things that can go wrong. Interestingly, there are more water damage claims than any other kind of claim. To prevent water from backing up into your basement – a common mishap, particularly in older homes – hire a drainage company every two years to check your building's drainage for breaks in the system.

I always recommend tankless water systems, as they contain little actual water. If you are away for the weekend you don't want to return home to a swimming pool in the basement. In addition, a water endorsement is a good option to consider. Based on the many water claims I have dealt with, I believe everyone should have a water endorsement.

Always buy as much liability coverage as you can afford – it will help you sleep at night. Most policies come with $1 million in coverage, but you can acquire more. I recently wrote the insurance for a $6 million building whose owner had previously been covered for only $2 million in liability. His losses could have been staggering if things really went awry. A judge could have awarded the full $6 million value of the building to someone else.

Keeping your insurer well-informed is among the simplest damage prevention measures.

For example, notifying your insurer should be on your to-do list when planning a vacation. Most policies, and particularly those in Canada, state that your property must be properly and regularly inspected while you are away on a holiday. Without regular inspection, the coverage for your home may be void. Where a policy includes a "freezing clause," someone will have to ensure that no pipes in your home burst while you are sunning in the Caribbean.

Some firms specialize in rental insurance policies. My firm has insured hundreds of apartments, rental condos and multi-family rental homes. Some insurance companies have programs for rentals and others don't. Many rental property owners aren't aware that they are only insured for 30 days after a rental unit becomes vacant, unless they inform the insurance company of the vacancy. Upon learning of the vacancy, an insurance company may limit your policy somewhat, but at least you have fire insurance. Always get proof of insurance from your tenant. Remember that you are ultimately responsible for your asset. Most renters forget to insure their belongings, even though it's relatively inexpensive.

During my 30 years in insurance, I have seen every type of claim: big claims, small claims and just plain weird claims. Claims happen. A good insurance policy will put you back to the place you were before the claim happened.

Do:

- Be certain that your property is insured to value, and get a RTC replacement cost evaluation tool, particularly in a fast rising market.
- Place rental income on your policy when you carry a mortgage.
- Make sure that your heating, roof, plumbing and electrical is

inspected and updated if your home is more than 20 years old.

- Get Contents Coverage, which insures such things as appliances and furniture. It's optional, but nice to have if there is a fire.
- Ask about improvements and betterments that have been done since the building was originally constructed.
- Check on any bylaw issues with the local municipality. You can buy bylaw coverage for homes, but you must ask for it.

Don't:

- Have less than 100-amp service for your building.
- Put-off replacing all knob & tube wiring, aluminum wiring, galvanized plumbing or fuse-equipped stoves with modern day equivalents.
- Hesitate to call your broker if you uncertain of an issue.
- Neglect simple property maintenance tasks such as cleaning the eaves trough or having the chimney swept. These tasks may sound innocuous, but many water damage claims are a result of clogged eaves troughs. And a chimney fire will burn for days.
- Forget that you – not the broker – are ultimately responsible for your asset.

8

Fred van Hunenstijn

Founded Advantage 24 Hr Emergency Services in
1972. He holds a Red Seal Plumbing License, Gas
Fitting License, Dip'T in Electrical - Electronics, and
is also a Licensed Residential Builder in BC.

BEST ADVICE: *When you buy – inspect the plumbing systems with your home inspector.*

"Water, water everywhere, nor any drop to drink." Great words in the poem by S.T. Coleridge but not so great when the water is in your basement! How did it get there? Where is it coming from? Where will it go? Two thirds of the planet is already covered in water, why my basement as well? These are all good questions but in the midst of a problem is not the best time to be asking them.

While plumbing has existed since about 2500 B.C. in Egypt, things have changed significantly over the last 50 years or so. There was a time when all you needed to know to be a plumber was —it flows downhill and payday is on Friday ! Those days are gone. Now there are a multitude of materials, adhesives, solvents, specialized piping systems, fire codes, building codes, electrical codes and plumbing codes not to mention energy and water conservation issues and regulations.

Sanitary Drainage:

But I checked the toilet and it seemed to flush OK:

A good test to be sure, but there is so much more. Let's start at the city connection which will be at the property line. Note - we said property line, not fence line, which may or may not be in the correct place. In some cases, certainly with newer homes, an inspection chamber (IC) will be conveniently provided right at the property line. This will be an eight inch pipe with a red cap, which when removed will allow a visual inspection of the sanitary line. This is also the demarcation point for line maintenance responsibility. **Down stream is the city's responsibility and upstream is the homeowners responsibility.** When searching for the IC, be sure to check neighbouring houses since they will be in line with yours which should help you find it.

The IC is very useful to the plumber as he can use a drain auger (sometimes called a snake) or jetting with a high pressure water stream, to clear a blockage by entering the line through the IC. Moving upstream, we will want to consider if the building has had any renovations, additions or suites added after original construction.

Beware the raised toilet in the basement, a good sign of do-it-yourself work. If these were done without permits, there is a good chance that the plumbing is not to code and may require more maintenance than normal, or complete replacement. Be sure to discuss this with your home inspector.

Branch lines, serving kitchen sinks and bathroom sinks, tubs and so forth can be augered with smaller equipment in case of a blockage, but usually cannot be inspected with a pipe camera. History is important here since the lines will be entirely concealed in the walls and floors. Once you own the property it is wise to use an enzyme product such as "BioSmart" (available from Advantage) on a regular basis to keep your drains clear.

Storm Water Drainage:

What Storm? I'm checking out the property in the summer.

The house will be protected from ground water with a perimeter drainage system. As the name implies, this is an in-ground piping system around the building which is discharged into the city storm drain, a city combination drain (in some municipalities storm and sewage water are combined) or in rural areas, an open ditch. Roof water may also be directed into the perimeter lines and can often cause problems by overloading the system in heavy rainfalls. It is counter productive to be pouring water into the lines designed to keep your basement dry and the current plumbing code requires a two pipe system around the building, keeping the roof water separate until it reaches the sump. This round concrete chamber is designed to intercept debris and sand before it discharges to the city. The sump lid can be removed and the debris removed from the bottom every few years with a vacuum truck. The sump is also an excellent access point for the perimeter system and both drain cleaning equipment and the drain camera can be sent down the lines from it.

Water Supply:

I turned on all the taps so what else?

Plenty. Is the piping copper, plastic or perhaps, in a very old home, iron ? A few older homes may be found with iron piping and a substantial budget should be reserved for updating if a purchase is being considered for anything other than "lot value". Copper was very common until about the late 70's when various plastics took over in Single Family Dwelling (SFD) construction. Older copper pipes had thicker walls and can sometimes outlast copper installed after the 80's . Copper generally will fail with pin holes, which allow for a tiny spray of water to escape. This is caused by a combination of chemical action, temperature and erosion within the pipe. Once a leak forms in one location, others will generally follow and the piping will need to be replaced, a costly procedure. This is particularly prevalent in high rise construction, which is discussed later.

One of the earlier plastic piping materials was polybutelyene, or Poly-B, while this was initially permitted in SFD under the plumbing code, it soon became apparent it was not a suitable material. Poly-B crimped fittings failed frequently, particularly on the hot side, resulting in a major flood from uncontrolled water flow from the full diameter of the pipe. Always check for poly-B plumbing, which is easily identified by it's grey colour. As with pin holed copper, the only satisfactory remedy is a complete re-piping.

Cross-linked Polyethelyene or Pex, is the currently accepted and very successful material. Developed around 1960, its useful life has been extrapolated to be 50-100 years.

Hot Water Supply:

I checked the tank and it's not leaking now, but how long should it last?

Many factors can affect the life of the water heater, including the incoming pressure, amount of cycling, frequency of using all the available hot water, chemical composition of the water and even the temperature setting of the tank. The age can be determined by qualified plumbing companies who maintain a database of the various manufacturer's date code systems embedded in the serial numbers. Beware of relying on warranties, as these are pro-rated and typically are for leakage only after the first year and usually do not cover labour. Most SFD construction will use natural gas water heaters, with their faster recovery time, while many Town Homes will use electric water heaters with their flexibility of installation locations. **Gas fired Tankless Water Heaters are now becoming popular** with their energy and water saving features.

Condominiums:

I have a condo so the strata looks after the plumbing, right ?

Only partially, and even then, you, dear owner, will be paying for its upkeep. Water supply in a high rise is a complex engineered system with booster, pumps, re-circulating pumps, boilers, pressure reducers, water storage tanks and more. Furthermore, the copper pipes age more quickly, due to heavy flow rates, than in SFD and when a building re-pipe is necessary it will likely result in a special strata levy. Read all the strata minutes carefully, going back as far as you can, for plumbing issues, past, present, or anticipated, and review any concerns with your home inspector. An alternative to the pipes is an epoxy based internal coating system. While this is promoted as an economical alternative to re-piping, the savings can be disappointing. Walls still need to be opened to isolate various fittings and valves which cannot be allowed to be coated, furthermore, the reduction in pipe diameter may require higher pressures to deliver adequate flow to all units. Consultation with independent engineers will be required before an informed decision can be made on re-piping a high rise. Allow for both time and money!

Note that most strata by-laws will provide that plumbing fixtures within the unit, such as toilets, faucets and garbage disposal units are the responsibility of the unit owner. Always use the services of a professional, licensed, bonded and insured plumbing company to service these items. Otherwise, you could be held responsible for flooding of units below and beside you.

Do:

- Inspect the plumbing systems with your home inspector.
- Get as much history as you can from owners and strata minutes.
- Check that any additions or renovations are done to code with permits.
- Have a proper evaluation of requirements before changing your water heater.

- Maintain your drains with an environmentally friendly enzyme product such as Bio-Smart.

Don't:

- Do-It Yourself with your condo plumbing.
- Ignore Poly-B piping.
- Assume your water heater will last forever.
- Ignore drainage issues just because it wasn't raining when you checked the property.

9

Doug Johnston

President and owner of Mustang Contracting
Electrical Installations.

BEST ADVICE: *Beware of the electrical contractor that will work for cash or, even worse, beer.*

I discovered early on that there are no short cuts in electrical work. Codes must be followed, regulations obeyed and the lights simply have to work. Business deals can be negotiated and contracts abbreviated, but electrical work is non-negotiable.

Of course, in business you also need to have personal principles. My dad used to say that your handshake is your bond. I made that my business motto, although sometimes that hand had to be a fist.

When inspecting the electrical in your new or prospective home:
- Watch out for cover plates that are warm to the touch – a telltale sign of a loose connection on a receptacle or switch.
- Keep in mind that aluminum wiring – common in older homes – is rated differently than copper wiring and that different devices will have different symbols: Al for aluminum, Cu for copper. Flickering lights and the discoloration of receptacles and switches may be a sign that aluminum wiring is in contact with a copper-rated device or that a connection is loose.
- Replace broken receptacles and other devices in disrepair with devices that meet today's wiring and cable codes.
- Find out if any renovations have been done to the home. If so, were permits taken out? Who did the work? Call city hall to

find out if there are any outstanding renovation permits. The seller is responsible to correct defects in a building, but a buyer can negotiate to assume responsibility of those defects.

- Be mindful of knob and tube wiring, which is common in homes built between 1900 and 1940. Some insurance companies will require that this wiring be upgraded to current standards.
- Check the hot water tank. If it's an older electric tank, you can either buy an insulating blanket for it or upgrade to a newer tank. In either case, make sure you insulate the pipes coming from the tank. Also check the date the tank was installed – tanks typically have seven-year life spans – and don't risk over-extending a tank's life, change it out.
- Found a great investment that was previously a marijuana grow operation? Make sure you do your due diligence with respect to all the documentation required to make the home safe. Not only electrically safe, but environmentally and structurally.
- Have a licensed contractor inspect the home before you buy it. It will give you great peace of mind.

Some people notice the lipstick rather than the lips when buying a home. As you become savvier in real estate investing, you should begin to look past the lipstick. It is there that you will uncover the real value of a home, be it an undiscovered gem or a money pit.

In the negotiation stage of real estate investment, knowledge is a key weapon.

For the real estate developer. Do:

- Have high expectations of contractors. Legitimate contractors come with knowledge and resumes and will provide you with customer references. Learn to negotiate.
- Shop mindfully for licensed and qualified electricians and contractors. Ensure that they follow all local building codes and provide permits and licences.

- If you do your own contracting, it's likely that you will have employees who do not show up for work; fail to return your phone calls; forget what you tell them; and neglect to confer with you about important decisions. It is not easy being your own contractor, but it can be very satisfying when you overcome the many challenges.
- Always pay better than standard wage. It's one way to ensure that when you find talented workers, you keep them. The cheaper price is not always the cheapest price, as costs can rise uncontrollably with inexperienced contractors.

Even though I've been an electrician for 30 years, I still take great pleasure in learning new things about the electrical field and real estate development. And while electrical work is often described as "simple pipe and wire work," there are many different wiring methods and products available to contractors and homeowners. For example, there are several ways to reduce your power consumption by purchasing energy efficient light bulbs; getting involved with your local power supply company; or investigating a cost-saving energy program like Power Smart. Don't hesitate to contact your electrical contractor for some cost saving tips or direction.

Some final common sense advice for the real estate developer: Educate yourself by asking questions and reading about basic electrical, plumbing, roofing and general trades. Don't be scared to ask for someone's professional opinion. Know your construction crew, inspect with respect and enjoy the journey.

For the Home owner

Do:

- Make sure the wiring in your home meets current standards and don't forget that aluminum and copper materials are rated differently.
- Ensure your light fixtures can house energy efficient bulbs, as

some energy efficient bulbs are larger than conventional incandescent bulbs.

- The prevailing school of thought is that you should install a larger electrical service if you know your power needs will rise in the future. For example, adding an addition, a garage, a hot tub, a basement suite or even air conditioning will increase your power requirements. It costs much less to install a larger service before you move in, than it does to add one later.

- When laying out your lighting plan, group your lights on different phases, so that in the event that you lose a phase of power, your house is not in total darkness.

- If you've discovered that your new home was previously a marijuana grow-op, make sure you do your due diligence to ensure the home is safe electrically, environmentally and structurally.

- Beware of the contractor that will work for cash or, even worse, beer.

- Shop mindfully for licensed and qualified electricians and contractors – and don't be afraid to pay a higher price for quality work.

10

Steve D. Miller, CRA

President of Bakerview Realty Appraisals Inc., a firm specializing in residential valuations and various other real estate consulting services.

BEST ADVICE: *Do not be afraid to spend a little to save a lot when it comes to Real Estate. Do your research and employ the proper professionals and the long term savings can be tenfold along the way.*

Understanding the role and benefit of a qualified Professional Real Estate appraiser is invaluable to your real estate investment portfolio. As an appraiser for the last 17 years I have experienced so many situations whereby I could have saved a purchaser and/or seller from embarking on a poor decision had my opinion been sought earlier in the transaction. I have found that many people are unaware that modern day real estate appraisers are subject to extensive schooling requirements, certification and recertification processes and are required to carry liability E & O insurance. We are continually required to stay on top of market changes and are well positioned to have greater insight and knowledge on current real estate trends than many of our other partners in related fields. But what many people don't realize is that **many of the tools to real estate appraising that we employ from day to day are also available to the general public, and often at little to no cost.**

Recent reports estimate that computers and internet access are now present in 75% of Canadian homes. Over the last several years most municipalities have or are in the process of developing web based mapping and property information websites that provide fantastic information to real estate investors and home owners. Information that in the past would only be available to you by taking a number and standing in line at the counter of your local civic office. If you have never attempted to research information on a property through a local municipality website I encourage you to practice with your own home and you will likely be surprised at how much information is available. Some of the most common, and information we utilize daily in our appraisal practice, includes mapping software that outlines lot dimensions, land uses and zoning, detailed and easy to read land use maps that highlight community plans and proposed land uses for certain areas, sanitary and water locations, and one of my favourites, satellite imagery. Satellite imagery, particularly for larger parcels and acreages, gives you a very clear bird's eye view of a property and its related site improvements and is available for most properties throughout North America. Google has their own free version of the satellite images and many websites actually link to theirs.

Having the benefit of being able to quickly search a municipality's mapping software for potential unknowns such as hidden underground services protected by registered right-of-ways or easements can save future heartache when you realize these hidden encumbrances now prohibit the space you once thought was available to put in that dream pool. This is all information that our appraisal profession use daily and is now easily accessible to the general public and can serve as an invaluable tool to the savvy investor.

While appraisals are often needed for many reasons including estate purposes, divorce settlements, and estimating market value for re-sale, the most common purpose for an appraisal still remains the financial appraisal used by lenders to secure financing. The lending institutions rely on our expertise and our appraisal reports to provide security for underwriting their loans. Over the years I have seen countless purchasers stung by financial/appraisal related guidelines that most people are simply just not aware of until it is too late. Lenders often have different guidelines for different types of properties and the interest rates they will associate with these properties. For instance, most of the major lenders in Canada restrict residential mortgages to the main house and 5 acres only for semi and rural properties. If you were purchasing that dream acreage just outside town and the property included a large shop and 10 acres you may be very surprised in the end to learn that you will need to come up with a lot more money down as the appraiser had to exclude half of your property and your dream shop in his/her analysis.

Another real world example that I often see is related to older homes with fair or poor maintenance and upkeep. One of the most important parts of an appraisal to a lender (and there are many) is a number we put in the report called "Remaining Economic Life." Simply defined, it is the estimated period the existing improvements will contribute to the property value. In urban centres where there is little or no remaining land for development and new construction is fed through an inventory of older homes that get demolished to make way for newer custom residences, we see "land" sales that occur with homes on them, however, there is little or no deemed value in those existing improvements. Many lenders restrict their loan-to-value rations on vacant land and even though there may be a liveable house present, there may be no intrinsic value in that home to adhere to lending guidelines. Sometimes in situations like this there still may be economic life in the home but perhaps for no longer than a period of 15 years. In a situation like this there is a good chance your lender will not amortize the loan for anything more than 15 years meaning your payments over that period will be significantly higher than if the home was amortized over 25 years or more. If you had not budgeted for this when making your initial offer this can obviously have dire consequences in the end. These are scenarios I see happen all the time and while there are often solutions and alternatives for financing on every deal it is important to know what the potential roadblocks are before laying down that non-refundable deposit and learning the sad truth later.

If there is one thing I have learned over the years is that we cannot all be professionals in everything we do and we must employ those who are to assist us in making the informative decisions. As an appraiser I have a real solid background and knowledge of building construction and quality, however, any time I am purchasing a property I still retain the services of a building Inspector to provide their unbiased opinion of potential pitfalls. I have access to MLS services beyond the level of the general public, however, I am still going to employ a realtor for negotiating and purchasing a property and why would I drive to 5 different banks to get a quote on mortgage rates when I could have a mortgage broker do that for me. You will find that mostly all lending institutions and brokers already have established relationships with local appraisers they deal with daily so go ahead and ask them for a referral and then make that call to an appraiser whenever you have that question that needs answered. Whether you are a seasoned real estate investor with a large portfolio or a young new home buyer eager to leave your parents domain, the key to success and peace of mind is often only a phone call or email away so never be afraid to embrace the vast resources available to you. All the best!

Do:

- Use the Internet to do your research through a local municipality website.
- Satellite imagery, particularly for larger parcels and acreages to get a very clear bird's eye view of a property.
- Check out financial/appraisal related guidelines ahead of your purchase.
- Understand that lenders want to know the "Remaining Economic Life."
- Hire a professional accredited appraiser.

Don't:

- Assume that vast research resources are not available to you.
- Assume every property purchase you make will carry with it easy financing options. Look for potential pitfalls or unique characteristics of a property and seek advice on them before purchasing.
- Try to do everything yourself. Employ professionals along the way to assist in the decision making process.

11

Randy Cowling

Owner of Mortgage Alliance – Meridian Mortgage
Services Inc. Mortgage Alliance is the highest
volume mortgage brokerage in the country, with
over 1,700 brokers processing almost 40,000
mortgages annually.

BEST ADVICE: *Make sure you can lock in your variable rate at the bank's best rate.*

B ack in the seventies and eighties, mortgage brokers were primarily a last ditch effort to finance borrowers who had been refused a loan at a local bank. These clients were routinely charged a heavy fee by the mortgage broker who would place the mortgage with "B" lenders, such as trust or finance companies. These "B" lenders would often charge their own fees on top of the broker's and would be at interest rates much higher than standard banks. Suffice it to say, mortgage brokers were not always the most respected cog in the real estate wheel.

In the early to mid nineties, a shift occurred in the Canadian lending community. Reputable and large lenders began to view mortgage brokers as a legitimate source of premier "A" business. With internet growth the lenders saw the need to provide higher and better service to a more knowledgeable clientele. Television and radio advertising promoting the lowest and best mortgage rates could now be easily confirmed by borrowers on their home computers. Banks needed a way to compete in the new marketplace. Why not outsource the loan application to a mortgage broker who could be educated not only on rates, but the features and benefits of each mortgage product as well.

Under this system, banks, credit unions and other lenders would pay the mortgage broker for mortgages as they funded. The fee paid by the bank to the broker was much less on a per mortgage basis than the costs of procuring a mortgage through a local branch. At a branch, the bank has to pay rent, staff costs, marketing costs, management, etc. All of these costs need to be factored into the interest rate of a mortgage. Using a mortgage broker, lenders could set up one central location that would accept applications via computer from across the country. This location could process thousands of applications with very little overhead. The savings are passed on to borrowers, resulting in lower rates for clients who used a mortgage broker than for those who walked into their local branch.

In the early nineties approximately 5% of mortgages in Canada were processed through a broker. Today, almost one third of all mortgages processed in Canada will be through a mortgage broker. The industry has progressed to one with large national brokerage firms and franchises much like the real estate industry transformed in the 1970s. The Re/Max and Royal LePage real estate offices compare to the Mortgage Alliance and Invis offices of the brokerage industry. Today, lenders look to high volume brokers and brokerages in order to process more mortgages with even less overhead. Not all brokers are created equal. Only the top producing and most reputable brokers have access to all the available lenders. Now the best and largest national firms are even beginning to offer their own original mortgage products exclusive of the major banks and credit unions.

A top broker today can offer not only the best rate, but the best terms as well. For example, variable rate mortgages are very popular at the time of writing. Rate, however, is not the only issue to consider with this type of mortgage. All variable mortgages allow for the borrower to "lock in" their interest rate should they wish protection from rising rates over time. The rate a borrower locks in at varies drastically between lenders. The difference between a posted rate lock in and a broker discounted rate lock in can be as much as 2.5% or more on certain terms. A broker can ensure the client is protected with a preferred lock in discount in writing at the time the borrower takes the mortgage. This can save the client tens of thousands of dollars in interest over the course of a mortgage.

The posted rate on a mortgage is the rate usually advertised by a lender at branch level, whereas a discounted rate is the rate offered by the same lender through a mortgage broker. The high production brokers and brokerages regularly get a better discount based on volume. Borrowers are well advised to check the reputation and rates offered through a broker prior to making an application. Once a broker has been chosen, the borrower should not seek the services of other brokers or apply individually at banks or lenders. Each application will create a hit on the client's credit bureau, and too many hits will adversely affect their credit. A broker can pull the credit bureau once and then forward to numerous lenders, safely sidestepping this possibility. A good broker will usually ask for a commitment from the borrower not to use other brokers. They know that shopping among brokers is not in the best interest of the client.

Brokerage should continue to grow in popularity as the system allows for a true win-win scenario for all parties to the transaction. Today the trend is for banks and other lenders to spend more time and effort supporting the larger and more reputable brokers. This will ensure only the most informed and full time brokers will remain in the industry. When choosing a mortgage broker, take the time to research both the broker and the brokerage he or she works for. A reputable broker will not only save you money on your mortgage but can also help you pay off the loan faster than otherwise possible. A good mortgage broker always has your *best interest* at heart.

Do:

- Hire a broker that has access to all the available lenders.
- Get not only the best rate, but the best terms as well.
- Never use more than one broker to shop your mortgage.
- Make sure you can lock in a variable rate mortgage at the bank's best discounted rate and not the posted rate. Get this in writing from the lender prior to funding the mortgage.

12

Harvey McCallum

Owner of Centum Creative Mortgage Ltd. specializing in creative mortgage development. He has been a top producing real estate agent and mortgage broker since 1981.

BEST ADVICE: *There is always a way to finance a transaction – but you must keep an open mind.*

Find a way to get it done. It's a simple credo, but one worth adopting if you're a real estate agent. I've held fast to it throughout my 28 years as an agent, doing the most I could for the seller, buyer and anyone else involved in the transaction. It wasn't always easy, particularly during the lean years in the 1980s when I – in spite of the market – made my first forays into the mortgage financing side of the business. Money was scarce; mortgages expensive (interest rates had climbed to 18%) and many a real estate deal foundered. Nonetheless, I took particular care to learn as much about the mortgage business as I could. In fact, after leaving real estate sales in 2000, I joined a mortgage brokerage business and, five years later, founded my own brokerage firm.

In days long gone, few transactions were actually required facilitation by a broker. But today some 40% of all mortgage-lending in the United States, and roughly 28% of mortgage-lending in Canada goes through a broker. With more than 100 varieties of lenders out there, take care in finding the one that suits your particular transaction.

There is the simple financing, like that of a client's personal residence. Even the financing of a second home or holiday home is relatively straight-forward. But then there are the deals that require a more creative approach, particularly if the buyer is investment-driven.

With a little ingenuity, you can gain the upper-hand in real estate negotiations, especially in non-conventional deals. Creative posturing can be essential to present the investor or borrower in the best possible light to the bank or lender.

Unfortunately, not all mortgage brokers are the same. Some of them simply don't know the business, or at best, are not up to date about all the mortgage options available.

For example, a few years ago I was peppered with calls from real estate bodies and dozens of brokers about a supposedly brand-new product, the 100% mortgage - no down payment mortgage. None were aware that a company known as Xceed Mortgage Corp. had been offering the 100% mortgage to investor clients for some time. But brokers simply weren't aware that they weren't aware. And as a result, they certainly could not suggest the product to their clients.

In addition to staying on top of new mortgage products and lender criteria (in 2009, lender criteria changed on a weekly basis), it's also important for real estate investors and their brokers to not be defeated by the typical setbacks in the hunt for the ideal mortgage. For instance, many investors will discover a great deal, but don't have capital for the down payment. They will get turned down by their bank, but fail to consider approaching Mortgage Investment Corporations (MICs) or other private pools of mortgage funds that – while expensive – might fit their bill. It's a matter of deftly maneuvering past the obstacles that appear between you and your investment.

In 2003, a client approached me wanting to buy a small subdivision out of foreclosure in the Interior of British Columbia. He wanted to close the deal immediately but couldn't muster the cash for the down payment. His only solution was expensive private money. I found him 100% mortgage financing at 10% interest rate.

There was also a 2% brokerage fee and a 2% bonus for the lender. An expensive proposition? Yes, but it was vacant land. It was in a small interior town, he had been turned down everywhere and my client did not have to put down any cash. For my client, it was perfect. Since the subdivision was comprised of lots that had already been individually serviced, he was able to buy the subdivision out of foreclosure and parcel it out to individual buyers within six months. Even though the $500 he paid to finance each lot appeared steep, it was meager considering the tens of thousands of dollars in profit he exited the deal with.

Today, you can take money out of your RRSP and put it on your own house or invest it in an MIC, which will then invest it in mortgages. You can use conventional or high-ratio mortgages. The level of creativity required depends on the deal. The good broker will steer you in the right direction and guide you through the myriad of mortgage options. Transferable or non-transferable mortgage? Variable rate with lock-in provision? And if you can lock-in, is it at the best rate? What are the penalties for early payout?

Some of the basics:

The investor mortgage:
The benefit of this mortgage is that the property, not the investor, qualifies for the mortgage. In 2009, you can get 95% financing – and get it insured. **You'll need:** Proof of income, proof that your taxes have been paid and a good credit rating. A minimum beacon score for 95% financing is 680 (get your free beacon score online at equifax.com). Your score can be as low as 600 at 75% loan-to-value.

The self employed (proprietorship or limited company) mortgage:
These were once easy to obtain. Not so easy after the financial

debacle of 2008. Nonetheless, they are still available and can be attractive to certain buyers. You must either be self-employed or a commissioned sales person with good credit who cannot meet the gross debt service ratios based on reported verifiable income from the Income Tax Notice of Assessment. **There are currently four different self-employed mortgages available.** Two are insured and two are conventional (don't require insurance). You can get up to 95% on a purchase and up to 90% for a refinancing of your property. These are available for up to four units. One unit needs to be occupied by the owner him or herself. **You'll need:** Copies of tenant leases; proof that you've been self-employed for at least two years; up-to-date income taxes; a minimum beacon score of 620; and a down payment that is from your own resources.

The rental property mortgage:

This would be a mortgage for a rental property you do not live in. **You'll need:** A 25-year amortization; 85% financing; minimum tangible assets of $100,000; three or more rentals; and a minimum beacon score 620.

The renewal mortgage:

When banks send out renewals, 65% of people sign them as they are offered and send them back. Don't get caught! Explore different options. And keep your bank honest: Get a second opinion on a renewal. Don't sign it until you talked to a professional mortgage broker.

As a borrower, you want to be excited about getting the right kind of mortgage. Certainly your broker should be excited about finding the mortgage that is tailor-made to you and your investment portfolio. There are many new ways to make old boring mortgages interesting and profitable, but don't ask your banker. He or she may want to slot you into their particular corner. At the risk of subjectivity, my advice is to talk to an independent mortgage broker.

Do:

- Adopt the credo: *"I'll find a way to get it done"*.
- If you're a broker or realtor, do the most you can for the seller, buyer and anyone else involved in the transaction.
- Take care in finding the mortgage that suits the specific transaction.
- Stay on top of new mortgage products and lender criteria.
- Look to independent mortgage brokers for advice about mortgages.

Don't:

- Be discouraged by the obstacles you'll most likely encounter in your search for an ideal mortgage.
- Automatically sign mortgage renewals, as many people do. Explore your options. Get a second opinion on the renewal.
- Depend on your banker for objective and sound advice about mortgages.
- Take for granted your broker's knowledge of the real estate trade. Many brokers simply don't know the business, or at best, are not up to date with all the various mortgage options available.

BEST ADVICE:
Understanding the purchase

13

Eppich and King

Lis Eppich is project manager for EIG Investments
and a real estate investor in Vancouver
Vikki King M.D., F.R.C.P.(C) is a physician and real
estate investor in Vancouver

BEST ADVICE: *Buy small, think big.*

The toughest part of turning a dream into reality is taking that first step. By deciding on a $48,000 townhouse in Prince George in 2005 as the first step towards our goal of buying at least five units per year over five years, we made that first step a baby step. Here are some of the key lessons we learned while achieving our five-year goal in less than three years.

Buy the ugly duckling, not the swan

Most people don't have the cash needed to start investing and, therefore, need to borrow money. Often, the easiest way to initially obtain credit is to build equity in your own home. As you cannot depend on a rising market to build that equity, learn to love and see the potential in ugly ducklings. Most homebuyers will overextend themselves by buying something as close to their dream home as they can afford. They buy the swan. Instead, buy the ugly – but sturdy –

duckling in an up-and-coming neighbourhood. That's right, the home with stained carpets, old paint and blackberries taking over the back yard. This is the house that you are likely to get the deal on while other buyers clamour to make offers on the swan down the road. As you typically can remain less emotionally attached to the ugly duckling, you are less likely to overextend yourself on it. This leaves money on the table for future investments.

Educate yourself

If you want to make a future out of buying and selling real estate, you need to educate yourself. Take courses, join real estate groups and subscribe to real estate newsletters, magazines and newspapers. Learn where new mines are being developed, which airports are expanding, and where new ports are being built. Attend conferences and seminars not only about real estate, but about local and global economic trends. Look at the big picture. How will the growth of China, retiring baby boomers, peak oil theory and global warming impact regional real estate markets? Use the Internet as a research tool. There is a wealth of information on the web about various communities that may be worthy of investment. Provincial government websites publish major projects inventories; city and municipal websites post information about jobs and economic development; and the Canada Mortgage and Housing Corp. publishes vacancy rates. Don't be afraid to spend on your education – the return on your investment is priceless.

Mingle

Get to know others in your field. Go for drinks with your teachers, mentors and fellow students. Meet your pillars at functions: your mortgage broker, real estate accountant and potential partners in a joint venture. Find out who is doing what, where, and how you can get involved.

Do what you love

Once you've immersed yourself in the world of real estate, you may be overwhelmed by all the potential markets and investment strategies. Be the type of investor that suits who you are. While shaping your investment strategy, keep in mind how you love to spend your free time. If you like to garden, buy the overgrown property. If you like to ski, look at resort opportunities. If you are tapped into the resources industries, buy where mining, forestry, or oil and gas companies are expanding. You are more likely to succeed if you focus your energy on what you are passionate about.

Exhaust your fears

Once you have educated yourself and researched what and where you want to buy, it's time to do the actual buying. Fears of unforeseen problems and of not choosing the best property often prevent people from making that first investment. By choosing to buy a small property – making that first step a baby step – these fears and risks are more manageable. Besides, if you have done your due diligence, what have you got to lose in making an offer? Remember that it's an offer with the subjects that make you comfortable. Once your offer is accepted, then you can have second thoughts. What if the economy goes bad? What if I lose tenants? What if the pipes burst? What if, what if, what if? If you are like us, you will spend a few weeks losing sleep, questioning and recalculating the figures and pouring over the home inspection report. By the time the subjects are to be removed – and presuming you have not unearthed any deal breakers – you will be so exhausted from all your research and so familiar with the property that you might as well buy the damn thing! With each new property, the process becomes easier and the fear mitigated.

Spread your risk

To thrive as a real estate investor, it is essential to keep your risk level tolerable. For us, that meant buying a basket of smaller properties in various communities that were driven by differing demographic and economic trends. This takes more work than buying a solitary apartment building in a single location. However, by diversifying into different communities it is easier to sleep should a sawmill close or a town flood. And, should you need to sell, it is always easier to sell a single-family home than it is an apartment building.

Find the win-win

No job is truly worth doing unless you feel you are contributing to a greater cause. Real estate is no different. Whether it's being a good landlord, bringing a house back to its former glory or leaving some money on the table for a first time homebuyer, finding the win-win in all of your endeavors is fundamental to loving and growing in whatever you do.

Do:

- Make your first step into real estate investing a baby step.
- Educate yourself: take courses, join real estate groups and subscribe to real estate newsletters, magazines and newspapers.
- Align your investment strategy with other interests that you are passionate about.
- Keep your risk level tolerable by diversifying your portfolio with different properties in different communities.

Don't:

- Overextend yourself by buying something you can't afford.
- Depend on a rising market to build equity.
- Get too emotionally attached to an investment.

14

Doug Ferguson

Copy Editor - Recreation and Investment Properties section of the *Calgary Herald*

BEST ADVICE: *Those who make a success of recreational real estate, as in life, are the ones who put in the time and do the work.*

One day, when my girlfriend and I were driving on vacation along the California coast near San Francisco, we happened to stop near the beach of a small town.

We were eating some peaches from a farmer's market when a man slowly came by pedaling a bicycle.

Nothing too remarkable about that, except that the bicycle was covered in little flashing lights, it was playing tinny, electronic disco music – and the man looked so relaxed.

I turned to my girlfriend and said: "So, tell me again why we're in the rat race?"

I work as a copy editor for a daily Canadian newspaper in Calgary, Alberta. I usually eat lunch at my desk, and my girlfriend has become resigned to me cancelling our dates.

Relaxed, I am not.

Part of my job involves editing stories about relaxed people buying a dream home in some mountain paradise in B.C., in the tropical rainforest of Costa Rica, or near a golf course in the Arizona desert.

So, it's not unnatural for me to think about how I could have my own version of a bicycle that plays disco. What makes it even more attractive is the thought that while I'm at play, what I bought could be quietly at work, growing in value.

Exactly the opposite is what's happening to that money I'm slaving away to earn.

When I was a kid in the early '70s, I could buy a chocolate bar in Calgary for 10 cents. As of this writing, if I want a bar from the candy machine at work, I have to shell out $1.35.

It's even worse when I consider that I'm actually getting less bar. Compared to my childhood dollars, the buying power of today's money is a fraction of what it was.

But if I buy some recreational real estate, I am potentially purchasing something that will not only hold its own as spending power declines, it will actually increase in value, weathering things like the recent economic storm that hit my mutual funds.

One of my friends likes to vacation at the family retreat his parents bought in the early '60s in B.C. for a few thousand dollars.

What was once a secluded area with no roads has become home to mansions. My friend's family shake their heads at the thought that their property is now worth hundreds of thousands of dollars – that they wouldn't be able to afford their own selling price.

I don't consider myself an expert on recreational real estate. I pay a mortgage on a gray-coloured house in the city and I dream.

That dream has recently become even more tempting as sellers cut their prices to attract gun-shy buyers, and mortgage rates hit new lows.

Yet, I'm still feeling cautious. Maybe I have an idea of the real estate world being something like what I learned as a kid with the board game, Monopoly.

If I can get the dice to roll just right, maybe I could end up on Boardwalk and win the game. But what if the dice roll wrong? Unlike Monopoly, I would lose money in the real world.

But in the real world, those who make a success of recreational real estate, as in life, are the ones who put in the time and do the work – not only making sense things like "timeshares" and "bareland condominiums," but an endless list of projects that, depending on your finances, could be almost anywhere in the world.

One of my friends recently bought some land in a remote part of B.C. Not only is it several hours' drive from Calgary, it's across a lake with no roads. He has to take a boat to get to it.

His land doesn't even have a cabin on it, but he's happy to own a bit of peace and quiet in the mountains that he can slowly improve.

That dream would be a nightmare to the guy I work next to. Not to knock him, but I suspect his idea of roughing it would be owning a place he couldn't drive to in less than a couple of hours – where there was only one bathroom instead of three.

That's why it's first important to figure out what it is you really want – and then get to work to find out what it will take to achieve it.

In order to placate my mom, my dad reluctantly spent a few vacations with her over about 10 years looking at places near the Kootenay and Shuswap lakes in B.C.

He once came close to buying a half-acre lot in the late '70s for about $35,000, only to turn it down. Considering it didn't even have a house on it, it seemed like too much money for a policeman and a nurse raising two kids.

When my parents went back to the area in the '80s, lots, alone, were selling for more than $100,000.

Now, even that price would seem like a steal.

Do:

- Figure out what kind of buyer you are: mostly to enjoy the purchase, or primarily as an investor? The mix of these two will help shape not only your property's location, but what type it will take: condo, fractional, cottage ... new or resale ... and so on.
- Calculate how much free time you have. Remember how long it took to get the flowerbeds and furniture in your new city home

up to snuff? Your recreational property will have time-intensive items, too, plus you'll have to travel to it.

- Ask yourself how much you mind that your property is by itself when you're not there. There could be thieves, forest fires and even squirrels to consider, and insurance required for protection.
- Now that you have a better idea of where, and what, you might buy, nail it down by figuring out what you can afford. Talk to a financial expert, such as your banker, accountant or mortgage specialist. Get pre-approval on a loan.
- Relax; take a deep breath. This may even be worse than buying a car, and no one listens to realtor sales pitches for fun – but think of it as an adventure.

Don't:

- Avoid the bad attitude that all the good properties were taken years ago for peanuts. Today's high price can be tomorrow's bargain.
- Everything looks good on vacation. If you haven't first done your homework, buying on a moment's impulse can mean plenty of long-term repenting.
- Don't just sit there and do nothing, either, because that's a decision, too. Make sure you've studied all the angles before deciding recreational real estate isn't for you.
- Never assume that you'll start making money on your purchase immediately. The smart buyer is often in for the long haul, so plan accordingly.
- You shouldn't ignore the need to leave some wriggle room in your budget for extra or unexpected costs. These can range from home inspection fees to lawyer's bills.

15

Willi Fisher

President Blue Creek Properties
Real Estate Investor

BEST ADVICE: *Build Solid Long Term Relationships.*

During my experience as the owner of a number of chain stores, I developed solid work habits, the ability to build and maintain strong business relationships and the know-how to negotiate a successful sale. However, my largest growth phase as an entrepreneur came later and in a different field: real estate.

All my life I have had the privilege of being surrounded by people that have faith in me. When I wanted to buy a pizza business at the age of 19, my dad – without knowing anything about the business – advanced me $25,000 on faith. To justify that faith, I have always felt that I had to work twice as hard, and that when I made a commitment, it had to be one of absolute trust.

The pizza business was successful and a good stepping stone for future in business. Like most entrepreneurs I was hungry for new challenges and faster growth. I found that in the Dollar Store industry, as owner/operator and as an Area Franchisor for the South West Corner of British Columbia. After 5 years in the business I decided to make a change and sell the territory which gave me some capital to finally invest in real estate.

I had always been interested in real estate, borrowing my mother's credit card at the age of 14 to sign up for a no-money-down real estate course. My first real estate venture was built on a handshake and personal relationships. Three silent partners and I each invested equal amounts into our first partnership. The partnership came together without any kind of written joint venture agreement – which I do NOT recommend – but was successful nonetheless. This is where faith and trust come in.

Some 5 years later – with the same original investors still participating in the deals – I am successful beyond anything I could have imagined. After five years of investing in multi-family and land, my partners and I have participated in roughly $70 million worth of transactions.

Build Your Team

Identify early on the professionals required to execute a deal properly and quickly. These people are your lawyer, accountant, banker or broker and certified due diligence professionals. Never have a team member that you can't trust. As in most things, success is a team effort.

Always have a plan – and an open mind

What's your goal? It's a simple question, but one that requires a thorough answer. In the early stage of any potential transaction, I consider whether or not the deal fits my business model. Is it a short term or long term hold? I have flipped several deals that would have worked long term for a quick profit – before the purchase agreement closed. If you plan on quickly flipping an investment, ensure that you have an alternative strategy planned in case your quick flip falls through. Will the investment have cash flow if I am forced to hold it? Real estate markets are cyclical. They can turn fast. You want to be able to weather any storm.

Develop personal relationships

Getting to know people on a personal level seems to be a dying art.

Make relationship-building a priority. Try to meet face to face with people. It takes more effort than a simple phone call, but can be enjoyable and pay unexpected dividends down the road. For example, one of my business relationships started over drinks and without a business deal in mind. The relationship evolved into a joint venture that generated us a profit of $1 million. You never know where a great deal may pop up.

Get it in writing

While personal trust is a major factor in relationships with partners, buyers and sellers, I have also learned that its best to reinforce trust with a piece of paper. Property managers must be checked out and joint venture agreements and all other deals, including buy offers, must be in writing.

Remember: IN WRITING. This is a big one. In my rookie years, not following this simple rule cost me several deals worth many a Harvard education. Never, ever, discuss a deal you are negotiating before signing a contract. Include subject clauses, get it signed, and then you can talk about it. I have had good deals slip through my fingers by not inking it with a realtor or friend.

Treat your investors like gold

If you want to quickly grow your real estate portfolio you need two kinds of investors: a joint venture partner and an end user, or buyer.

The joint venture partners can help raise capital and sniff out deals. It's vital that their personal and business traits – risk tolerance, expectations of returns, exit strategies – are aligned with yours. In your rookie days, you will have to put more chips on the table than your partners. That will change once you have proven yourself. Remember that investors want to play with a proven performer.

I like to develop long term relationships with my end users. Buyers can help you court new investors if their experience with you is a positive one.

A general rule: always under-promise and over-deliver. The delivery will look that much more impressive in the face of risk.

Do your homework

No matter what type of investment it is, always thoroughly familiarize yourself with your candidate investment before signing on the dotted line. This includes physically visiting the property. Also consider the property's surrounding environment. What is the outlook for long-term employment there? Who is the local government and what's it like to deal with? Is the area growing or declining in population? I will never buy any property, no matter what the price, if it's in an area where the population is declining.

Be passionate

My definition of passion is: "I can't fall asleep because I am thinking about it." I believe that you should love whatever it is you spend your time doing. If you don't, quit! Ask anyone who is in love, or sky dives, or thinks about real estate in bed. All they want to talk about is what excites them. Embrace your passions. Think about them, long for them. Not only will you be more successful, you'll have more fun.

Think big

There is a saying that you are your only obstacle. To knock down that obstacle, do something everyday that scares you. Get comfortable living outside your comfort zones. Sure you will have a few sleepless nights, but the best experiences have an edge to them. The best holidays are off the beaten path; and the best deals are found outside your comfort zones.

Do:

- Embrace your passions.
- To knock down that obstacle, do something everyday that scares you.
- Physically visit every property.
- Treat your investors like gold.
- Get it in writing.

Don't:

- Buy in an area where the population is declining.
- Have a team member that you can't trust.
- Never, ever, discuss a deal you are negotiating before signing a contract.

16

Lori-Ann & Lawrence Keenan

Owners of C.S.L.I. – Canadian as a Second Language Institute. C.S.L.I. was the first school to be recognized with the Consumers Choice Award.

BEST ADVICE: *Timing is everything when buying your own business space.*

Most people don't realize that McDonald's and Starbucks are really in the business of real estate. By owning your own space you have the benefit of capital gains as real estate prices increase while having greater control over your business' financial destiny, as well as a buffer when times may get tough in your market. Further, lenders generally are not keen to lend on a small business itself but will against a solid asset, like commercial property. Besides, why rent when for the same operating costs (or less) you can own? After all, through rent you already pay for your landlord's property taxes, overheads and mortgage (it all just comes as one monthly bill) so why not just buy the place and pay the bank direct!

So much simpler.

Getting there can be tricky but we now know that **timing is everything**. Here's our story where we made this possible **with no money down but using abundant creativity, something having no money gives you.**

My wife Lori-Ann and I worked hard slowly developing a very successful private language school for adult foreign students. We named it C.S.L.I. Canadian as a Second Language Institute, English classes with a unique Canadian flavour and with the winning motto *"Uniting the World with English"*. Like most businesses we struggled through our early years, learning the typical valuable but expensive lessons that young enthusiastic companies make, especially when dealing with landlords. Rents were our greatest expense. We learnt quickly that zero wasn't where a business stopped trading: we flew way past that to owe tens of thousands of dollars and survived only because our first landlord went out of business before we did. But our real opportunity came at a time when we were most vulnerable: when it appeared our next landlord had no interest in renewing our quickly expiring lease, and we were forced to look elsewhere.

And urgently.

This was in 2000 and real estate had been in the doldrums in British Columbia. One saving grace was that I had been an avid student of real estate, following the strategies of such gurus as Ozzie Jurock, which helped develop a contrarian mentality in times of pessimism. Despite this we were still relatively broke and with a business on a very short lease.

Few leasing options were available until we came across a Concord Pacific development in Yaletown with over 10,000 sq ft on the corner of Nelson & Cambie Streets: three commercial strata units on the ground floor with great visibility. The Concord Pacific Group is largely credited for transforming Vancouver City's inner core through creating quality living communities.

No school can normally afford the luxury of a ground floor location in downtown Vancouver! Who can afford that? The developer's challenge was that the commercial market had been beaten senseless by a less than sympathetic provincial government, and this office/retail space was without easy access to parking (Nelson Street is a busy thoroughfare), making it unattractive to many. What added to the seller's motivation was that despite the sold-out condos above (to a burgeoning new market of inner-city yuppies), the building appeared dark, and empty from the street due to this unfinished, unloved ground floor area.

Opportunities started to emerge once our vision took hold: our first god-send was a remarkable gentleman named Dan Ulinder, the developer's then VP of Marketing, who in an earlier life, was a professor at the University of B.C. It was to Dan that I first sang our story of how we could enrich their Yaletown community with a place of learning. He loved the idea and was willing to negotiate a lease to bring us there. To Dan and to Terry Hui I remain eternally grateful, as I know without this personal connection our dream would never have materialized. Our joint challenge turned out to be that Concord were not in the business of leasing, and after weeks of to-and thro' negotiating we would end up with them insisting that we buy the place instead. How absurd! We never had that sort of money. Did we? With a motivated vendor there had to be a way...

Of course C.S.L.I. couldn't qualify for a commercial mortgage, especially one in the millions and each time we were rejected our vendors would send us back for another attempt with the banks before finally introducing us to their own financiers who, somewhat reluctantly agreed to back us. How could they disappoint their largest developer client? With some solid advice from negotiator Tom Matzen, we structured a large vendor second mortgage in the form of a two-year balloon payment, along with early access to the property to begin improvements plus a cash-back of the original deposit to cover these costs. The building was purchased as a shell and required extensive outfitting. The gamble of course would be that if we didn't complete, all our investment would go back to the vendor, with all covered by personal guarantees. And even if we did complete, the deal was contingent on our new business being a success and real estate prices increasing, otherwise refinancing of the mortgage and repayment of the balloon payment would be impossible. Recent economic times clearly show the downside of such risks.

Did I tell you it was a tough real estate market? This had affected the housing market as well and after sorely missing out on a wonderful foreclosure opportunity for a condo on Stanley Park, Lori-Ann and I lucked out a month later by purchasing our dream home for half of the original listed price in West Vancouver's British Properties from an even more motivated seller. The deal was done the day the vendor was to leave for overseas for good, using our credit card limit to cover the deposit and closing costs. We had been looking for years to buy but the timing just wasn't right. Until now.

Our home purchase happened 60 days before this commercial opportunity but it was sufficient time to have our residence re-appraised to create additional equity to invest into the school deal. Remember this additional mortgage was a business expense to CSLI too. And this is where timing played an even bigger part: with a weak BC economy contractors were readily available, flexible and willing to negotiate terms. 30 days credit in fact, including supplies, which allowed us to recover all of the GST taxes from the property purchase and improvements, in time to make partial payments.

Needless to say that business grew and the real estate market boomed with an invigorated new government, and we were fortunate enough to restructure the commercial mortgage to a more manageable one. In time, this deal alone made us millionaires with most being made on the day we bought. This was a huge opportunity but one which could have easily buried us. But it was a risk worth taking. Buying at an optimum time, an opportune time, creates the best insurance.

Do:

• **Add the human touch to your deal:** Share your spectacular dream with the vendor as it may support their own. We asked our vendor to help create a centre of learning in their community. At least you will stand out from other deals, and remember the vendor's best deal is not always the top price. I once bought an aging home from an aging woman on the promise that I would return it to its original beauty (the house I mean). I was outbid in price but still got the house. I fulfilled my promise and had her over for tea before she passed on.

- **Maximize leverage:** Nothing provides access to capital like real estate. Be creative and structure deals to take full advantage of those you are working with, negotiating vendor finance or using their credibility to access funding. Help the vendor to solve his problem, especially during challenging times. Remember they still get to hold the property as collateral so it's up to you to do what you are good at: your business.

- **Timing is everything:** Isn't it amazing how perception of the real estate market and the economy can change so dramatically? This provides incredible opportunity, not just with vendors and competitors, but also with bankers, contractors, city and government policies.

- **Surround yourself with success**: It's harder on your own. Most successful people I know are only pleased to share experiences **in their area of expertise** and the best of them consider it an obligation. Yet few ask, and worse, listen to those who have least to offer. Accept responsibility for everything that happens to you and celebrate the good. I owe much of my success to those around me especially my amazing wife Lori-Ann.

- **Credit is king:** As long as you can manage it! As shown, credit doesn't need to have a cost, and can also be leveraged. Our deal allowed us to, in effect, use a little credit card credit to leverage a multi-million dollar deal.

- **Buy is best:** We have rented and leased apartments, homes and commercial properties before but buying is so much easier. Not only do you have greater control over your life and a business with less surprises, it is far less complicated. Just compare the size of an actual lease document versus the contract of purchase/sale for the same property. The first has more conditions, terms and is definitely harder to understand and to maintain and that's why it costs more in legal fees. If the property is yours, you may do as you wish, within legal reason, and without requiring consent. Commercial strata title makes this much easier for smaller business. We are grateful to be in a country where law protects property more than anywhere else in the world.

17

Peter Meribian
and Astrid Gottfried

Owners and directors of Turning Point Investments,
a real estate investment company. They provide
investors with easy ownership of fully managed
investment properties with excellent returns.

BEST ADVICE: *Buy – as long as it cash flows.*

The best real estate advice came to us, like a jigsaw puzzle, in
bits and pieces from many smart investors. We don't pretend
that we *"got it"* right away because putting a puzzle together, particularly one of this magnitude, takes time, but once we put all the
pieces together we saw the big picture.

**To ride out any market, a property needs to provide you with
three returns - equity growth through appreciation, equity growth
through principal reduction, and most importantly, immediate
monthly return through cash flow** (an ongoing surplus of income
over and above costs). As long as it cash flows, it will ensure the
ability to ride out any market cycle with the added bonus of a tenant to pay off the mortgage over time and essentially buy the
property for you.

This cash flow is a form of passive income, essentially money
that you don't need to work for. It supplements or replaces your
full-time job and allows you to lead the lifestyle you desire.

It doesn't matter if the property values go down (although in
Canada, over time they have always gone up) as long as you are still
cash-flow positive. This economic position will allow you to sail

through any real-estate storm and safely reach your equity harbour. If you keep in mind your destination, by applying simple real estate investment rules, you can persevere and make it to the big reward in the end - equity growth, your financial nest egg.

As long as you have a system in place, no matter where the market is you'll be able to sleep at night. If the market is down, you are able to stick it through. Downturns end. They always do. If you plan your purchases wisely, when the market heats up, your bank account follows suit. **Here are ten simple rules of analyzing properties for maximum return.**

Do:

- **Make sure it cash flows.** If the property doesn't cash flow, don't buy it. Not only would it be a financial drain, you would give up the benefit of adding a net-positive amount to your gross income. This net-positive addition to your income is what makes it possible to borrow more money from the banks to acquire more properties down the road.
- **Don't choose a location just out of convenience.** If the market in your backyard does not show the economic strength and cash flow you need, consider investing in a different location. Canada is a large country with many sub-markets, some performing much better than others.
- **Invest in a diverse economy that is creating jobs.** Economic strength is key. Current real estate markets cannot tell you what the future market will do. Only the economic strength and indicators provide you with this information. Some of these indicators include average wages, wage increases, disposable income, inward migration, housing affordability, and vacancy rates.
- **Remove your emotion from the equation.** "Investing" in real estate should be dispassionate. It is all about the numbers and fundamentals. Remember, this is an investment; your plan is to rent, not live there.

- **Cater to the rental market.** Always bear in mind the type of tenant you want to live on your property and the type of home they are accustomed to renting. Never over renovate; often fresh coat of paint and good scrubbing will suffice. Never personalize; cater to the masses by using neutral colors and design.

- **Screen your tenants carefully.** A tenant will make or break your investment. Be sure to carefully investigate a potential tenant by checking references and doing a credit check. Never rent to an unscreened tenant just because you need to have the place rented by the end of the month. Treat the renters as your customers - after all, they are paying for your investment.

- **Rent the garage/ parking spot.** Garages and other storage areas can provide a great deal of added revenue. Often tenants will rent a house for the same amount regardless of whether it has a garage or not. Why not rent it to someone else and fetch the extra income?

- **Manage the property manager.** You may have the best property manager in place but no one will have the same vested interest in its performance as an owner. Communication is the key. Make sure you are aware of what is happening to your property on a regular basis. Make it a team effort to come up with strategies to retain tenants while maximizing rent.

- **Time your purchases and sales wisely.** If the circumstances allow it, buy when a real estate bottom has been hit and an uptrend is on the way. You sell when that particular real estate market has hit its peak and a downtrend is being established.

- **Take on a partner.** Be honest with yourself. Do you want to be an active or a passive investor? If you don't have the time and/ or expertise, take on an experienced partner that does. It will save you a lot of grief and provide you with a higher return on your investment with little or no work. Weekend warriors are often first to fall.

18

Rob Osmond

Founder of the musical group, Pennan Brae
(www.pennanbrae.com), which has received airplay
on 120 Radio Stations in Canada & the U.S.

BEST ADVICE: *Buy what you like.*

My 1st Purchase: It was a snowy day when I pulled into Kimberley, a small Rocky Mountain town in the East Kootenay Region of British Columbia. I rented a car from the airport and made the twenty kilometre sojourn to the city gates. It was like some type of hallowed ground for me; I had an image of the city and what it might be like and now it was coming to fruition before my eager eyes. Snow-laden trees roadside bent under their heavy burdens, multicoloured metal roofs echoed the area's mining past and billowing smoke spiralled ambitiously upward from rows of chimneys. Instantly I was charmed.

Why had I come to this peaceful alpine center? For one reason; to find an attractive piece of real estate I could fall in love with.

I checked into a hotel located smack dab in the center of town. It was retro 1970s-style inside, but that bothered me little; for from my window I was able to observe the comings and goings in all four directions from the main intersection. Best of all, I was directly across the street from the real estate office where I would be going the next day.

That night I plugged in my laptop and snagged a wireless signal wafting somewhere in the midst. I reviewed the listings for Single Family Homes and checked if anything new had popped up during my commute. I was strictly interested in this type of dwelling.

I had nothing against condos, except, well, the condo fees. Plus, a patch of grass in the backyard to call one's own is always appealing. As for big apartment complexes, I had little capacity to crunch such big numbers. I still do. As for duplexes, three's and four's; baby steps, folks! This was my first purchase; I had to learn to walk before doing cartwheels and somersaults.

As a side note, no new listings for Single Family Homes had been submitted.

That was fine, for I previously had created a shortlist of properties which I found appealing, both from a financial and aesthetic perspective. For admittedly, I can be a sucker for aesthetics.

Thus, I trudged out ungrudgingly into the chilly dusk and put a face to some of those intriguing pictures I had seen on Multiple Listing Services for so long. And some of the houses complimented those photos quite well while others were less flattering. In fact, there were even a few which were quite unrecognizable!

After covering some good ground, I grabbed a hearty dinner, returned to my room and snuck under the covers. I had an early morning meeting with the realtor whom I was meeting for the first time and I wanted to be well-rested and ready for the education which lay ahead.

Dave (the realtor) was a warm guy and we quickly struck a friendship. We reviewed and compared our perspective shortlist of properties and eliminated a few immediately while highlighting others with potential. We then set forth on walkthroughs of notable ones of interest. Exciting!

The process was an eye-opener for this rookie. In some houses, you knew immediately they weren't for you. They typically were unkempt, unclean and unlevel!

The next step-up was middle-of-the-road-type properties; they were better maintained but lacked any unique, amenity-type features (such as waterfront or view) I sought something really special;

a property I'd be passionate about.

So we maintained our quest. We explored a two-story grey rancher, but nope; not a fan of leaky basements.

Next we entered a snazzy log chalet; it sure was pretty, but was also way out of my price range.

And then, like Goldilocks optimistically searching for something 'just right', low and behold there it stood before me; a charming red-roofed bungalow with a detached garage also bearing a red metal roof! The home sat squat on an ample 75x95 square foot lot. My dream palace was 835 square feet on the main floor (hardwood, by the way) with an equivalent-sized footprint in the half-finished basement. It was not The Trump Tower or the Taj Mahal, but it was exquisite and beautiful to me.

To further elaborate, the feature I loved most was the rushing river which ran rapid along the rear lot line. It provided a wonderful, soothing sound, especially this time of year when mountain snow began its melt, empowering the water's flow.

And would I want to buy this place? Heck, I was already wanting to move in. Fortunately, the best of both worlds lay before my enthusiastic eyes.

It just so happened to be this property's first day on the market. And during this stretch, the Kootenay area's real estate market was starting to heat up. Thus, though it was still the comparably quiet early Spring market, this property already was attracting a lot of attention, with other besotted buyers driving by and scribbling down contact information from the 'For Sale' sign firmly planted in the soil out front.

In that moment, I was clear what I had to do. For the purpose of my trip was not sightseeing, and I was ready to write. I thus put pen to paper and, in a nutshell, wrote:

Dear Seller, my offer; full asking price, no conditions.' (PS: dear readers, please use conditions; I was young and a touch brazen then...though I'm pleased how it worked out!)

We offered at 9 in the morning and requested an answer by 5

that evening.

The result? Offer received!

I was ecstatic to celebrate that wonderful event in my life with Dave.

In that moment, the little red-roofed house with the matching red-roofed garage became my pride and joy. And know what? Years later, it still is.

Do:

- Fall in love with your first purchase.
- A lot of research before you go house hunting.
- Hire a quality realtor that understands your needs
- Take action.

19

Liesl and Kevin Staley

Liesl and Kevin Staley are a 30-something couple with shiny new Masters degrees who work in post-secondary education in BC.

BEST ADVICE: *To start, decide precisely what you are ... an investor or a flipper. Clarify your objectives.*

First time investing can feel a little intimidating in the beginning. As a young professional couple, we questioned whether investing was a smart idea at all.

We worried about risking our savings and taking out another mortgage. If we had extra finances, why not use it to pay down our current mortgage? We were concerned about finding the right property to invest in. How far would we need to travel to get something in our price range? How would we know if we were getting a good deal? Then we knew we'd have the ordeal of finding "good" tenants and maintaining a property from afar. With both of us being academics, rather than handy or businesslike, these were real concerns.

But we couldn't help getting excited about the idea of investing. We saw that real estate had the potential of bringing in a better return on our investment than our measly 2.5% "high-interest" savings account. We could keep a property short term and bring in a chunk of money to apply to our next home purchase or another investment. Or, we could keep it longer and guarantee ourselves some regular passive income. If we kept the property until after the 25-year mortgage was paid off, whatever money came from tenants would be like free money! Either way, we could not pass up the opportunity.

Where to start?

To start, you need to decide what to invest in and how much money you want to put into it. Do you want to get a property that is priced low or needs fixing, do some work on it and resell it – in essence, flipping it to make a profit? Or do you want to find a property you can sit on for a while and let time increase the value of it if nothing else? It also depends on how much risk you are willing to take. In our case, as people who generally avoid risk, we decided on finding something we could afford, where the rent would pretty much pay for the mortgage. For us to feel secure, that meant looking for out-of-town older residential apartments.

Finding a property

Finding an area was our first challenge. We looked at small towns with properties in our price range, and tried to locate places where big companies were moving to, growth was projected, and vacancy rates were low. We chose a small town up north which had opened a ski resort and had an airport close by. The only problem... it was 12 hours away!

This meant we had to get our ducks in a row before visiting. We had to get pre-approved with a good mortgage broker who could act from afar if necessary. We had to do our research – check out what had been selling, what the average prices were, what units were renting. And finding a good realtor was essential.

One stumbling block was in remembering that the property we were buying was not for us to live in. We wasted some time getting distracted by nicer places rather than what we could afford. On the other hand, it was still important to do the work to find a unit that would be easy to rent at a decent rate. So, we spent a lot of time understanding the area, looking for an accessible building with a great location and amenities nearby. We viewed a lot of units, made a few offers, and did our due diligence – read the minutes, walked the suites, got a home inspector in, talked to neighbours, and collected as much information as we could. Eventually, we landed on our first investment property – a 600 square foot unit on the ground floor of a low-rise building which was walking distance to town centre and a short drive from the ski hill.

The real money involved

Even though we had bought our current residence, we were still surprised by all the costs we hadn't anticipated with our investment property. In the end, the rent we received did not cover our costs and we had to subsidize it by about $100/month when the suite was rented, and $500 when it was not. Think about how much you are able to put into this at the beginning and throughout. At the outset, consider not only down payment, mortgage, and legal fees, but any potential upgrades you may want to do to attract a higher rent. On an on-going basis, remember you'll need to cover strata fees, maintenance, insurance, property taxes, and we found city utilities in a small town astronomical compared to our residence in the city. In addition, don't forget to set aside money for emergencies – months when your unit sits vacant when a tenant bails, replacing appliances, or special levies. And don't forget about capital gains tax when you sell.

Finding & managing tenants from afar

To attract a good rental income, you want to make the unit look as good as possible.

This means getting it properly cleaned, painted, and perhaps replacing cupboards or appliances that are outdated. This can be easier said than done when you are not in the same city as your property. We lucked out by finding that the building caretaker's sister could clean our suite between tenants, and our realtor knew a good painter and was willing to manage the painting process for a small fee.

Although we could have directly managed the tenants, we decided to get some help as we were so far away. During the four years we owned the suite, we had three different rental experiences – a rental pool, and two different property managers. In the rental pool, several units pooled their rents together and then split it proportionally (by square feet), regardless of whether units were rented or not. This allowed for a regular income stream, but in the end felt frustrating to those of us whose units were always rented. We went our separate ways and eventually found a solution that worked for us – an independent property manager. He charged us 10% of the rent, but found us a tenant who never left. He also had excellent relationships with service providers, including a plumber, electrician, and carpenter, so when anything went wrong, it was quickly rectified.

Although having a property manager was an extra cost, it gave us the peace of mind that our property was being looked after. Other ideas include befriending some of the locals who can check in on your place, making regular visits to the town if possible, and being on the strata council. Above all, we found that one of the best methods to ensure that our unit was looked after was to show extra appreciation to everyone involved. We sent chocolates to the caretaker and the property manager and even the tenant!

Selling your property

In the end, no matter how pleasant your situation is, you are still looking to make money on your investment. Once you've bought, it's important to keep an eye on the market there, and ask your realtor to send you regular listings of similar properties, so you can follow the trends and consider timing for when you want to sell. Keep an eye on when there is little on the market, or when places are selling quickly. When the price is right, it might be time to sell. For us, as we saw prices rising, we allowed our place to sit vacant, got it repainted again, and put it on the market. We were delighted to sell and made quite a good profit, something that never could have happened in four years with a savings account!

Overall, buying and selling our first investment property was a scary but exhilarating process. We felt a steep learning curve every step of the way, but benefited from the expertise of fellow investors in our building and our realtor and property manager. We are very aware we are not "business-people", but this experience gave us the confidence that we can buy and sell real estate. In the end, we made a chunk of money (on an $8,000 investment, we cleared $35,000) that we never would have if we didn't take the risk, and look forward to taking the plunge again.

Do:

- Decide precisely what to invest in.
- Research the town you invest in – collect as much information as you can.
- Get yourself pre-approved, so you can move fast when an opportunity arises.
- Consider not only the down payment, mortgage, and legal fees, but any potential upgrades you may want to do to attract a higher rent.
- Make your apartment as appealing as possible to tenants.

Don't:

- Forget to keep an eye on the market, and ask your realtor to send you regular listings of similar properties.
- Forget all costs: strata fees, maintenance, insurance, property taxes (with no homeowner's grant), and utilities.

20

Bryan Woolley

President of Maverick Real Estate Corporation, a specialist real estate project sales and marketing firm that currently operates in Western Canada and the United States.

BEST ADVICE: *Purchase Early in the Pre-Sale Process.*

I've been in the new home development, marketing and sales business since 1992. During that time I've made money from owning new condominiums and I've watched thousands of other people make profits with new condominiums in both up and down markets. I've also worked with many developers and have seen some of the things that the best ones do that the other ones don't. Here are my tips for you:

Profiting from Purchasing New Condominiums

A. In Any Market:

1. **Take Advantage of Pricing Mistakes** – Pricing isn't an exact science and some people are better at it than others. If you're astute and understand what sells in your market, you can often make money by knowing what is underpriced and buying it, then holding for the long term or reselling for a profit. Things to watch for are:

• **View premiums** – some views are worth more than others. Sometimes the developers miss it and in most cases they don't have enough of a premium on the best views.

- **Balcony or deck premiums** – some markets will pay huge premiums for a great deck or balcony. We've seen developers under price some decks by as much as $250,000. I know someone who bought a suite with a huge deck and immediately turned around and assigned his contract for a $200,000 profit.
- **Directional premiums** – sun in the evening, afternoon or morning. Or very little sun at all. What sells best in your market?
- **No recognition of plan design** – all other things being equal, you should have to pay a higher price for a great plan. Many developers miss this.
- **Is the whole building off** – sometimes the developer just prices the whole building too low. If you've been paying attention you can profit from this.

B. In a Stable or Buyers Market:

1. Buy a Great Deal and Rent or Resell – When it's a Buyers market the power is in your hands. Negotiate hard to get a great deal from a developer that wants to close his units out. Buy a foreclosure or purchase an assignment of contract from someone who can't or doesn't want to close. Some people will let you take over their deposit for free and pay you to take their contract because they can't, or don't want to close and don't want to mess up their credit rating. Don't be bashful when you make your offer. You can then:

- **Resell** – sell for all cash at a profit, or consider taking a small mortgage back for part of your profit if you get a better price.
- **Rent, then sell** – If you can find a condominium that will provide positive cash flow you can hold it long term or rent it until the prices move up and sell then. If your condo is in the right location you can rent it on a furnished basis for a substantial

premium. I know a woman that rents out her downtown condominium on a weekly basis and makes substantial positive cash flow. When prices move up significantly you can make big profits.

C. In a Rising or Sellers Market:

1. Leverage on Your Deposit – If you purchase on a pre-sale basis you typically have to pay a deposit of 5% to 25% of the purchase price. Ideally you want to keep your deposit as low as possible. If you purchase a $400,000 condominium that will close in two years with a deposit of $40,000 (10%) and the market goes up $150,000, you have substantial equity if you choose to close or if you can assign your contract to someone else for a $150,000 profit. On a $40,000 deposit a $150,000 profit equals a simple return of 375% over two years or 187.5% per year. During the run up of prices in the mid to late 2000's many people made phenomenal gains on presale condos some in the hundreds of thousands of dollars per unit.

2. Purchase Early in the Pre-Sale Process – If you know someone or are just aggressive and diligent enough to get in on the developer's family and friends event or the early events that are typically held before the project is released to the public you can often get a better deal. In some cases it's just lower deposits, in others it's lower prices and some incentives. Developers want to secure some early sales to show the project is a success and will raise prices regularly as demand continues, particularly after they've hit their pre-sale target for bank financing. We've moved prices up 10 times in a day and someone coming in early might save from $10,000 to over $750,000 depending on the unit selling.

3. Use the Concentric Circle Theory – Pricing tends to be on a relative basis to other areas. Here is a simplistic example, but it will illustrate the concept. Let's say that downtown hi-rise con-dos are selling for $700 psf. In the next ring of communities, pricing for similar product may be at $625 psf and then $550 psf for the third ring of communities and so on. There are locations that com-mand the highest prices and if people can't or won't pay those prices, then to some degree they move to the next ring of communities at a lower price, trading off location for price. If the price rose $100 psf in downtown, then ultimately the whole market would re-price again so that it made some relative sense. In theory it works. In practice, it never works perfectly. If you pay attention to pricing you'll see the price movement in several communities in action. You can make money by buying in a community where the prices haven't re-set, but knowing that they will if you wait for it. Then you can sell and take a profit.

4. Know Replacement Cost – sometimes when the market is moving up quickly, land costs, construction costs and all the com-ponents of development move up as well. If you're paying attention you can make huge money. For example. When construction costs moved up in Calgary in approximately 2005/2006 so that for a de-veloper to build a concrete hi-rise meant that they had to sell at $500 psf plus to make money, there were some projects in Edmonton that were still selling at just over $200 psf. They weren't paying attention. You could go to Edmonton and buy almost anything be-cause they were still selling based on their old land costs and construction contracts rather than what it would cost today. Ulti-mately prices jumped significantly in Edmonton as the costs came in line with Calgary. Some people made a relatively quick $100 to $250 psf in profit by buying in Edmonton at the right time.

5. Watch for Big Price Jumps – a big price jump in a project in one area is an early sign that other projects in that area will follow suit and that it will move to other areas as well. For ex-ample, if the market of hi-rise condominiums is at $500 psf and someone brings a new building on at $650 psf, then all the buildings in the area that are already selling start to increase their prices. And new buildings will start at $650 psf or higher, all things being equal. But, not all developers are watching closely and it may take them a few days or weeks or even months to change their pricing. Just by paying attention you can buy into a project or projects that haven't moved their prices yet and win as they do.

6. Buy Existing Condos Near a New Development That Will Move Prices – This works best when there hasn't been much recent development in a specific area. If your resale condos are selling at $250 psf and a new project is pricing its units at $600 psf it will drag the price of the existing condos with it. So as the new project starts to sell the existing condos may move to $300 psf, then $350 psf and ultimately to $400 psf or more. There is a new measure of value provided by the new project and everything tends to price off that. We had an expensive project in the Denver Colorado market. It was selling at an average price of $1,100 per sq. ft. A nearby older project jumped $150 per sq. ft. the day we started selling. If you'd bought quickly you could have made a quick profit.

Do:

- Take Advantage of Pricing Mistakes
- Use the Concentric Circle Theory
- Rent it on a furnished basis for a substantial premium
- Purchase early
- Buy Existing Condos Near a New Development

Don't:

- Assume that all premiums are the same
- Buy without knowing the replacement cost
- Underestimate deck premiums
- Don't be bashful when you make your offer

21

Michael Wintemute

Manager, Re/Max Sea To Sky Real Estate, Whistler

BEST ADVICE: *Capitalize on the appreciation and revenue generation possibilities of recreational real estate.*

Most of us dream about spending our golden years in a vacation or retirement home. How about a bungalow shaded by palm trees on a white-sand beach that leads to a clear blue ocean? Or perhaps a log cabin nestled in snow-covered evergreens, a warm fire burning in the river-rock fireplace? For the past fifteen years, I have been fortunate enough to call such a place home.

Up the mountain from the Southern Coast of B.C. you'll find Whistler, the top-rated ski resort in North America. For me, it's a place of both work – I'm in the real estate business – and play.

When I was growing up, recreational property was a place for families to spend time together away from the city. An aunt and uncle of mine had a cabin on Keats Island across from Gibson's Landing, which is a short ferry ride from Vancouver. I don't think they gave any thought to capital appreciation or how to generate revenue from their property – it was purely a lifestyle investment.

While lifestyle remains a big consideration for recreational property buyers, capital appreciation and revenue generation have perhaps become even more salient factors than lifestyle. Population growth and increased demand have greatly driven up the value of recreational property. But recreational real estate is a strange animal. Zoning laws, by-laws, and other regulations are applied differently in each resort and municipality. Value becomes even more of an issue in such resort municipalities as Whistler, where regulations limit development.

Here are a few of the many questions that need asking when buying recreational property:

- Do you need to produce revenue in order for your purchase to make financial sense?
- What are the zoning issues, if any, regarding the short-term rental of your property?
- What tax implications are there if it is an income-producing property?
- Does the property meet the guidelines required in order to get adequate insurance?

Resorts, timeshares, timeshare points, tenth-shares, quarter-shares, condominiums, hotel condominiums and single-family homes are among the most attractive recreational real estate properties to invest in. So how do you decide what is right for you? Every buyer must ask themselves, firstly, how much can they afford to invest? Secondly, with consideration towards commute times, work schedules and so forth, how often will you use the property? Usage will help in determining the type of property that suits you. If your ability to use the property is limited, then your money may best be put toward a rentable suite or one that is maintained by a grounds manager.

Timeshares and timeshare points:

Traditionally, timeshare buyers are designated a particular week or multiple weeks in their resort condominium.

The timeshare will include such costs as property taxes, strata fees and other incidental expenses. If you make adequate use of your timeshare, you won't worry much about costs. However, if you don't use your allotted time, the additional costs become a burden. In recent years, timeshares have lost much of their lustre and become difficult to sell, particularly if its owner's time allotment is during the off-season. It can be difficult to find real estate agents willing to help unload a timeshare because the commission on the relatively small properties is not very enticing. Timeshare points have become a popular alternative, as they can usually be traded for time at other resorts, allowing for more travel options and less commitment to a single location. In any event, unless you buy your timeshare or timeshare points from the resale market, you will likely experience a loss at sale time.

Tenth-shares and quarter-shares:

Recreational real estate has become more affordable and accessible to the masses thanks to the proliferation of tenth-shares, quarter-shares and other fractional real estate. But these properties tend not to appreciate much, have high management fees, and cost more per square foot than comparable properties that are not parceled into shares. In quarter-shares, the time slot during Christmas is only available to each owner every fourth year.

Condominiums:

While some recreational condominium agreements allow owners to rent out their units month to month, many don't. And most condos are not zoned to allow for nightly rental. These restrictions are to preserve the residential status of the building and area. While condos that have no rental restrictions tend to be very popular, additional considerations and hassles, such as noise and property damage, come into play when you rent out your suite.

Condominium-hotels:

These are typically operated by hotel chains like Best Western International Inc. and Hilton Hotels Corp., and usually include policies that restrict owners from occupying their suite for more than 120 days each year. Condo-hotel suites are attractive to overseas investors because they are fully managed. Revenues generated by condo-hotels are usually pooled and divided equally regardless of how often your particular suite is occupied. These properties have hotel management contracts associated with them, so make sure to understand the management fees. And to determine if the investment indeed makes economic sense, take a good look at net revenue the hotel generates. Also be aware of tax complications that come with owning a property that is both commercial and residential.

Townhomes:

There is always a strong demand for townhomes in resort communities, as they offer large space without the hassle of property maintenance. Some resorts are zoned to allow townhouse owners to rent their units nightly. But, again, there can be issues that arise when renting your suite to strangers. A common misperception is that the value of townhouse increases if it is zoned to allow nightly rentals. Not true.

Single family homes:

As with townhomes, there is no relationship between the value of a single-family home and zoning that allows nightly rentals. Ownership of a single family home in a resort community usually requires someone to manage the property when the owner is not there. Some insurance companies even require owners to provide proof that their home is being maintained while they are absent.

Like any slice of real estate, recreational property should provide you with years of enjoyment and capital appreciation. Typically, single-family homes, townhomes, condominiums and other properties that are without restrictive-use clauses or fractional ownership agreements offer the best investment opportunities. However, fractional ownership and condo-hotel properties may suit your lifestyle and pocketbook. Whatever you decide, ask many questions and do plenty of homework before signing.

Do:

- Think of recreational property not only as a lifestyle investment, but one that can offer capital appreciation and revenue generation.
- Remember that zoning laws, by-laws and other regulations vary from municipality to municipality.
- Before buying, consider how much you can afford to invest and how often you will be using your recreational property. These factors greatly influence what types of recreational property suit you.
- Many recreational properties include management contracts, so make sure to understand the management fees.
- Renting out your recreational property to strangers creates additional responsibilities, so make sure you are prepared to play the landlord.

Don't:

- Get locked into a long term rental contract as it can make re-selling more difficult.
- If income is your number one priority leave your emotions at home and focus on revenue first.
- Purchasing revenue properties can have GST implications. Make sure you get the GST position before you buy.
- Like any city parking is always an issue. Don't purchase a property that doesn't have dedicated parking.

22

Shell Busey

The HouseSmart Guy

BEST ADVICE: *In home improvement - use a professional at all times.*

Why move when you can improve? Indeed, the demand for home improvements is endless, with billions of dollars spent annually in North America. I've seen many ups and downs in the home improvement business in the last 45 years, but two things remain constant: the appetite for skilled tradespeople and proven products.

When the real estate market is strong, so is the renovation market. In a strong economy, people tend to invest in such major upgrades as new bathrooms, kitchens and finished basements. But demand for home improvement doesn't stall when the economy falters. In an economic downturn, homeowners tend to stay home, spending more on improving the quality of their home life and less on luxury items like travel and vehicles. Renovations can range anywhere from a $10,000 bathroom upgrade to a $300,000 addition.

Appraisers are finding that homeowners are staying in their current residence as the cost and affordability of homeownership skyrockets. Mortgage brokers and lenders are ordering appraisal assignments that reflect two values: the "as is" value and the "as if renovations are completed" value.

A chain reaction of events is set off when a homeowner wants to upgrade their new or existing home. For starters, there are renovation products to buy, and carpenters, plumbers, electricians, landscape designers and project managers to hire.

Communication among all parties involved is fundamental to a renovation's success. Homeowners are faced with questions like: How much should I spend on renovations? What will be the return on my investment? Into what project should I direct my dollars?

Over the years, professional networks sprouted up across Canada that became trusted to accomplish renovations properly. In the 1960s, there was Blue Army. Later, there was Mr. Build and Mr. Renovator. For a time, even BCAA, an automobile advisory network, had a renovation services network for its members. The reason for such networks is simple. Homeowners demand quality products and professionals. However, to refer a company, tradesman, or product, one has to understand how the job has to be done. Companies and individuals have to be checked out before they can be recommended. A steady hand is needed at the helm that knows every detail of home improvement, from the building envelope to the minutest repair. In 1998, recognizing the demand for renovation expertise, I created a home services referral network known as HouseSmart. It has since grown into one of the most recognized referral programs in the home improvement industry, counting 170 certified professional contractors and building industry suppliers across Canada as its members.

Homeowners often think that they can go it alone – that they can be their own renovation contractor. Some can succeed in this, but more often than not, it has been my experience that homeowners-turned-contractors fail. I am constantly invited into homes and guided through this or that horror story in which renovations went terribly awry. In one instance, an owner hired the wrong engineer. Wanting to save money, the homeowner had become his own contractor and, in the process, saw their costs more than double. A pricey eight-foot cantilevered sundeck was built, but the deck's tiled surface wouldn't adhere to the underlining and was too great a load for the deck. If the owner had even a small gathering, the deck could have collapsed. Aggravating the situation, no building permit had been obtained. The problem was that the full scope of the job had not been considered at the outset. Had it all been mapped out correctly up front, it would have been much less than the $60,000 white elephant that resulted.

People often think that referral services can create an unnecessary expense when dealing with home improvement projects. But how much more does it cost if the job isn't done right? Getting caught by an inspector attempting to band-aid a repair can be plenty more costly than having professional do it right.

Don't be referred to home inspectors by realtors. I have seen inspectors miss drainage problems (the property was sold in dry weather, but when it rained, major problems flooded to the surface). Get your home inspector referred from a professional organization independent of the real estate transaction.

People working with friends: in my experience it seldom works. Some detail gets overlooked, or found not to be necessary (like a building permit). In one case, a client had a deck extension built by a friend in offence of a bylaw and, as a result, the deck had to be reduced to its original size.

When considering investing in an older property, be on the defensive when you see new carpet or a newly painted wall: what was the reason for that particular carpet or wall repair?

Have a clear, set budget for any project that is more than $50,000. Ensure that the contractor's rates are understood and that all materials and other costs are documented and approved. Feel comfortable with your budget.

Check out the contractor. Get his or her references. Contractors that are part of the HouseSmart network require 10 testimonials from home owners. Stay on your contractor's case. What are his or her work habits; where is he or she buying materials from; and are the bills being paid to the materials' supplier? (Remember, a contractor's supply store can lien your house.) Does your contractor have third-party liability insurance? Are they properly licensed? Did they get a building permit? Get everything in writing. Are the builders covered under the Workers' Compensation Board? They should be.

Do:

- Get your home inspector referred from a professional organization.
- Check a contractor's reference before hiring him or her.
- When considering an investment in an older property, be on the defensive for cover-up jobs like new carpet or a newly painted wall.
- Make sure you are certain of the full scope – costs, time, supplies – of a job at its outset.
- Have a clear, set contract and budget for any project that is more than $50,000.

Don't:

- Be referred to home inspectors by realtors. Go to a home inspector totally independent of the transaction.
- Be your own contractor. More often than not, homeowners-turned-contractors fail.
- Hire friends as contractors. Some detail usually gets overlooked, or found not to be necessary (such as a building permit).
- Hesitate to stay on your contractor's case throughout a job. After all, you are the one who has to live with the results afterward.

23

Marv Steier

President, TVS Tenant Verification Service Inc. , Marv is a retired Police Officer and former Fraud Investigator who had an idea that evolved into a successful business which provides a valuable service to the Residential Rental Industry across North America

BEST ADVICE: *Protect Your Real Estate Investment - Screen Your Tenants.*

Successful Real Estate Investing requires a due diligence process called tenant screening; this minimizes the risk of renting to individuals who use landlords as a revolving line of credit. High risk tenants or **tenants from hell** can turn real estate investing into a bad experience if allowed to happen. But it doesn't have to!

Where there is a tenant screening system in place, then Real Estate Investing can be a pleasant and profitable experience.

Why do High Risk Tenants use landlords as a revolving line of credit? Well let's examine the facts:

- Are they charged criminally for fraud or false pretences? **No.**
- Do they go to jail if they don't pay a court awarded judgement? **No.**
- Do the major credit bureaus allow landlords to report tenant pay habits? **No.**
- Is there any consequence when a tenant leaves a landlord stuck with unpaid rent? **No!**

So will High Risk Tenants ever stop using landlords as a revolving line of credit? **Yes!**

When landlords network to identify High Risk Tenants and deny tenancy based on bad pay habits, the revolving line of credit will stop. Not being able to maintain a roof over your head would be a strong incentive for most High Risk Tenants to change their irresponsible ways and pay rent as stipulated in the lease agreement. These tenants don't pay simply because there isn't a consequence.

For many Real Estate Investors it is imperative that rent payments are on time because there is a mortgage that needs to be paid. It is important that the tenant who gets the key to your investment property is credit worthy, tenant worthy which means paying rent on time and has a stable job and a level of income that ensures timely rent payment. This should form your **Criteria**!

The biggest complaint that I hear from Landlord Associations is that many landlords do not treat the rent process like a business. Furthermore they don't know the tenancy laws in their Province or State, they don't complete the proper forms for tenancy or lease and they don't screen their tenants. But... they do complain about the system when they have a problem. Go figure!

Having tenants is a lot like raising kids; many of them need to be reminded of their responsibilities, and they need to be made aware that there is a consequence for not being responsible which includes not paying rent on time. Most tenants will obey the lease rules when there is a consequence, particularly when they know that it could affect future tenancy. Consequences should be in writing and the tenant should acknowledge them by signing so there can be no argument later. This would be called a **Deterrent** and it is a form called **Notice to Tenant** which is available at www.tenantverification.com

Reporting tenant pay habits to a Credit Reporting Agency at the beginning of each month is also a strong **Deterrent**. Let me ask you this... knowing that the Credit Card Company reports late payments to the Credit Bureau, do you pay on time or do you wait for 2 or 3 months before making a payment or not pay at all? Okay a rhetorical question...so if the tenant knows that you report pay habits to a Credit Reporting Agency on the 3rd day of each month do you think they would be more likely to pay? In most instances yes, reporting tenant pay habits to TVS a Credit Reporting Agency will minimize risk of late and non rent payment.

OK...Kids get sick and tired of rules and so do tenants; there should also be incentives and rewards. Many landlords & property managers have strategies to affect this throughout the year. One strong incentive for a tenant to pay rent on time would be a **Certificate of Satisfactory Tenancy.** Why? Many tenants do not have a good credit history and are denied tenancy based on bad credit, landlords are mostly interested in rents being paid so the Certificate of Satisfactory Tenancy might be the ticket to a better rental accommodation. The landlord would issue this at the end of the lease period where tenancy is completed as per lease agreement.

This incentive is a win win situation for tenant and landlord!

Education is one of the key elements to a successful real estate investment business and where landlords take the time to educate tenants about responsibilities and rights; there is mutual respect, fewer hassles and less income loss. There is a greater chance of a tenant receiving the aforementioned Certificate when they know their responsibilities.

Tenantsinfo.com is an educational website for both tenant and landlord. Tenants can be advised to visit this website if they are not aware of their responsibilities or if you are not aware of your responsibilities as a landlord.

Many landlords at seminars have told me that they rent to an Individual based on gut feeling. Okay... that works when you have a tenant that has intent to pay rent and fortunately most do, however where your mortgage payment is dependent on the rent, are you willing to take that chance?

Tenants, who are **Systems Users**, look for landlords who ignore the tenancy laws, ignore their landlord responsibilities and don't complete the required forms. These tenants can make real estate investing costly for an unsuspecting landlord as the system usually works in their favour where the rules & regulations of the Residential Tenancies Act haven't been complied with. This type of tenant can be avoided, just **follow the rules**.

So, I mentioned landlords & property managers networking to identify High & Low Risk Tenants. What if every landlord and property manager reported tenant pay habits to a Credit Reporting Agency such as TVS? Would that affect the way High Risk Tenants use landlords as a revolving line of credit? Absolutely, they would be identified... what landlord or property manager would rent to them?

Can reporting tenant pay habits benefit Low Risk Tenants? Yes, many tenants do not have a good credit history, but they pay their rent on time and complete a satisfactory lease term. A **Certificate of Satisfactory Tenancy** would benefit them as TVS can verify the good pay habits.

If you follow the rules & guidelines for screening tenants as you do for real estate investing, you will minimize risk of income loss and allow yourself a greater chance for success.

Do:

- Familiarize yourself with the Tenancy Laws in your Province or State.
- Screen your Tenants as you don't want to be stuck with the Tenant from you know where.
- Join your local Landlord Association, they are generally experts in the tenancy arena and can help you with a problem Tenant or the Residential Tenancy Office.
- Have a checklist that ensures you have completed all due diligence & proper forms.
- Visit www.criminalfraud.com for valuable Tips & Advice on ten-

ant screening.
- Ensure that the Management Company you hire has a good tenant screening process in place and completes periodic site inspections.

Don't:

- Extend tenancy based on gut feeling.
- Discriminate as per Human Rights Act as this could be costly.
- Rent to Individuals who insist on paying cash only.
- Rent to Individuals because you feel sorry for them.
- Forget to document in writing all formal contact with tenants.

24

Scott Ullrich

President and CEO of Gateway Property
Management. Scott has a Bachelor of Arts, a
Diploma in Urban Land Economics, is a Certified
Property Manager and a Chartered Accountant.

BEST ADVICE: *Making money is 50% increasing your revenues and 50% decreasing your expenses.*

Property management 101. Prior to joining Gateway Property Management in 1983 I was a Chartered Accountant with a firm then called Touche Ross and Company. Although I was involved in auditing, accounting and consulting, when introduced as an accountant in a social setting, the conversation always turned to what advice I could give someone regarding their personal or corporate tax situation. As a Property Manager, I still enjoy the occasional cocktail party but invariably the conversation leads to what advice can I give about increasing ones real estate bottom line. The answer has always been simple, "making money is 50% increasing your revenues and 50% decreasing your expenses". When further pressed I would expand by saying; "make sure you find a good Property Management Company".

Great Property Management companies will always increase your bottom line but the advice I'm about to give will help you achieve at least a portion of that increased cash flow yourself.

If nothing else, get yourself a good Resident Manager.

At Gateway we spend several thousand dollars every year profiling our Resident Managers. Of course it is important to have staff who understand leasing and maintenance but if they don't have the personality traits to properly deal with residents and their concerns, you soon find that you are the "proud" owner of a very troubled building. When interviewing site staff, you should spend the time necessary to find out how they deal with difficult situations, and whether they enjoy interacting with residents and suppliers. If they indicate that they can be patient and understanding, yet firm in their approach, you may have found the right person. If they are qualified to do minor repairs that would normally be handed by a contractor, by all means, let them do it. You can either adjust their salary to include this work or you can pay them a little extra for each additional job they perform. The cost to have a Resident Manager repair a leaking tap is always going to be less than calling in a plumber.

Find yourself a good handyman and/or a good plumber

The majority of your repairs and maintenance work can be easily handled by a qualified handyman or a good plumber. Plumbing issues always seem to be the most common maintenance issue with carpentry work number two. Spend the time to interview a good contactor and let him or her know that as long as the quality of work is good and the price is reasonable, they will be your preferred contractor. Every three years or every time they approach you with a rate increase, let them know you will be checking the market and ensuring that you are still getting the best price. And pay your contractors on time. At Gateway we do a cheque run every Friday so that no contractor should have to wait more than 10 days to get paid. By doing this we get the best prices and have the most loyal contractors. It's a win-win for everyone.

Join a local Landlord Association

When it comes to volume discounts and industry knowledge you will never beat a good Property Management Company. As an individual you will not be able to get the kinds of pricing discounts from suppliers that a Property Management Company can get. Your best option is likely the volume discounts that you can get through your local Landlord Association. In addition you will also gain access to necessary forms, advertising signs and advice. All of these benefits will be more than worth the cost of membership.

The 30% rule

You've heard the expression "throwing good money after bad". Well this relates to being a landlord as well. Any decision to repair equipment whether it is a refrigerator or a furnace should be analyzed on a cost/benefit basis. If the cost to repair a 10-year-old fridge is equal to or greater than 30% of the cost of replacing that item, you should consider replacing that item. The new item is going to last much longer than the repaired item and in some cases (fridge, furnace, lighting etc.) additional energy savings will also be achieved to reduce the payback of a purchase. The short term price is going to be more but the long term maintenance costs much less.

Be energy efficient

Expanding on the previous point, always look at what potential energy saving can be achieved and what the benefits are compared to the costs associated with that efficiency. We all want to do our best to ensure we are taking care of the environment but we also need to achieve that bottom line. When a repair is required you should consider the 30% rule and if replacing something, you should look at the benefits of replacing that item with something more energy efficient. Sometimes it also makes sense to replace something that is not broken. At Gateway we are always looking at what government or utility company subsidies might be available to retrofit a building, whether it be energy efficient lighting, heating, cooling or insulation options. If you are given an opportunity whereby someone else is going to pay a portion of the cost for you to save more money, you will definitely want to look closely at it.

Inspect your suites regularly

Throughout my many years in Property Management I've been exposed to all sorts of residents. When one of our clients purchases a building I've always insisted that we go through and perform a suite-by-suite inspection of each unit. I've seen suites that you literally cannot move around in due to the junk that has been collected. I've seen a suite where the tenant removed the door to one of his bedrooms and installed a screen door allowing the second bedroom to be used as an aviary for about 50 pigeons. I once tripped over a boa constrictor in the same suite where a baby was crawling around. Add to that the drug labs and gang hangouts you hear about today and you should consider yourself warned that you need to know what your residents are up to. When these problem residents move out or get evicted the damage they leave behind can be as much as the one year's rent. Inspect your suites at least once a year and make sure you have good residents.

Pass on as many costs to the residents as possible

When I first started in this business, almost every apartment had cablevision included as part of the rent. Today most residents pay their own cable cost directly to the cable provider. This allows the resident to pick and choose what services they like and of course they pay accordingly. The same can hold true for other utilities as well. Electricity, gas and water rates fluctuate quite a bit and as a landlord you typically are the one at risk with these fluctuations. There are times when you win at this game but over time you are typically playing catch up on the rate increases you are handed. It is not uncommon to see tenants open and close their windows as the sole source of adjusting the heat to their unit. When that cost is passed on to them the windows are miraculously closed more often and the thermostat becomes much more useful. The same holds true for water and electricity. Whenever possible and economically feasible you should consider metering your building and passing these costs on to the residents. Even if you have to lower your rents to achieve this, the cost savings over a year may be more than worth it.

Use the Internet for advertising

Not that long ago Gateway was spending in excess of $1,000,000 per year in newspaper advertising for all of our clients. With more and more potential residents looking to the Internet we have reduced our newsprint advertising to 40% of what it was while increasing our Internet advertising by only 10% of that (less then $100,000). For half of what it used to cost, we have actually increased our exposure to more potential residents and of course you can do the same. You have to be careful of which Internet advertising source you use however, as your ads might just be perceived as spam and actually reduce the number of serious enquiries. If you're not using a professional Property Manager, check with your local Landlord Association for their recommendations.

Consider allowing pets

Most landlords prefer not to have pets in their buildings due to the additional costs associated with them. I used to be in that camp but today I believe that it's not the pets we need worry about, it's the pet owners. For every bad pet owner out there I feel there is at least one good one as well. How do you control the bad ones? Well one way is with their wallets. In some of our buildings we allow pets if the resident is prepared to pay an additional pet deposit (if allowed under the tenancy laws in your Province) as well as a premium on their rent. So we might charge an additional $50.00 per month for the resident who has a pet. At the end of one year we have a pet deposit plus an additional $600.00, which should cover any damages but most likely will actually result in a better bottom line for you.

There are of course many ways to improve your bottom line. More ways than the space in this chapter allows. In the end, you should recognize that real estate investment is not as the Canada Revenue Agency puts it, "a passive investment" but a business like any other where the more time, effort, and determination you put into it will reward you with a good return on a good investment.

Do:

- Look for ways to improve your bottom line.
- Consider allowing pets.
- Pay your contractors on time.
- Inspect your suites regularly.
- Whenever possible and economically feasible you should consider metering your building.

Don't:

- Repair – if the cost to repair is equal to or greater than 30% of the cost of replacing.
- Forget to spend time interviewing staff – find out how they deal with difficult situations.
- Assume. Go inspect every suite you buy or manage.
- Forget to pass on extra costs to your tenants.

25

George Vernon

President of Park Place Investments Inc., a family owned company

---

BEST ADVICE: *Make a Fortune by Never Selling Real Estate.*

Everybody wants to be successful and make money. We had kicked around ideas for revenue generating ventures for two or three years. Real estate was constantly at the top of the list or close in all of our thoughts, but how would we get started? Discussions about investment opportunities one day resulted in a family meeting, which in turn led to a refresher course in real estate investment. The result of that meeting was the beginning of a new family real estate investment venture.

We quickly determined that we wanted to build a real estate investment business that was sustainable, one that would continually grow and expand. Our credo became, *'Create an ever increasing income stream by never selling real estate'*. While we might make money more quickly by flipping, we knew we wouldn't be building something of substance, something that would endure. We really wanted to build wealth for our family for the long term, own investments that would have longevity. We wanted our efforts to provide opportunities for ensuing generations.

Our Mandate:

Our goal is to create an endless income stream by holding, not selling our investment real estate. The most important aspect of making money in real estate investments is actually finding good investments. Our premise has been to find and hold those good investments, using the equity gain generated to help finance new purchases. By retaining our real estate investments, we continue to build our revenue producing portfolio. This will enable us to be in the position to take advantage of business opportunities that arise or are presented by old fashioned digging. We also believe we can build a wealth generating organization that will give us the opportunity to channel some of the income to help and give back to others. If you help someone else, you also help yourself.

Our Strategy:

Our strategy is to search for and buy in growth areas, areas where people want to work, retire or holiday. We constantly monitor and re-evaluate our 'focus' on where to invest. While we might not want to live in a particular area, others will for many reasons... changing real estate values (generating positive cash differential from selling in one area and purchasing elsewhere), climate preference, living closer to children, relatives or friends, retirement, job transfers, etc. We subscribe to the axiom that in order to be successful, we will buy the deal, not the market. A good deal in any market remains a good deal.

How We Do It:

We have found that, with any venture, to expect problems. In real estate, problems are normal. Learn to deal with them. Always have some cash reserves, because you will need them. Buy in different geographical, socio-economic, climatic areas. Some areas will experience downturns while others will enjoy growth. By diversifying our investments, we have a better chance of balancing our income stream.

Be Your Own Banker:

As mortgage terms on your investments expire, re-mortgage and use the money from the equity gain to purchase more investments. Make sure your down payment is large enough so the revenue stream will cover mortgage payments and other expenses. Hold your investments. Never sell. That building or unit you purchased 5 years ago has helped finance other investments, and will continue to help with more in the future, while continuing to pay the mortgage down.

Building a portfolio in this manner will make you very successful, and you will be surprised at how quickly your investments and your equities grow while continuing to provide an increasingly larger income stream. Maintain your investments. You may not own the most expensive real estate in town, but you will always be able to demand the top dollar in your area if your unit or building is well looked after. As well, this will ensure you will have fewer vacancies. Time is your friend. In most instances, time will help to increase your equity gain.

Lessons We Have Learned:

By far the most important decision you can make is to purchase your first investment. Until you do that, all of your real estate investment courses, accumulated knowledge, discussions, literature, pontificating and procrastination... will mean absolutely nothing.

Real estate investment is a waiting game. Purchase, and then 'wait for the gain'. Only work or partner with people you trust implicitly. Life is too short to do otherwise. If the deal is 'too good to be true', it usually is. Deals can be similar, but no two deals are exactly alike. Never stop learning. Attend seminars. Ask questions. Seek information. Help others. Others helped you.

Remember, **'The teacher always learns more than the student'**. Be positive. Avoid negative people at all costs. If you listen to negative people, they will drag you down. Spend time with like minded people, entrepreneurial people, people who share your vision.

Our investment decisions are enhanced by pooling our individual strengths and differences, which sometimes makes for boisterous meetings! Don't be afraid or too proud to learn from others. You can always expand your knowledge and your skills by getting help. Most successful people will be willing to share if you demonstrate that you are serious and won't waste their time. Over time you will find that you will have valuable information to share with others.

Lessons We All Can Learn:

As an investor, you are in a very small percentage of the population who has the foresight and the fortitude to invest in and take control of your own successful future. Remember, you won't get what you want in life without a lot of help from a lot of people. This axiom also holds true in real estate investing. Once you have some success and have gained good solid knowledge, be willing to help others on the way up. Success will always come because of it. Have fun. Be proud of your accomplishments. Good luck!

Do:

- Act and buy that first property.
- Create an endless income stream by holding, not selling your investment real estate.
- Buy in growth areas, areas where people want to work, retire or holiday.
- Expect problems. In real estate, problems are normal. Learn to deal with them.
- If the deal is 'too good to be true', it usually is.

Don't:

- Sell ... keep your real estate investments for cash flow.

- Buy the market, buy the deal.
- Listen to negative people. If you listen to negative people, they will drag you down.
- Lose patience. Real estate investment is a waiting game.

26

Andrew Westlund

President of Apex Wireless Inc., one of the top five Telus Mobility resellers in Canada. The company has 10 stores in Metro Vancouver and employs 100 people

Best Advice: *Consider each piece of property as a small business in itself.*

I treat my real estate portfolio as a passive income play for the long-term. My principal business – a wireless communication company – is my cash machine, while my real estate investments are what will keep me going in my golden years. I always keep the two entities separate. My cash machine provides me with enough money and credit to buy additional real estate.

Although I thoroughly enjoy running my wireless communication business, it requires my full attention to run it efficiently. Its success is directly related to the amount of time I am willing to put into it.

Like many industries in this fast-paced marketplace, the wireless industry is continuously evolving. Therefore, constant vigilance is needed to stay competitive. Furthermore, there is no guarantee as to the future success or value of my business.

Market conditions continually change and every business goes through spikes and drops in earnings. If my business declines, so does the value of my company and the amount I am able to sell it for when I retire. Subsequently, market conditions could dictate when I sell rather than my own preferential timing. In other words, if my income is tied to this single asset, I could end up with less financial security in my later years.

Many people expect much more out of their job or business than it is capable of giving. They expect their job or business to last them for 40 years and then give them a pension for the rest of their life. Those were the good ol' days! I have business colleagues that think they won't have to work hard at their business when they're old. My personal experience in business is that it's full-on all of the time. I predict that as I get older, it will be harder to maintain the risk ratio.

I don't expect my business to ever provide me with enough passive income for retirement. This may sound discouraging but it isn't. I love what I do, which is why I've stayed with it for more than 20 years. I employ roughly 100 people and enjoy working with them, particularly during strategy sessions. I get a lot of fulfillment out of creating a winning strategy with a group of people that is all working toward a singular goal. Different personalities with different perspectives are all contributing as a team.

It's particularly challenging leading a group through these tough economic times, but one of the roles of an entrepreneur is to take risks. As long as I enjoy leading a group the way I do now, I will stay in business. If it becomes overwhelming, or if I get to a point in my life when I want to slow down, I want to know that I will be able to transition to a business that requires less of my time, but that can generate income for me. I know that at that time, I will want to be involved in a business that is less risky but nonetheless exciting – one that requires less of my time but that still gives me a sense of fulfillment.

To have this option in the future, I began planning well in advance.

I believe my 20-plus year real estate acquisition plan gives me a solid footing for developing my "passive income" business. My wife Phebe and I have a real estate portfolio composed of commercial, residential, raw land and resort property. We are particularly attracted to resort properties because of the level of engagement required. The marketing of these properties requires both of us to be creative.

It's been a great business to develop as a husband and wife team. Together, we strategize and discuss the pros and cons of different types of property purchases. One of the most enjoyable aspects of our real estate ventures is their tangible results: our real estate investments provide us with a greater sense of security than our other investments.

As a family, we love seeing the enjoyment our resort properties provide other families. We're always thrilled to read the comment cards that guests leave detailing the memories they made during their stay. We encourage our guests to join our property's Facebook site and add pictures.

We consider each piece of property as a small business by itself. Our goal is to make each business generate enough revenue to pay for its administration, marketing and overall upkeep. If we break even financially on each property we can then move ahead to the next project.

It's exciting to think of all the possibilities we have to acquire additional properties in the coming years. We are not presently trying to make cash machines out of our real estate acquisitions, but we are careful to avoid "boat anchors."

While we are wrapping up one project, we are already considering our next move. We search for property that we will be proud of. This is a very important criterion: the property has to make us feel good. There is a great sense of satisfaction in experiencing success now, while simultaneously planning for success in the future.

Do:

- If real estate isn't your primary income stream, consider treating your real estate portfolio as a passive income retirement project for the long-term.
- Keep your real estate portfolio separate from your principal in-

come or business.

- View each piece of real estate property as a small business – make it generate enough revenue to pay for its administration, marketing and overall upkeep.
- Always have an eye to the future: while you are completing one project, consider what your next purchase will be.
- Get a great sense of satisfaction from your purchase: when considering real estate investment, search for property that you will be proud of.

BEST ADVICE:
Understanding the sale

27

Jennifer Berkeley

Jennifer Berkeley has developed a successful staging business that started with staging her own investment properties. Her company, Urban Presentations, stages homes throughout Greater Vancouver

---

BEST ADVICE: *Set the Stage for better results.*

The best piece of advice I can give anyone who is about to sell their home is to accept that it is not your home anymore! Nearly everyone has an emotional attachment to their home, especially after living there for many years; but the house that you are selling now is a product that you have for sale, your biggest asset! It's not about you anymore!

The most common question that home sellers ask me is "Can't the buyers use their imagination?" The answer is "No, they can't". Buyers can't use their imagination and see a lovely guest bedroom where you have your home office. No, they can't see past your clutter and imagine a spacious interior and no, they can't imagine what an empty room will be like with furniture in it. When you are selling a product, you want to make sure it appeals to the greatest number of prospective buyers.

Staging prepares your house for sale, for marketing the dream to your potential buyer. Given two properties with similar prices and amenities, buyers will choose the one that looks better. Statistics show that staged homes spend less time on the market and generally sell for a higher price. Although staging is relatively new in Canada, and you may think 'We never had to do that before, so why should I do it now?' Times have changed, our Real Estate market is highly competitive, and buyers are educated and discerning.

The Process...

Exactly what a space needs in order to look great and sell quickly will be different for each property I look at. Professional stagers work in the Real Estate industry, they follow design and market trends, they understand what features are most desirable, and what features will sell your house. Stagers create a fantasy for the buyer, showing off your home's best features. They take into consideration what needs to be noticed about your property: architectural features and details, open space, logically purposed rooms or an amazing view. Stagers remedy what they hope buyers will not notice: small or challenging spaces, poor natural light or limited storage.

The following are the most important steps in staging your home for sale and the things that most homes need:

1. Highlight Your Home's Best Features.

Often, if you've lived in your house for a long time, you stop appreciating its best features. A feature that isn't important to you may be one that buyers will love. A wood burning fireplace is a great example. Lots of people have fireplaces that they never use, but buyers generally love them; they add a feeling of romance and coziness to a living room.

• *Tip: If your living room has a fireplace or a stunning view, make sure buyers will notice it. Arrange the furniture to lead the eye to the fireplace or the window.*

2. Make Your House Move-In Ready!

Buyers are attracted to move-in ready spaces. If they have to choose between a house that needs new paint, a new kitchen faucet or minor repairs and one that all of these issues have been attended to, they will generally choose the house that can be moved into right away.

- *Tip: Some simple updates that you can do without spending very much money include:*
- Fresh Paint
- Updated Light Fixtures
- Updated Bathroom and Kitchen Fixtures
- Updated Electrical Outlets and Light Switches
- Updated Cabinet Hardware

3. Make Sure Rooms Show Their Function!

Remember that buyers are going to be comparing your home with others in your neighbourhood in the same price range. If your house has 4 bedrooms, you need to show 4 bedrooms. If you are using one bedroom as a sewing room and another as an office, buyers will only see 2 bedrooms. If your home has a formal dining room that you are using as a TV room, buyers will walk away with the impression that there is no dining room.

You may ask "But can't buyers see past that?" No, they can't. At least, most buyers can't, and the goal is to appeal to most buyers, right? You need to set these rooms up to clearly demonstrate the intended function. You can rent furniture for staging for a reasonable price; you can borrow from family or friends; or you can get creative. No one needs to know you have an air mattress under that beautiful bedding...

4. Declutter, Declutter, Declutter!

Most people have too much stuff in their homes, and this only makes a home look smaller than it really is. Too much furniture in a room will make the room look small and buyers will not be able to walk freely through the room. Remove extra pieces and the flow will be improved and the space will open up. Bookshelves that are over-flowing and plastic storage bins stacked up to the ceiling in the garage will make buyers think that if there isn't enough room for all your stuff, then where will all their stuff fit? All I can say is get the stuff out of there. And don't hide the clutter in the closets or cupboards. Buyers will look inside! A self storage facility is a very economical way to store extra stuff while your home is on the market. Remember, I said it won't be easy...

5. DePersonalize!

Buyers don't want to be constantly reminded that they are in some-one else's house. Family photos stare down buyers and remind them that 'Somebody else lives here!' Think about how you feel looking at a show suite or luxurious hotel room. You are totally comfort-able moving through the space and wouldn't hesitate to open a closet door and have a look inside. You start to imagine what it would be like to live there. Now think about how you feel touring a home that someone lives in. If you walk around seeing family photographs, personal items, a shower full of shampoo, razors and tired towels are you totally comfortable moving through the space? Even though you know the house is for sale and you are allowed to be there, you feel a bit uncomfortable and unsettled. Now, is uncomfortable and unsettled the way you want buyers to feel as they walk around your home? No, of course not. So the closer you can get your house to looking like a show home, the better.

Stagers Sell the Dream!

Stagers know how to create luxury touches that would only be expected in high end homes. How about a master suite that has a peaceful sitting area where the homeowner can imagine herself escaping the chaos of her day with a good book and a cup of tea? Even the most modest master bedroom has room for an upholstered chair, small side table and a lamp. It doesn't matter that you have never sat there, or that your potential buyer will never really have time to sit there. It's about creating the dream, the fantasy, that in this home, it might be possible. Stagers add these touches and more throughout a staged property.

Staging services do not have to be expensive. It can be as simple as hiring a stager to come in and give you a list of suggestions and executing them yourself. If you don't have the time or inclination to do it yourself, a stager can take care of the whole job for you, from packing up your clutter, and rearranging your furniture, to shopping for a few new accessories to create a stylish, pulled together look for your MLS photos and showings!

Do:

- Always remember you are selling the dream. Make sure buyers will fall in love the moment they walk in the front door.
- Always take out the excess stuff – Declutter. Pare down and simplify the home to make the space look larger.
- Always make sure all rooms show their function. And make sure it is a function that most buyers will be looking for.
- Always show off your home's best features. The décor should direct the buyers eye towards that beautiful fireplace or stunning view.

Don't:

- Let buyers see your personal, intimate items. The property, not your life, should be the focus of the buyers' attention.

- Take decluttering too far and strip your home bare of all decorative accessories. You don't want your MLS photos to look like your house was robbed.
- Expect that buyers can imagine what your home would look like with less clutter, or better décor, etc.
- Try to do all this on your own. Hire a stager, even just to get a few tips and suggestions. They have experience creating homes that sell.

28

Ryan Donohoe

Owner and operator of Nor-Wes Landscape and
Design Ltd. in greater Vancouver

BEST ADVICE: *Find out what inspires you in the garden.*

Why is landscaping such an important aspect of real estate? Because we judge a book by its cover! Curb appeal can increase a home's value by up to 15%.

Whether you are a home owner or thinking of selling your home, creating a beautiful landscape is like highlighting a work of art in the perfect frame.

Here is some advice for those of you considering a landscape project in the future.

First, research different styles of landscape design. Are you interested in contemporary, traditional, formal etc. Find out what inspires you in the garden. Are you an enthusiast who loves to get your hands dirty and play in the garden, or are you someone who wants a low maintenance approach? Read various books and magazines, go to the local trade shows and search online. Maybe you're inspired by a garden that you enjoyed visiting while you were on vacation or the garden your parents created when you were a child. Take your time with it and enjoy the possibilities that evolve. You can almost look at this project as an opportunity for self discovery. A landscape often reflects your personality and style, so whatever you create will invite your true colours to come out.

Once you've covered the groundwork, the next step is to hire a qualified designer. Designers are trained to think outside of the box. A good designer should offer ideas and opportunities that you haven't even considered. He or she will recognize the problems and possibilities within your landscape and execute the design process that will create a design solution to fit your budget. Be sure to check their portfolio, references, testimonials and qualifications before you sign a contract with a landscape designer.

A landscape designer can save you time, money and frustration. They can even discover aspects of your landscape you never realized existed. Recently while completing a landscape design in West Vancouver we discovered the client owned an additional 2,200 square feet beyond their property line. Often structural failures on a property are discovered during the design process. On a past project we uncovered the need to rebuild a large hidden retaining wall on the property line. We were able to adjust the landscape design to include replacement of the retaining wall, while staying within the installation budget.

So, you now have a great design and you are ready to implement the plan. It's important to note at this stage that design and installation are treated as separate processes, often with different contracts and personnel. Again it's critical to research the different companies. Whether the company is large or small is often of less consequence than the scope and type of work they do, which is why it's important to review a company's portfolio and make sure that they meet industry standards and qualifications. As long as you have done your research, you should choose the company that you feel comfortable with, as the installation process can be a lengthy one.

Landscape Installation companies must know local building codes and bylaws regarding construction and excavation, to avoid utility damage and fines incurred by not having the proper building permits. They should be familiar with their provincial landscape standard (a publication that contains guidelines for acceptable landscape installation practices). They must be registered with their local workers compensation board and have liability insurance that protects you from any accidents or damages that occur on your property during construction.

Landscapers consider themselves as the original green industry, environmental initiatives should be important to them. Ask the installation company if they are using organic fertilizers. When building the hardscape can they use recycled products? During the design process were pro-environment installations such as green roofs, green walls and water catchment systems considered?

Last but not least, it is critical that you sign a detailed contract between you and the builder. The contract should contain information regarding all aspects of the installation including but not limited to scope of work, warranty, time line, fees, payment schedule, progress reporting, and sub trades used on the site.

I am fortunate to work in a field that I am passionate about. I enjoy sharing ideas with other professional landscape designers and installers. Together we work to educate our clients and continually raise the standard of landscaping in our neighbourhoods.

Do:

- Find out what inspires you in the garden.
- Research different styles of landscape design.
- Hire a qualified designer. Check their portfolio, references, testimonials and qualifications.
- Sign a detailed contract between you and the builder that you understand.

Don't:

- Underestimate the value of a good design as it will save you money and time in the long run.
- Rush into a project without doing adequate amount of planning beforehand.
- Expect the job to be completed right away. Depending on the scope of the work it could takes months (sometimes up to a year) from the beginning of the design to the end of the installation.

29

Dan Eisenhauer

Real Estate Investor

BEST ADVICE: *The very first thing you should know about your investment property is who your target market will be. Allow yourself to sleep well at night, read **in detail** and understand every contract you sign.*

So, you own an investment property...What is the first thing you need to know about that property? Surrounding rental rates? Important, but the wrong answer. Maintenance contracts? Wrong again.

The very first thing you should know about your investment property is who your target market will be. In fact, you should have that firmly established in your mind before you even make your offer. There have been two classic cases of major firms not knowing their target market before launching new products. The first was Ford's introduction of the Edsel. The second was Coke's retooling of the Coke formula into "New Coke". While these were extraordinary corporate blunders, landlords also need to understand target marketing.

When buying, you should know what kind of people live in the area you are considering. Is it downtown, or in the suburbs? Is the area a beehive of activity, or is it rather sedate? Are there schools and universities around that could make the property attractive to students. Is there industry with transient workers, such as in Ft. MacMurray, where the employees come in for a month at a time, and then go home for a month? These are all important answers to have because a house or an apartment is different from every other house and apartment, and your marketing should not be cookie cutter marketing.

But market also includes adapting your building to the needs of your target market. Let's look at some examples.

You have just acquired a small building six blocks away from a major hospital. It would make a lot of sense that nurses would make an ideal target market. So, what would - probably - single women want in their building. Security is probably a high priority. If you equipped your building with upgraded doors and entry systems, well lit parking, and maybe some ground floor security over windows, you would go a long way to aiming at one group... a group that might pay a premium for feeling safe.

Many landlords shy away from students. Would you have rented to yourself when you were a student? Most would have, yet many seem to avoid this target market. Students want internet access, extra storage for their toys, like bikes and snowboards. Some may have cars; some may take public transit. Some post-grad students may be married. Each of those would be a different segment within that market. When trying to learn what students want, take the time to visit student union buildings and survey your potential clients. You may be surprised.

Seniors are another target. As our population begins to age, that market will be growing exponentially. Seniors are looking for security, quiet, easy access to the building and to amenities. Would it be worth it to you to install call buttons and alarms in each room, or offer your clients a community bus to get them to appointments, etc? Are the halls wide enough to handle wheel chairs? Low nap carpet would make a wheel chair easier to move than higher nap.

As seniors get older, some of them have problems opening doors, whether to rooms or closets. Replacing knob type door handles with levered handled would overcome that problem.

Falling in a tub or shower is another concern. Installing non-slip surfaces, grab bars, or seats would add a feeling of security. Although they are expensive to buy and install, walk-in tubs can be a nice feature.

Pay attention to the outside of the property, as well. Many seniors enjoy gardens and nicely landscaped properties. If your property is large enough to create them, use walkways that are wide enough for a wheel chair, and connect them to gardens in different parts of the property.

Perhaps your property is close to a major large employer, such as an oil refinery. Does your building have enough space to add more rooms, and to rent as a rooming house to single employees of the local plant? Creating common areas, and large kitchen, along with some of the features students might like, such as cable TV, internet access, etc. would make it attractive. Contact that employer to see if you could get a contract to house some of its employees.

Targeting a given market segment also means directing your marketing at that segment. For example, it would make little sense to advertise your student housing building in a suburban area, ten miles away from the closest post-secondary school. Your audience will not be there. However, today's students are very internet savvy, and rely on the Net for many things. Creating marketing schemes that use social networking sites such as Facebook and MySpace would likely generate numerous leads.

Seniors may frequent shopping malls, or churches. If there are bulletin boards offered there, make use of them for your marketing.

As a general rule, many advertisers are veering away from newspaper advertising these days. The younger generations look at other media. Seniors may still rely on their old stand-by, the newspaper.

In addition to finding the correct media, you also need to talk the language of your target market. The senior and the student will speak very different languages, and see different meaning in the same set of words in an ad. Target your copy to your audience. With seniors, talk about security, ease of access, emergency help, etc. The student will want to know about the space for her toys, internet access, ready access to her classes, etc.

When you target your property to a given demographic, you can often get premium rents for that suite. Tenants do not buy on price alone, but on value. When you offer greater value, you are able to charge more for it.

In closing, the identification of your target market should become clear as you are doing your diligence on a property you are interested in. This outlines just a few possibilities in finding your target market. But, if you miss your target, you could end up owning an Edsel, or trying to sell "New Coke".

Do:

- Read and understand every contract you sign. If you do not understand the contract, have a lawyer explain it.
- Understand landlording legislation in your area, especially if you are a residential landlord.
- Pay attention to the basic fundamentals of real estate investing, and do your homework when going to a new area.
- If you are working with a Realtor, be loyal to that person. If you find a property on your own, bring your Realtor in on the deal somehow.
- Treat your joint venture partners with respect. Invite your better JV partners in on the sweet deals, as well as the rougher ones.

Don't:

- Fall in love with a property. It is an investment, not a spouse.
- Try to nickel and dime the other side when buying or selling. Try to make every deal a win-win for everyone involved.
- Accept the seller's word about zoning, or income and expenses, etc. Do you own analysis.
- Necessarily buy in your backyard, or be able to drive to your

properties. Investigate towns and cities that you may have to fly to.

- Don't buy new construction pre-sales. That is not real estate investing; it is speculating.

30

Frank O'Brien

Award-wining editor of *Real Estate Weeklies* in Vancouver; editor of *Western Investor*, a commercial real estate publication, and editor of three other publications related to real estate

---

BEST ADVICE: *When you try translating the media coverage of real estate, keep in mind that statistics are lagging the market.*

A few years ago, Regina newspaper readers were treated to a news update from the local home builders' association headed: *"housing starts soar 300 per cent."*

The information was true, but the facts were that housing starts had increased from 7 homes to 21 homes, hardly the signal of a booming real estate market that the headline would suggest.

In April of 2009, newspapers in Vancouver and Victoria, British Columbia – where the housing market is often a lead news item – were decrying a 0.5 per cent apartment rental vacancy rate. Tenant advocates were quoted, all warning that greedy landlords were driving renters from their homes. The reality, however, was that vacancy rates had actually hit near 15-year highs of 5 per cent and even 6 per cent and landlords were capping and even reducing rents to keep tenants in place.

The newspapers, and their chosen sources, were citing what they took as the most accurate apartment rental information available: the annual surveys from **Canada Mortgage and Housing Corp**. (CMHC). These surveys are released in June with a more detailed survey, which also tracks condominium rentals and suites in private homes, in December of each year.

The CMHC survey being quoted had been conducted in October of 2008, and the market had changed dramatically over the following five months as the housing market slowed and more homes and condominiums came up for rent.

Distortions of the Canadian housing market, indeed the real estate scene globally, are quite common in media, where editors are continually bombarded with information on the ups and downs of sales and housing starts. Unfortunately for consumers, most editors and writers depend on outdated information, and on input from sources who have their own agenda to defend.

For anyone not intimately involved in the industry it can be difficult to translate what it all means.

The most stunning example is the media response to the rollercoaster real estate market during 2008 to 2009.

In the spring of 2008, Canadian news outlets were running articles about roaring housing sales, despite the fact that, as early as March, residential sales had been tracking lower, month-over-month. One widely circulated release in April of 2008 from a major real estate company was headed: "Rising housing values and lack of inventory challenge first-time buyers." Housing prices and sales by then, of course, were already tanking.

The reason for the misread is that editors, and most of their sources, rely almost totally on statistics from Canada's real estate boards, which invariably compare the previous month and the same month a year earlier. The resulting article is often bolstered by self-serving quotes from real estate board presidents.

The problem with media coverage of real estate is that once a trend is spotted, that remains the news despite what is really happening.

This is being seen as I write this – in May of 2009 – where Canada's newspapers and TV are reporting on the collapse of the housing market, when in fact sales have been rising month-over-month since February in most cities and prices, while below a year earlier, are still near the highest in history.

As an editor and writer who has covered Canada's real estate market for 30 years, I offer the following advice to investors on how to translate what you may read or see in media coverage of the market.

Do:

- **Keep in mind that statistics are lagging the market.** Around the 5th of each month you will see a blitz of housing related articles, because this is when Canada's real estate boards release their statistics based on the Multiple Listing Service. This will be followed a few days later by a comment from a major bank or analysts reacting to the statistics. What you must **keep in mind that these statistics are lagging the market by one or two months,** because of the time it takes from when a home sale is made to when it is officially reported on the Multiple Listing Service. For an accurate reading of what is going on in the market, ask your Realtor or Real Estate Board for the sales-to-listing ratio, which shows the ratio of homes listed for sale to those that actually sold. In a robust seller's market, this ratio may be 20 per cent or more; in a strong buyer's market it will be below 8 per cent. In May of 2009, for instance, this ratio in Greater Vancouver was 19 per cent, a sign the market is moving towards a sellers market, despite sales being down 10 per cent from a year earlier.
- **Consider the source.** A real estate company spokesperson will always spin the statistics to make the market appear better than it is. A tenant advocate or opposition politician will virtually always try to make it look worse than reality.
- **Remember that many newspaper reporters and editors are pressed for time** and, unfortunately, can also be lazy. It is easier for them to parrot the statistics and the quotations than to get out on the street and find out what is really going on.

Don't:

- Count just on Canada Mortgage and Housing Corporation's annual vacancy rate surveys for information on rentals. A more immediate gauge is to check out craigslist.org a free online bulletin board now widely used by landlords. Search mid-month for "available now" and you will get a fairly accurate snapshot of not only how many rentals there are, but how many are not rented two weeks into the month. This provides a valuable clue

31

Pete Ryznar

Real Estate Advertising Sales Manager at Pacific
Newspaper Group, publishers of the *Vancouver Sun*,
the *Province* and *West Coast Homes & Design
Magazine*

BEST ADVICE: *Advertising is an investment, not an expense.*

One of my most memorable calls was to a developer of a 60 unit townhouse complex on the North Shore. It was early spring and I had arranged a meeting to discuss some advertising opportunities for their latest project.

I arrived at the developer's home adjacent to the construction site and was greeted by a husband and wife team who were in their late 50s. Over tea, we discussed their needs and objectives before taking a stroll around the property. We walked through a number of the units that were nearing completion; a high-end development targeting business professionals and retirees – large suites, custom finishings yet a reasonable price tag. We went back to the house where I presented them with an overview of our products. I explained that I couldn't promise them sales but I could guarantee them exposure and traffic. *The Vancouver Sun* has a very high penetration on the North Shore and reaches an educated and affluent audience; high-income earners – the truly qualified buyer. The couple was initially uneasy about the cost of advertising but recognized our strengths and, after further discussion, committed to run a series of ads in our flagship product, *West Coast Homes*.

The first ad ran on a Saturday and the first call I received Monday morning was from the client, "What the hell did you do?" he asked. "We had 200 people show up at our front door on Saturday morning."

"Hey, I promised you results, didn't I?" I replied, elated by the news. The response to the ad was phenomenal. The client did not anticipate the huge spike in calls or surge in traffic but agreed it was a great problem to have. The project sold out before the second ad ran.

"There is no better feeling than serving a client well."
-Jim Smith, Realtor/Broker

With the media landscape evolving and constantly changing, many feel that newspapers are less effective than in past years. The truth is, newspapers (in print and online) are a more powerful advertising medium than ever before. Whether you're a realtor, developer, marketer or investor, newspapers get results. Contrary to what many believe, readership has stabilized. Recent studies show that 77 per cent of Canadian adults have read either a printed or online edition of a daily newspaper in the past week* Why? Because Canadians choose to get their information from a reliable and trustworthy source, especially during times of crisis and following major events.** It is worth noting that among Canadian Internet users the greatest percentage of total time online spent is on news sites.***

Whether in hardcopy or digital form, newspapers offer superior reach.

A $2.5-million Canadian property recently sold after a realtor placed an ad on one of our sister newspaper's websites. The buyer, from Saudi Arabia, saw the ad online while surfing the editorial pages and purchased the property sight unseen.

For investors and out-of-town property buyers, newspapers have become a valuable tool when searching for real estate. Perusing the local newspaper sites can provide buyers with a wealth of information about the communities they are targeting. Price comparisons, rental and vacancy rates, employment and migration information is readily available on these sites. Localized content can also reveal municipal/political issues that allow investors to make more informed buying decisions.

For realtors, newspapers are the perfect vehicle for increasing sales and building brand. It's a fact: 84.8 per cent of people who have purchased a house, condominium or co-op in the last year have read the newspaper in print or online in the last seven days.**** Advertise where the eyeballs are. A combined print and online campaign will help reinforce your message. Advertising in a daily newspaper will bring you credibility by aligning your business with a trusted and established brand.

So often, we'll hear from realtors who want to spend their entire advertising budget on a full page print ad for one day only. It is much more effective to run a series of smaller ads in print and online over a longer time period, maximizing reach and exposure. The secret to successful advertising is consistency, not size. Keeping your name in front of the public is important. It will help build your brand and your client base.

My investment partner and I were recently interested in viewing a unique waterfront property that he had noticed while boating in the harbour. Unfortunately, he was too far from shore to see the Realtor's name on the sign. We searched the Multiple Listing Service (MLS) and couldn't find the property. We checked our local community papers, Googled the area, and, finally, after a time consuming search stumbled upon the realtor's website. The list price had been reduced by 40 per cent so the assessed value was now 50 per cent higher than the asking price. Our jaws dropped when we arrived for the appointment – an amazing property–not waterfront but water's edge – panoramic views, south facing, and a massive lot. The home itself was in need of an update but you couldn't deny the value.

Why was the seller taking such a hit? Sure, the market conditions had changed and the listing had gone stale but the truth is, there was a lack of marketing/advertising. This home had huge potential. It should have been marketed as an outdoor paradise, a kayaker's dream, a potential fishing lodge, bed and breakfast, a spa or corporate retreat. Intrigue the buyer: Sell the dream and the lifestyle - not just the bricks and mortar. A consistent print and online campaign would have driven traffic through the roof. Well designed creative with an ocean view photo would have been enough to generate excitement on this property. I often hear from realtors that their marketing strategy consists of listings on MLS, a sign on the lawn and an update to their own personal websites. It's not enough – in real estate you have to cast your net wider to catch potential buyers.

Don't suffer from a lack of exposure. Stand out, brand yourself and make yourself known in the marketplace. Run your ad in print and online adjacent to other blue chip advertisers. It will bring you instant credibility. Remember that advertising is not just a cost of doing business. It's a proven sales tool that returns many times your investment in traffic and sales.

*Nadbank 2008

**Ipsos Reid, December 2008

***Ipsos Canadian Inter@ctive Reid Report, Quarter 4 - 2007

**** Scarborough Research, Release 2, 2008, Multi-Market Report

Do:

- Advertise where the eyeballs are – a combined print and online campaign will maximize your reach.
- Advertise consistently. A frequency campaign is the key to success.
- Sell the dream and the lifestyle - not just the home.
- Use your local newspapers for price comparisons, rental and vacancy rates, employment and migration information.

Don't:

- Just rely on MLS and a "For Sale" sign for your marketing strategy – cast your net further.
- Look at advertising as an expense – it's an investment.

BEST ADVICE:
Understanding development and the larger deal

32

Mark Betteridge

President and CEO, Mark Betteridge & Associates (MBA) Inc.
Specializes in the development and management of complex real estate assets in both the private and public sectors, including public/private arrangements.

BEST ADVICE: *When employees are happy, human resource management costs drop and productivity goes up.*

W(h)ither Green Buildings? Is green, sustainable, low/zero carbon footprint building a good investment? And by what measure?

Since humans started wandering this earth, we have sought and created shelter from the elements. Caves, shade trees and crude tents provided temperatures and dryness needed for pure survival. As societies became more organized, we learned to build larger and more complex structures that made storage and manufacturing of agricultural and industrial goods feasible. Passive solar structures, sometimes called mud huts, stone houses, pyramids and barns, improved living standards, health and commerce. Active energy (managed and designed gravity, water, wind, electrical, hydrocarbon and nuclear systems) then took us to yet higher levels of social structures permitting the standards we have taken for granted.

Distributed energy coming from hydrocarbon sources, primarily, has helped us live longer, in more places, in more ways with ever increasing impact on the 'environment' – a term that has taken on connotations to say the least.

Then things got a little crowded. Now, perhaps seven billion souls on this little rock are competing for a life that, we are told, may fry or freeze us, so green and sustainable development and buildings are de rigeur – required even (and this is the key).

Permit me to narrow this down to some direct experience. In the 1970s, courtesy of the first oil crunch, virtually air tight homes were promoted but this raised issues of interior air quality and moisture problems. Tough on breathing, good for mould, bad for re-sale.

In the office market, most buildings have been boxes premised on cheap energy with success being measured by low operating costs and therefore lower rents for tenants. Buildings have been valued (for the balance sheet and for borrowing) based on capitalizing net rents excluding operating costs so there has been little incentive, monetarily, to do much more than install average cost, average performance heating, cooling, lighting and humidity systems. But would tenants pay more net rent (hence more valuable buildings) if the operating costs were lower? In other words, is it the sum total gross rent that counts?

Ten years ago, we built a suburban office building with a full ground source geo-thermal heating and cooling system with a projected seven year payback. We installed opening windows and individual office HVAC controls. We estimated that the operating cost would be about $1 per sq. ft. lower with the gain coming to us as net rent. The market did not pay us this $1 so we had 'over-invested'. Because our net rent did not increase, our building value did not increase.

About eight years ago, we built a similar building but with photovoltaic panels to run a back-up electrical system. Same story – more capital cost, no gain in rent or value.

We attended many of the green building conferences and listened for that nugget of wisdom as to why we should build green buildings. Turns out there may be a couple of nuggets. One carrot and one stick.

Employers are finding out that **when employees are happy, human resource management costs drop and productivity goes up**. Post baby-boomer generations are increasingly attracted and retained by work environments that offer that happy feel provided by high air and light quality, individual control and truly smart systems, such as rain-water harvesting. Some of this is measurable, some is perceived. For example, we are finishing our Discovery Green building (at least LEED Gold) which has been leased to HSBC. This company adopted world-wide corporate environmental policies supporting their employees' health and requiring buildings with high green standards. The bank adopted a policy of being carbon-neutral in 2005. Given how long it takes to design, finance and build an office building, this standard has just arrived in our marketplace.

The other nugget? Some governments, such as the Province of British Columbia, have figured this out too so most are now requiring LEED standards, or similar, for all new facilities. Whether they really understand LEED and its competitors is irrelevant – they are mandating it. Whether it is for political appearance or is based in science is irrelevant. Reminiscent of the first automobile pollution controls mandated in California on an industry that claimed it would die if it had to meet such standards. It appears that this will be the case for both new and existing buildings which will drive green retrofit standards too. By setting green standards, which will inevitably rise, combined with an appropriate government tax and incentive regime (such as British Columbia's 30% tax credit system), we are seeing the creation of clean/green technology companies that can export into much larger jurisdictions where energy costs are higher (such as California).

It would seem that the lending industry and the insurance industry will follow suit. Why loan money to the developer/owner of
a building that does not meet prescribed green standards? Why
insure the financing/construction/operation of a building that may
not meet the perceived standards of its users and may not maintain
its value when compared to competitors that are appropriately green?
And wait until the lawyers represent aggrieved employees 'dam-
aged' by their air and light quality, desk-top.

In British Columbia where we have one of the lowest energy
prices in North America yet some of the most progressive green
standards (carbon tax, alternative energy technologies and power
production for starters), the pure financial payback calculations
for new buildings have, until recently, not justified the investment.
However, given these shifts, these two nuggets, Discovery Parks is
trying to stay on that leading edge, just behind the bleeding edge,
because we want to and we have to.

So, fellow rock occupants, if you want to stay in this game...

Do:

- Decide now to build and/or retrofit everything to LEED or
  equivalent standards or be left behind regardless of your views
  on global warming. All will be happy too.
- Talk to the HR manager for your current and potential ten-
  ants/occupiers to learn what 'green' attributes are most prized
  by their employees.
- Watch for green requirements creeping into financing and insurance documents.
- Keep learning. The clean technology industry is hot.

33

Bill Iles

Owner of a construction and real estate company with real estate holdings in BC, Alberta and Arizona. Responsible for the formwork and concrete for over 30 hi-rise buildings in the Greater Vancouver area.

BEST ADVICE: *When you buy an investment property, check out the builder and get quality property management – and have some rules for yourself – such as the 1% rule.*

Many people think that if they buy a condo in a concrete hi-rise they have something solid that will last. While this is true of many buildings - you have to know the builder's reputation to be sure you are getting top quality. As a concrete formwork contractor I can tell you that not all concrete buildings are created equal. The structural concrete is tested, the re-enforcing steel is inspected to the engineered drawings, and the shoring is engineered and inspected. This is true for all concrete buildings. **The difference lies in the building envelope** and can make the difference in owning a strong asset or a cash drain.

The building envelope consists of the window or curtain wall system and all the membranes, waterstops and panels which either cover the concrete or form the connection between the concrete and the window system. Concrete on its own is not waterproof. Sometimes a builder will opt for a less expensive window system which may work in a drier climate but doesn't stand up to a Lower Mainland (Vancouver, BC) winter. What keeps the water out at ground level may not work 20 levels up in a 75 kmh wind.

Sometimes the waterproofing system used on the basement parkade walls is not adequate for the amount of water being protected against and water will seep through the inevitable cracks in the concrete walls.

I have seen buildings where the interior finishes that were delivered were not what was promised. Particularly the developer may be saving by providing lower end cabinets and fixtures. Although these types of items will not cause structural issues they detract from value and if a builder will cheap out here - where else might he have cut corners that will cause larger issues.

Even if the actual concrete structure is solid there can be large differences. For instance: Building A is a well maintained, low maintenance strata building with happy owners and tenants while building B has tarps draped all over it and the owners have an expensive assessment to bear. Same engineered structure - different level of diligence in the finish. **Investigate your builder**. Some are here for the long haul, some only for the money and are all too willing to cut corners to make an extra buck.

When buying into a concrete building make sure you are going with a builder that has a long and proven track record of satisfied customers and a strong warranty and don't end up buying in Faulty Towers.

Hire a competent property manager. We once purchased some apartment units in a Northern British Columbia town. All seemed well at first as the units were already rented. We had a property manager from Vancouver looking after all the paperwork and a live-in caretaker (hired by the property manager) to deal with the tenants. Over time we noticed the income dropping off. Upon investigation it turned out the property manager had hired a local barkeep to be the caretaker. She was not able to collect delinquent rents and actually avoided the other tenants. Without rules and good management the quality of tenants deteriorated. It was a mess. We hired a new local property manager who knew the town. He took charge, cleaned the place up and we were back to cash-flow in short order. Good property management provides peace of mind and profit.

When owning investment real estate one of the best bits of advice I ever received was the 1% rule of cash flow. Basically if you can get 1% of the value per month as rent (or close to that depending on interest rates) you have a wonderful thing called cash flow. You can sleep well at night knowing that someone is paying all the bills on real estate that you will someday own outright. When real estate cash flows you don't need to worry if the market goes up, down or sideways. When you are able to get 1% you can rest assured that you are getting in very close to the bottom.

Most importantly, to be successful in real estate investing **you must take action**. You can think about what you should do and could do and next year look back on what you should have done and could have done. Without action it is only talk and wishful thinking. THE best advice I ever received without question is to write down your goals, create an action plan, get into action and hold yourself accountable. Today.

Do:

- In a concrete high-rise check out the building envelope.
- Check out the exact quality of all interior finishing such as the kitchen cabinets – take pictures of the show suite.
- Check out the builder ... What has he built before? How are other buildings he built finished?
- Have some rules for yourself – such as the 1% rule.
- Have a plan, write down your goals and take action. Real estate is great for creating your own personal wealth.

Don't:

- Assume the property manager is good. Check him or her out.
- Assume concrete on its own is waterproof.
- Assume that all buildings are equal. They are not.

34

Ender Ilkay

Principal of Cedar Coast Properties, a Vancouver based land development company with over 6,000 acres of property holdings in waterfront communities across British Columbia.

BEST ADVICE: *Invest in land.*

I was on a ladder and had a can of paint in my hand when I experienced my first revelation about the wealth-building power of real estate. I was twelve years old and, together with my older sister, was painting the family home. I was putting a second coat on the aging wooden siding when the lady next door pulled into her driveway and greeted me in a particularly cheerful mood. She exclaimed that she had just paid off a six-unit apartment building she owned. I was amazed that this unassuming old lady next door – most any adult is old to a twelve year old – had six people paying her rent each month. I didn't know it at the time, but the seeds of my future had been sown. Since the age of eighteen, I have been immersed in the real estate world as a realtor, business coach, investor and developer.

I have owned a vast number of properties over the past two decades, and in my experience, the best-return real estate investment is land. It is one of the only segments of real estate that truly appreciates. Buildings, despite renovations, depreciate over time. A vacant lot, or a house with property, will outperform a similarly-located condo over the long run.

But vacant land generally offers no income, so location and timing are critical in a land-only investment. Of course timing the market is much easier in theory than in practice. In the late 1980s, as a twenty-something real estate agent in Toronto, it seemed that everyone was making a fortune buying and selling real estate except me. I was sitting tentatively on the sidelines, wishing I could have bought in 1985 when prices were low. I finally jumped in with both feet after watching more and more people make six figure profits buying and flipping homes with seemingly little effort. I acquired three houses and a condo in nine months. Days after my last purchase in April 1989, it was as if someone had rung a bell declaring the end of the biggest real estate boom seen in Toronto in generations. What followed was a vicious downturn, with house prices dropping 35% and condo prices dropping a full 50%.

It was certainly a great early lesson. Markets move in cycles, and "this time it's different" is never correct. Having no pressing need to sell, I held my investments and waited for the market to recover. After all, every downturn is followed by a recovery. I eventually sold the houses for a tidy profit. However, I sold the condo unit 16 years after purchasing it for less than I had paid, despite it being in a well-maintained building in central Mississauga, one of Greater Toronto's fastest growing cities.

A realtor colleague of mine made the same timing error, buying at the peak of the market. He vowed to never again buy real estate aside from his own home, and stuck to earning commissions instead. It's surprising that only a small percentage of realtors build any meaningful wealth through real estate investing.

With the Ontario market in the doldrums in the mid 1990s – and having learnt a few lessons about market cycles from my previous mistakes – I bought as much quality real estate as I could afford at the time. If the market took off again and prices rose, I would be rewarded. If the market remained flat or perhaps declined even further, I'd have the opportunity to buy additional low-priced properties. A slow market is full of great opportunities, and that's the time to act, even if our natural desire as humans is to have our decisions validated by others. At the height of the real estate bubble in 2007, people lined up in all sorts of weather at presale condo sites for the privilege of paying $500 to $2,000 per square foot (amazing but true) for a suite. They vastly overpaid, making the same mistake I made more than twenty years ago. If you're one of the many who got caught up in the marketing hype and overpaid for a presale condo or real estate of any kind, my only comment would be to not beat yourself up. Learn from it and move on. I've yet to meet an investor who has not made any investing mistakes.

The most important task that I do as a developer is analysis. I study multiple trends, statistics and data before making any land investment. Buying land in the path of growth seems like a sure-win strategy, but it's not that simple. I have a friend in St. George, Utah, a fast growing city set in a breathtaking red-rock canyon an hour and a half north of Las Vegas. In 2006, with construction underway on a new international airport, the area was ranked the fastest growing county in the United States. The population was expected to double from 150,000 to 300,000 in ten years. However, after analyzing the St. George market, I concluded it would be a terrible place to invest. There was a singular shocking statistic: every building lot required to house those extra 150,000 residents was either already created; in the process of being serviced; or had received final approval to proceed.

I look for scarcity in my land investments. Most of the land parcels I have bought are waterfront or have a great view of the water. Here's an example of the appreciation that waterfront property owners can enjoy: I recently looked up the sales history of a beautiful oceanfront property in West Vancouver. The property initially sold as a newly-developed lot in 1930 for $6,000. A modest home was built on it and periodically updated and expanded, although the value remains primarily in the land. The initial owners kept the property for 25 years and sold it in 1955 for $60,000. It sold again in 1980 for $600,000 and then in 2007 for $6.3 million. That's a ten-fold increase every 25 years! Will it be worth $60 million by 2030? Sounds outlandish, but who knows? After all, $600,000 would seem extraordinary to the buyer who paid $60,000 in 1955. Interestingly, to achieve this remarkable return, the property's annual rate of appreciation has averaged just below 10%. It doesn't sound like much, but that is the power of compound returns.

The only real estate I've known to outperform waterfront homes in Vancouver is waterfront and water-view property in small towns in rural B.C. An example is a one acre oceanfront lot on Vancouver Island that was purchased for $11,000 in 1973 had appreciated to $33,000 by 1982, and $800,000 by 2007. Has it gone up in a straight line? Absolutely not. There have been peaks and valleys, and as I write this in 2009, the value of this property has declined sharply to $500,000, a drop of almost 40% from the peak. These pullbacks in price represent tremendous opportunity, because the next high will be much higher than the previous peak and these non-urban properties will continue to outperform. Here's why:

- Demographics: As the population ages, there is a trend to moving away from the city to retire in smaller communities. There is also a greater demand for second homes.
- Improvements in roads and infrastructure: Recreational areas such as Whistler, Tofino and the Okanagan have become safer, quicker and easier to get to. Real estate values in the areas have increased as a result.
- Improvements in air travel options: When Westjet began offering flights from Calgary to Comox on Vancouver Island a few years ago, the flights were only offered three days a week. Now there are daily flights to Comox from Edmonton and Calgary. Albertans who are tired of -20C weather are flocking to Vancouver Island for a few days of golf in February, and to enjoy the sea and sand in summer. Airports in a number of rural B.C. cities have expanded recently or are slated to expand.
- Technology allows us to stay connected or work from locations that would not have been practical just fifteen years ago.
- Canada in general and BC specifically are seen around the world

as a nature filled paradise and a safe haven. People want to live here, own here and invest here in ever greater numbers.

I am fortunate to have visited many beautiful places in B.C., either camping, vacationing or scouting investments. It's a place where a well-researched investment in land will not only provide enjoyment and memories, but will be one of the soundest investments you make. Yes, be careful, do your research, and don't get caught up in hype, and yet don't miss out on the greatest wealth creation vehicle there is.

Do:

- Remember that markets move in cycles, and "this time it's different" is never correct.
- Look for scarcity in land investments. Waterfront or properties with a great view of the water have consistently outperformed the market in general.
- Understand the power of compound returns.
- Don't beat yourself up if you've made an investing mistake. Learn and profit from the lesson.
- Do your homework, research well but remember that rewards only flow to those who take action.

35

Cameron McNeill

Co-founder and president of MAC Marketing
Solutions Inc. In 2007, MAC sold more than $1.1
billion worth of new construction real estate.

BEST ADVICE: *Find and keep the MOJO! Start with a plan.*

When Oz asked me the question, "What's the best advice you ever gave a developer?", I was initially stumped. And I'm not often stumped. I wanted to say something profound, something meaningful. But the real estate marketing and sales profession is really a very complex concept. It's hard to distill into one or two quips. A successful sales and marketing program is really the synchronization of 10,001 details, all orchestrated in perfect harmony. I often use the following analogy to describe the role of MAC Marketing Solutions Inc., a real estate marketing firm I founded in 2000:

MAC is like the conductor of an orchestra. Our job is to ensure that all the components are playing in perfect harmony. One can assemble the best composer (architect?), pianist (interior designer?), string section (communications firm?), etcetera, but if not all the orchestra is following the lead of a charismatic and competent conductor, then the symphony won't be played to its full potential. On a competitive stage, everyone needs to play in perfect tune.

At MAC, when all the elements of a sales and marketing program are in perfect harmony, we call it the "Mojo." And you can tell when a project has the Mojo – it cannot be faked. It creates magnified results and a positive energy that is impossible to replace.

So, what's the best advice I can give?

Find and keep the MOJO!

How do we do that? Not easy. It's really about getting all stakeholders to execute every detail in near perfect harmony. Here's one key:

Start with a plan.

In order to maximize success – and regardless of the developer's attributes, vision and constraints; regardless of the market cycle; and regardless of any specific property characteristics – start with a well-defined and thought-out plan. The sooner a comprehensive strategy is in place, the better. Beyond that, a plan can add strong value at any stage of a project.

At MAC, we put such an emphasis on the planning process, that we created a proprietary process dubbed MAC ESP, which is an acronym for Envisioning, Strategy, and Plan. For each project, we create a stakeholder group comprised of minds that can best help bring the project to its optimum conclusion – a sale or multiple sales. This group can include research and intelligence experts, marketing and salespeople, developers, development managers, construction firm owners, architects, interior designers, planners and retail and hotel experts. As many as 15 participants share their thoughts and debate the project. After the brainstorm, a strategic plan in the form of a flexible and dynamic MAC ESP document is drafted to help all the parties involved understand the project's objectives and to move ahead to the next step. The brainstorm results in a deep understanding of the sales opportunity and has lasting positive impacts:

- It defines the customer (target market). All aspects of the project are consequently designed and targeted to that customer.
- It provides an opportunity for the developer (or visionary) to articulate his or her vision, and allows that vision to be captured and communicated to all those involved in the project. In my experience, regardless of the passion and vision of the devel-

oper, too many details are lost in translation to the multitude of project stakeholders. Even the best visions are meaningless if they aren't clearly communicated to everyone involved.

• It gives all stakeholders an opportunity to share and be heard, and to ultimately "buy-in" to the future direction of the project.

The MAC ESP document captures the critical thinking of **ALL** in the stakeholder group. It includes both macro and micro research, competitive information, design parameters for architects and interior designers, a detailed SWAT (Strengths, Weaknesses, Opportunities, and Threats) analysis of the project, communication information, key advertising and sales messages, and timelines and budgets for marketing and financial partners. As well, an overall marketing plan defines in detail the target market(s), right down to the lifestyles of each target market. The plan provides **CLARITY** to all involved. It also allows for confident and timely decisions and gives outside groups, such as financiers, greater confidence in the project. Furthermore, it allows MAC to disseminate a **COMMON VISION** to all stakeholders. Even the greatest vision or plan won't be successful if it can't be communicated to all involved, from architect to interior designer, developer to sales team. What exactly makes this location special? Will a quiet and peaceful location be desirable to a single twenty-something? Perhaps not! To what extent can the municipal planners be influenced? What is the dream that we want the customer to buy into? What differentiates us from the other guys? We "get it", but can the sales team communicate the right message?

And the plan needs to be flexible and dynamic. Variables are ever changing. Regular check-ins are required and key milestones need to be met to ensure the essence of the plan remains intact. Changes need to be communicated and the project's course continuously reinforced.

The majority of projects that fail do so because they weren't sufficiently planned right from the get go. A clear vision can be misinterpreted or poorly executed by someone down the line. MAC is often asked to step in and assist with the marketing plan of projects that have already been launched. In these projects, we often find that few members of the existing orchestra are playing in tune with each other. A detailed planning process and strategy at **ANY STAGE** can re-align the members of a team, identify problems and re-chart the best course of action.

To summarize, development marketing has less to do with science and more to do with thoughtfully bringing together the right professionals who can share and debate ideas and, ultimately, rally behind a common vision. This process, while not always flawless, maximizes the potential for a successful development. And let's not forget that **MOJO** thing: When you have many people all working in harmony towards a common vision (don't hesitate to inject a little fun into the process), the project will find the Mojo. And when you do, everyone involved will know it!

Do:

- Hire the right people. Surround yourself with the best planners, project managers, builders, marketers, salespeople, specialized lawyers, graphic designers, advertisers and financial partners. Spend plenty of time discovering and gathering your very own "A-team" that best fits with the scope of the project.
- Understand that certain expenses paid in one area will more than pay dividends at the end of the project.
- Start with a comprehensive plan and let every stakeholder participate in its creation.
- Provide exceptional customer service at **EVERY** step of the development and construction process.

Don't:

- Cheap out on the talents of lawyers, architects and others. I have seen developers try to avoid an architect's $50,000 fee and then waste millions on inefficient design and delays in the approval process.
- Sell your best units first.
- Let yours or any other stakeholder's real estate tastes and architectural biases trump the needs and wants of the target market.
- Skimp on the sales talent. The sales team is gold and can make or break sales success.
- Waste space. I recall a project in which the architect designed a typical apartment layout that designated 15% of space to hallways. We redesigned the ground floor with street entrances, eliminating the hallways and adding space. And the entrance from the street provided a more homey feeling to entice buyers with.

36

Randy Stark

Builder, Developer and Investor

BEST ADVICE: *Do your due diligence.*

Land Development and Subdivision:

For the purposes of this chapter, I concentrate on land development as it relates to the **average** real estate investor or speculator and how they can profit from it. Of course there are hundreds of potential scenarios possible in the development world and the following is by no means exhaustive or conclusive. I want to focus more on the parameters and building blocks of developing land rather than the technicalities, of which there are many.

Definition of developing: For our purposes, I am defining the word "develop" to "change into something other than it currently is" (i.e. different use), or "redefining the parameters governing the use of a property", and therefore hopefully its value.

For example:

- Changing the way we see the property being used;
  I.e., property usage is becoming more creative
- Foreseeing other usages;
  What are all the options for this property?
- Thinking outside the box;
  How can this property be best used (and therefore most efficiently)?

How to find properties:

If you are serious about developing, you must have a workable plan of locating potential properties. Following is a list of ways I have used to find properties of interest.

- **Relationship with realtor**
  A realtor specializing in development properties is an invaluable addition to your team. They usually have the information on what is available, what the area is like, and what the current values are. Most realtors specialize in their own geographic areas and this is good as the "shotgun" approach to finding properties can in my experience be very inefficient.

- **Be "development" minded** ... get into the habit of thinking like a developer. Always look at property with an eye to upgrading it. This will require you to know the basic rules of developing in your area of interest. Which brings me to the next one.

- **Get an OCP (overall community plan)** or equivalent from the city hall, and learn where there is potential for development. This can often give you a good heads up where future development will be as well as other useful information.

- **Look in the papers for fisbos** (for sale by owners) or realtor ads. There are also several online forums and websites that are very popular and full of real estate for sale.

- **Drive around the subject areas** you are interested in regularly... you never know when you will see a new "for sale" sign on a front lawn. Many people want to have a shot at selling their own property first and you may be the first to see it.

- **Talk to people**: neighbors, friends, etc. ... who may be a link to a deal. Many deals come from networking and people like to

deal with those they know. You want to make sure that everyone knows that you are in the market for development property.
A short true story may help to drive this point home. Several
years ago I had an application for a very simple and non-intru-
sive rezoning before a city council. Unknown to me, however,
the neighbors had taken a negative view of my proposal and
rallied several dozen people in the neighborhood to show up
with signs, petitions, and speeches all proclaiming the devasta-
tion my small rezoning would cause. Fortunately for me the
application was not illogical and so I did receive permission to
rezone, and it all ended up with good feelings because the end
product was positive. However, the lesson I learned was not to
assume anything and treat your neighbors in a "neighborly" way.
You can be sure that the NEXT time I will talk to any possibly
affected neighbors to clear any air before starting the process.

What to do when you find a potential development property:

A very important part of real estate developing is putting together
a deal that will enable you to explore the potential with minimum
risk. As I mentioned, all developments are different and each has
its own set of nuances and challenges. I want to mention a few of
the tasks you will usually need to accomplish in order to proceed
after you find an interesting property, but please remember that
this is a very technical and complicated business and all successful
real estate developers have a plan they go by that hopefully keeps
them from making errors.

When you locate a possible redevelopment property you will
need to move into action. Good properties usually don't stay on the
market very long but unfortunately this is where many people come
to a wall. They like the property, they think it has potential, they
really want to move forward ... but they hit a wall. Whether its fear
or not knowing how to proceed, there exists a wall between think-

ing and doing. How to get past that wall is not what this chapter is about, but a few steps to take are:

1. Get it in writing!

If the property is worth your interest, usually you will want to at least "tie it up" for enough time to enable you to explore everything relevant about that property and what you may want to do with it. This will require time, and the more you need to find out the more time you will need. You will need several days or even weeks, depending on the project. How you tie it up is to be worked out by your realtor or your lawyer, but unless you do, you stand the chance of someone else moving in on your find and scooping it. You need to have subject clauses that allow you to research the possibilities that exist and create a budget and time frame for a successful development.

2. Go to the City Hall

You will almost always want to take a potential development to the local city hall in order to have many of your questions answered.

- You need to find out all the possible uses
- You will need to find out the costs to develop and many of these costs can be found out from the city hall such as:

1. Application costs
2. Servicing costs
3. Development costs charges
4. Parkland acquisition costs
5. Permits and other fees
6. Business license
7. Inspection fees
8. Approval fees
9. Administration fees
10. Security deposits

11. Water service app fees
12. Utility connections
13. Any road work costs including driveway let downs, sidewalks road expansions etc.

There can be more costs and fees than you can think of, and so it is very important to exhaust every source to determine the potential costs you may be responsible for. It is a good idea to hire a development consultant to ensure you don't miss anything ... as usual; a good consultant can save you lots of time, effort and money.

Needless to say, you, the developer, will be responsible for paying many if not most or all of the costs to develop your property.

3. Do your due diligence

As in any business project, due diligence is a must. I cannot stress how important it is to have a good and thorough plan to execute all the due diligence and research that is necessary to be successful at developing. Please pay extreme attention to this as "surprises" tend to be common in any real estate developing. From underfunding and having insufficient capital, to overvaluing your final product, many a project has been torpedoed by the misuse of due diligence.

Real estate developing has been around since people have been around and as long as people need somewhere to live, there will be a need for developing. The world is becoming more fascinating every year, and I honestly believe that there are more opportunities today in developing than there were yesterday.

In conclusion, here is a list of my dos and don'ts (rules) that came at great cost to me. Stick to these rules ... they were expensive to learn!

Do:

- Act hastily on a potential property.
- Cultivate relationships with realtors who know development

potential.
- Look regularly and systematically for properties and have a plan.
- Look where others are not looking.
- Start to think like an entrepreneur, in that everything you see has opportunity.

Don't:

- Expect it to be easy and fast.
- Make enemies of the neighbors. If possible, include them in your ideas. Ask what they think. This can turn away future wrath.
- Ignore property because you don't think the city will accept a development, or consider your ideas. Many new ideas are becoming the norm, and higher density is necessary. Innovative ideas are welcome and so land development success also goes to those who think outside the box!

37

Freeman Yee

President of HighPath Capital Corporation, which offers alternative investments and real estate financing.

BEST ADVICE: *Big profits in real estate come from "changing the legal use" of land.*

In recent years, there have been more and more companies offering investments in land and development. They sound so enticing compared to stocks or GICs, but some are riskier than others. As part of my 18-year career in financing real estate, I spent four years working for the leader of this industry. Let's discuss what to look for, and what to look out for in these investments, from an "insider's" perspective.

There are several reasons to consider these investments. Firstly, an investment in a development can make you money, even if "prices" do <u>not</u> go up. This is because you are investing in the profitability of the development, instead of just hoping for price increases. Secondly, a well-run project will be completely passive. There are no tenants, no toilets, and no tradespeople for you to deal with. Thirdly, some of these investments are RRSP-eligible.

However, there are risks in these investments. Firstly, since you are investing in the profitability of a development, you are exposed to the risk of cost-increases and the ability of the managers. Secondly, most of these investments are not liquid – you typically have to commit your funds for several years without an easy way to get your funds out of the project early. Thirdly, some projects do lose money.

184 ··· REAL ESTATE ACTION

Before we analyze these investments, let's look at a couple of development examples.

In the mid 1990s while I was a mortgage broker, I used to think that land made a terrible investment because there is no revenue on bare land. Then one day, an accomplished homebuilder had me help arrange mortgage financing on a new subdivision. His projections showed that as each level of rezoning and planning is approved, the value of the land increases significantly. When services (water, sewer, power, communications, roads, etc.) are added to the property, the value goes up again. Subdividing the lots adds value. Construction of homes adds value. I quickly realized that the big profits in real estate come from "changing the legal use" of land.

However, a couple of years later, the BC real estate market slowed down. The developer couldn't get civic approvals, ran out of cash for mortgage payments, and the project went into foreclosure.

Today, some developers are not finishing the construction of their projects. Why not? Often, it's because of financing. Banks require that the developer pre-sells most of the building before they provide the necessary construction mortgage. However, pre-selling locks in the developer's sales revenue. If construction costs subsequently rise above the pre-sale prices, the developer would be completing construction at a loss. So they don't bother.

In both examples, it was mortgage financing that put the developments at risk. With this in mind, let's discuss what to look for when investing in land / development:

1) Mortgage Financing

Generally, part of the investment capital raised is set aside in an "interest reserve" for mortgage payments during the expected duration of the project. However, if a project run longer than expected, the interest reserve could run out.

The safest land / development investments have no mortgage

at all. If a project runs longer than expected, there are no mortgage payments to make and there is nobody to foreclose.

Also, if there is no construction mortgage, there is no need to pre-sell. This allows the developer to increase sale prices (market conditions permitting) in order to still make a profit if construction costs rise.

If there is a mortgage, find out how the payments will be made, or how the mortgage can be paid out in full. For instance, if the property can be rented out after construction, perhaps the rent can cover the mortgage payments. If the property is to be sold after value is added, look at how much of the "end product" has to be sold in order to pay off the mortgage debt, and consider how easy (or difficult) it would be to achieve these sales.

2) Cash Shortfalls

What happens if they don't raise enough money or if costs increase? Will the developer still be able to buy and develop the property, or will the project fail? Will the developer have to borrow more mortgage money, which puts the project at greater risk? Find out if the managers have successfully raised funds for previous projects.

3) How is value added?

Some managers collect investors' capital, congratulate them for being involved in a prestigious development, but never actually add value to the land. Be sure that value is being created for you, after you invest (by rezoning, servicing, subdividing, or construction).

4) Management Experience

Despite the compelling advertisements, glossy handouts, and slick websites, some of these deals have managers with little or no experience in land development. Many have never seen a real estate down-cycle. Don't let them learn with your money. Experience and strong relationships with city hall will greatly improve the likelihood of the development being profitable for you.

5) Management Compensation

Look for a compensation structure where managers make their money by sharing profits with you. This motivates the managers to keep costs down, and to sell the end-product for you at the highest possible price, as quickly as possible. The more profit you make, the more profit they make.

6) Specific Location

Find out exactly where the property is in relation to other developments. In order to build, you need infrastructure and services, which are typically brought from nearby developments. If services are too far away, your money may be tied up for many years. Realize that when the salesperson says a property is just 5 minutes from a booming prairie or desert city, a 5-minute drive in these areas can be a long, long way to bring services.

7) Economics and Migration

The best reason to build one more home...would be because one more family is moving to town. Even if every new family decides to rent, you still have to build more homes for them.

Invest in larger cities with strong and diverse economies. This creates a broad range of jobs, which attracts people of different backgrounds. Avoid small towns with few industries, no matter how pretty the location. There have been many failed projects that were very pretty. Recreational properties generally get hit hardest in slow markets because they lack jobs. Don't allow promises of a future resort, golf courses, or waterfront cloud your vision. Stick with strong economics and migration. Population growth creates the only truly sustainable demand for housing.

The two basic ways to invest in land / development are mortgage lending and equity ownership.

If your investment involves being a **mortgage lender**, the returns are typically 10-12% per year, paid to you as an income. However, there is no income from bare land to make the mortgage payments to you. Other mortgage investments can offer similar returns, with far less risk. Remember that mortgages put developments at risk, even if you are the lender. If the developer fails to make mortgage payments, you may have to get together with the other mortgage investors and hire a receiver to take over a half-completed development.

Also, look at your security. If the sum of the mortgage investment plus any other mortgages exceeds the current "as-is" value of the property, then your investment is not fully secured, and should really be considered an "equity ownership" investment, so you should earn a better rate of return as described below. Do not base your decision on the value of the property "upon completion" – use the "as-is" value.

Equity ownership investments typically involve being a silent, "limited partner", or a share-holder in a legal entity that owns the land. These usually pay you a percentage profits at the very end of the project, with a cumulative return of approximately 20% per year. For instance, if a project pays out in 4 years, your target gain should be 80%.

Conclusion:

Land / development investments can be excellent wealth creators for the investor who wants a truly passive, RRSP-eligible, real estate based investment that can be profitable even when prices do not go up. However, you do need to be able to sort through which ones have the best chance of being profitable.

Do:

- Understand that some investments may sound enticing compared to stocks or GICs, but some are riskier than others.
- Understand the financing of any project. The safest is a project that has no mortgage.
- Find out if the managers have successfully raised funds for previous projects.
- Be sure that value is being created for you, after you invest (by rezoning, servicing, subdividing, or construction).
- Invest in larger cities with strong and diverse economies, where there is sustainable population growth.

Don't:

- Let a developer learn with your money.
- Invest, if services are too far away.
- Be influenced by pretty properties, in the absence of sound economics.

BEST ADVICE:
Thinking 'out of the box'

38

Scott Berg and
Wayne Edgar

Owners of Western Canada's largest trading network with 800 business clients producing close to $10 million per year in Trade transactions

BEST ADVICE: *Don't pay cash for Real Estate, trade for it!*

There is a powerful tool for real estate investors that has been available for centuries. Using trade (also known as barter) instead of cash to buy real estate!

Selling a Property Using Trade:

I have spoken with real estate investors over the years that have had difficulty selling their real estate (especially in tough markets). Either it is a buyers market or the price they want to get does not attract any interest. For the creative real estate investor there are other options available. For example:

Your listed asking price is $500,000 and you are not willing to accept offers for less and are not getting any buyers who are interested at that price

BUT

You need a boat as well.

Solution?

Advertise that you are willing to accept a boat, car or something else you want (worth at least $50,000) that you will take for part of the purchase price!

I know of several real estate investors who have bought or sold on this basis. A real estate investor I know of accepted a $200,000 Ferrari towards the purchase price of a condo he was selling. With a little creativity anything is possible!

This tool will open new doors that aren't open with a full cash offer. Many people (especially business owners) are looking to move their excess inventory or distressed inventory and may consider turning it into a piece of property if they can get full value for the Trade.

If you don't really want to take something directly you can also use the services of a corporate trade company that will help put buyers and sellers together.

Buying a property with a Trade Component:

If you are buying real estate you can also use this same tool. If you find a property you are interested in and the seller is not willing to move on the price, you may have something to trade that could form part of the purchase price. You may even have some property that you are looking to move that they will accept in trade for what they have.

There are many options when dealing in trade that most individuals are not aware of. If you come across a distressed sale, ask what else they would take as a down payment, tie it up and use these ideas to find what they need and trade it!

Using a Trade Exchange to Buy or Sell Real Estate:

Another option is to use a corporate trade exchange to help you navigate the buying or selling of real estate using trade. Retail trade exchanges have been around for over 50 years with over 250,000 businesses in Canada and the US participating in one form or another. Their job is to bring buyers and sellers together in all types of business to exchange their goods and services without the use of cash.

A trade company is a clearing house for their business clients. They help find buyers for their product or service that is paid for in a trade credit commonly known as a Trade Dollar. These Trade Dollars generated from business they would not normally get is then used to offset existing and future cash expenses (usually at their wholesale cost). You can ask if they have any properties listed for sale that you can take a look at that are available with trade as part of the purchase price. All you will need is something to offer the trade company to form part of the trade.

A great example is for a hotel. If a hotel has 10 empty rooms tonight, tomorrow morning it is revenue they will never get back (a perishable asset). If the hotel trades 4 of these rooms into their local trade exchange, they get their regular price and don't have any incremental costs to take the booking other than maybe a cleaning fee of $15 per room. When they need business cards or other printing, they use their Trade Dollars to make the purchase (at a cost of only $60 – cleaning fee for 4 rooms) which is a massive savings every time they purchase on trade instead of cash.

This same concept can apply to real estate. A business that sells seminars at full retail price to our members at $1200 per seat. If these seats were left empty, it is revenue that would be lost forever. By selling the empty seats, he has generated close to $100,000 of additional business that he would not have received otherwise. This additional $100,000 was earned at a cost around $10 per seat in books, coffee, etc. giving him a 90% discount every time he uses Trade in lieu of cash. A rental condo came up for sale for $250,000 with a $100,000 down payment accepted in Trade that was cash flow positive. The purchase was made but using the example above, the $100,000 Trade down payment actually only cost $10,000. A $90,000 savings on the purchase which of course is now converted to real cash in a piece of real estate with rental income to cover the mortgage.

Do your Research:

There are many resources on the internet that can be researched to learn more about how a trade exchange can benefit any business owner or real estate investor. The key is to remember that you must have something of value to trade and need to be able to find goods and services or real estate to acquire with the trade you earn. Call your local trade companies and ask how long they have been in business, how many clients they have and the volume of transactions they are doing each month. Make sure to find one that has at least 500 business clients and has been in business – ideally - for at least 10 years.

Remember, on your next real estate deal don't pay cash, trade for it!

Do:

- Look at all your non-cash options.
- Think wealthier.
- Use your work as your down payment.
- Use old inventory to buy your real estate.

39

Bert Chapman

Celebrating 40 years as a Realtor. Former President (2007) Okanagan Mainline Real Estate Board.
Broker Owner Premier Canadian Properties Kelowna BC.

BEST ADVICE: *Use other people's money.*

The best Real Estate advice I ever received for residential investing came from my father some 40 years ago.

He said, "Use O.P.M. and let O.P.P.". You must be thinking the same thing I did. What is he talking about? "Use O.P.M. and let O.P.P." gobbledy gook! So I asked. What did you say, I don't understand? He said, "It's a long story....but I'll tell you!"

First you buy a house using money borrowed from the bank. Other people's money, O.P.M. Then you live in it for a while and build some equity by paying down the mortgage and the natural appreciation in value that happens through time. Next you buy another house. You increase the loan on the first house for a down payment and take out a mortgage on the second house for the balance. You move into the second house but don't sell the first one. Most people make the mistake of selling the first one. Don't! You rent it out to cover all or most of the mortgage. In other words you use other people's money – O.P.M. and you let your tenant make the payments. That's other people pay or O.P.P. "Use O.P.M. and let O.P.P." You see, if you are a tenant, someone else owns the house that you are paying for. If you are the owner, someone else is paying for the house that you own. Then you do it again and again. It sounds easy, but what if something goes wrong? Like what....Dad lived through two world wars and the great depression, what could be worse than that?

Let's look at some scenarios. If I buy, and Real Estate values drop but I let other people pay for my Real Estate, I gain. If Real Estate values remain the same and other people pay for my Real Estate, I gain. If Real Estate values increase and I let other people pay for my Real Estate, I really gain.

But wait! Where should I buy? Will some places be better than others?

Will Rogers said it best. "Find out where people are going, get there first and buy Real Estate." I wonder if he knew about O.P.M. and O.P.P.?

That's great but...where are 'they' going and will 'they' have any money for Real Estate when they get there?

The next piece fell into place when I attended a seminar by Urban Futures from Vancouver. I still vividly remember the presenter David Baxter. He managed to deliver what could be a very dry subject, demography, in a very entertaining manner. Demography is the study of human populations and the predictions of what they will do in the future. This information is very valuable to governments, municipalities, cities and businesses to predict future needs. David said there are 78 million baby boomers. Those are people born between 1946 and 1966. In Canada every day for the next ten years, 1000 people turn 60 years old. Every day! The boomers are unique. They have had a full working career without interruptions like wars or depressions. They bought Real Estate when it was cheap and can sell at a huge profit. Then to top it all off, their aged parents are dying and leaving inheritances. This will be the largest transfer of wealth in history. David said, 'boomers can go where they want and buy what they want and they will". They will drive the market in lifestyle Real Estate. They will choose from the places in Canada that have the best climate and the best recreational lifestyle. Boomers will live longer than their parents and be in better health. So....the best Real Estate investing advice

I ever received is made up of all these things. Buy lifestyle Real Estate in resort type areas like the Okanagan and Vancouver Island. Get there before all those boomers during the next ten years. Use O.P.M. and let O.P.P. CHA –CHING!

Thanks Dad.

Do:

- Find out where people are going, get there first and buy Real Estate.
- Do use other people's money.
- Do let other people pay for your Real Estate.
- Buy a second house and rent out the first one.
- Buy lifestyle real estate.

Don't:

- Wait to buy Real Estate. Buy Real Estate and wait.
- Sell any of your Real Estate. Just borrow against it to buy more.
- Use a relative as your Realtor unless they are the best Realtor for the job.
- Wait for the market to change. Just make the best deal you can in the existing market.

40

Ed Deprato

Has created a Rent-To-Own program where he provides investors a predictably profitable real estate investment without ever dealing with tenants, collecting rent, or maintaining property.

BEST ADVICE: *Rent–To–Own, rather than traditional renting is win/ win for tenants and investors.*

The best Real Estate advice I ever received came from a wise old Italian man who owned several houses for what appeared to be forever. Bruno was already in retirement when we met and we were in the middle of a friendly negotiation as I tried to get the best deal I could on his little 4-plex in central Edmonton, and he tried to get the highest price. After a few days of back and forth, we met over an espresso and finally papered a deal we could both live with. Once the deal was signed Bruno smiled at me the way a grandfather does when he sees a little of himself in his grandchild. He told me that I was going to be very successful and advised that if I continued to own real estate for the 'right reason', I would grow my portfolio to a higher value faster than I could imagine. Admittedly, I initially thought very little of Bruno's advice. It's just too simple… It wasn't until many years later that Bruno's simple words really began to mean something to me.

As we've seen and experienced over the past few years; a rapidly rising market attracts inexperienced speculators to simply jump in blindly buying property in any condition without any regard for what or where they buy, resulting in a buying mania which pushes prices to a level where little value can be found. What's worse is the rising euphoric market eventually produces another buyer willing to deliver a tidy profit to the first. Often their gratification and enthusiasm of having realized a seemingly significant and easy profit on their first adventure in real estate 'investing' causes them to do it again, and to also tell everyone they know how they too can find fortune – suddenly everyone's an 'investor'. For the true investors diligently trying to increase their holdings, this type of market is a challenge. Maintaining a focus on owning the right properties for the right reasons are especially difficult in a rising market. Too often, investors lose out on an otherwise reasonable deal to someone willing to be unreasonable. It's hard to put a fair deal together when herds of others are racing to outbid you simply because it's become fashionable to own real estate at any cost. A rapidly rising market is extremely difficult for responsible investors.

Often new investors are willing to compromise monthly cashflow in exchange for the opportunity to sell a property for more than they paid. It's an easy and profitable trade to make in a rising market. However, when prices are not rising as quickly investors often struggle to top up the rent in order to cover expenses, while the prospect of selling at the same or less than their purchase price causes unnecessary worry and frustration. Sometimes investors' concerns are further aggravated by problematic tenants not paying rent on time or possibly causing damage to the property.

Rent-To-Own can offer a solution which restores the opportunity to own real estate for the right reason while insulating the investor from the typical pitfalls of our business (vacancy, management concerns, problems of liquidity, and market fluctuation). Rent-To-Own as it relates to real estate is simply a facility from which the tenant is given the exclusive right to buy the home at a preset price for the life of their lease. Normally the renter pays a small premium on top of the market rent which accumulates over time to form a downpayment which they then use to buy the home.

A properly structured RTO deal benefits the tenant by helping them build a downpayment while they rent; and by offering a fixed price on the property which may (due to market forces) be more, or less than the actual value of the property when the tenant chooses to exercise their option. While some investors may not be willing to offer a tenant a fixed option price and an opportunity to buy the home at less than what it's truly worth, I feel that it's good business. Our company offers tenants an opportunity to move into home ownership, which makes it different than just renting from other landlords. We are also better positioned to create an open and profitable relationship with our tenant. Since our tenants have the intent of buying the home they rent, their mindset is more that of a buyer/owner and therefore they have a vested interest in maintaining the property – unlike a typical renter. Our tenants generally pay an upfront option payment (normally between $5000, and $20,000) which gets credited to their purchase. It is because our tenants have a vested interest in the home right from day one that we rarely (basically never) have to deal with a tenant that has skipped out. Our tenants pay a small premium (on top of the monthly rent) which accumulates monthly and is added to the initial payment to form together a sizeable downpayment over the life of their lease. This is applied to the final purchase price once the tenant buys the property. Obviously all of this monthly cashflow enhances our ability to service our obligations, during the lease period without ever struggling through periods of negative cashflow. We set an option price based on a modest rate of appreciation and comparable home sales. Of course our tenants are also our buyers, so we don't have to worry about finding a buyer when it comes time to sell. And because we already have a profitable price fixed with our tenant, we are not exposed to market volatility. We establish a fair purchase price with our tenant right from the start so we know exactly how much we'll make and when we're going to be paid. Nothing is left to chance and so we feel that if the market appreciates to a level where our tenant gets to buy our home for slightly less than true market value at the end of their lease – God Bless Them! This is an easy trade for us to make considering we've had little to no hands-on maintenance of the property; positive cashflow right from the start; our tenants haven't missed a payment; and we sell on a specific date without having to list it for sale or negotiate... This is the right reason to own real estate.

To be fair to ourselves, our option to purchase is available to our tenants for a fixed period of time, providing their account is in good standing. Our tenants are also told that if, in the event that they do not exercise their option, they forfeit all of the option money they've paid into our program – which makes sense to the tenant considering we are holding the property available exclusively for them for a set period of time.

Do:

- Try and set a target for a total downpayment to represent a reasonable percentage of the purchase price.
- Plan to sell the home; and not to simply keep the tenants' money and the home.
- Establish a fair purchase price with tenants.
- Take a small upfront option payment.
- Know your tenant – research their application thoroughly.

Don't:

- Transfer title to your property until its SOLD and your lawyer has all the money.

41

Ozzie Jurock

Deal making Toolbox I : Foreclosures

BEST ADVICE: *Sounds sexy ... but it is not as easy as it sounds.*

Generally speaking, I have seen better deals made at auctions (sometimes even those with reserved opening bids) than at foreclosures. Foreclosures have tremendous appeal to the 'shark' in us, but in most parts of Canada you have to be a very patient shark indeed. The foreclosure dance in this country is carefully choreographed to benefit the homeowner as much as possible.

If you are trying to find a foreclosure property, be patient and don't expect anything to be easy. The real successes in the foreclosure game come during the order nisi period (i.e., the grace period the owner is granted before he is foreclosed – often dealing directly with the owner) and consummate a deal before it gets to court. In Canada – with our new privacy laws – it is difficult to find these kind of 'pre-foreclosure deals.' In the US, where courts are not nearly as nice to defaulting owners ... it is much easier. In the tough markets of 2009 you have hundreds of foreclosure listings advertised in the United States – a handful in Canada.

Despite all the press write ups to the contrary, we see very, very few investors who are consistently successful in this particular area. The same goes for the much touted "tax sales" you sometimes see advertised on late night TV. Usually, the situations being talked up are in the U.S., where foreclosure and repossession laws are much tougher on sellers. In Canada, properties are rarely sold for taxes owing.

Of course in life we do not get what we deserve but what we

negotiate ... so remember all 'great deals' - ALL – are negotiated. Not just because they are a foreclosure. In fact we have seen some foreclosures, that – after much work – were really very average deals. **The main thing to remember is, that in all 'hard tough' situations there is always work involved.**

While there are many ways to research foreclosed property, generally it is best to deal with the financial institution or the lawyer that has an order for sale. Particularly if the property has been on the market for a while, it may be a burr under the lender's saddle – one they'd like to move off from.

Foreclosures work well in tough markets, not very well in hot markets ... although people will be people and some will get into trouble in ANY market.

If after all you have read, you are not discouraged – follow these steps:

1. **Identify an area that you like to own property in.** (Remember, you will be going back and forth.)
2. **Get Realtors that are given the task by CMHC**, GE Capital and by financial institutions to sell their foreclosures. They vary between area and banks change them from time to time. CMHC has Realtors bid on their total foreclosures annually by area. You can call their office to get the latest list.
3. **Find out which lawyers and appraisers specialize in foreclosure** mortgage portfolios on behalf of financial institutions (may also vary by area).
4. **List your name with all realtors** in your area telling them of your interest.
5. **Talk to YOUR bank and or banks** in the area and ask them "Do you have any foreclosures or court ordered sales in your branch?"
6. **Yes, every court house in the province publishes its list** of foreclosed properties daily. You can buy these addresses just by going there.

General Rules:

1. **It is better to deal with the Realtor that has the foreclosure listed**. (He/she has the inside scoop and human nature being human nature will like to double end his/her own deal.)
2. You can write a 'subject to financing' offer...if the lawyer or bank will accept it...but before it goes to court for approval...all subjects have to be removed.
2. **Your opening bid is just the entry into a court date**. That bid will be known to all.
3. **Expect on the court date to have many competing offers**, including possibly from the old owner. Have another better one ready yourself.
4. **Always add $100 or $200 to the price** ... such as $120,100 or $99,200. Judges will grant competing bids even for $100.
5. **Always take your Realtor and/or a lawyer with you**. On larger deals a lawyer may make a better argument on your behalf.
6. **Foreclosures are generally sold as is / where is**. Be sure to take a home inspector/ appraiser with you when you get granted access for viewing.
7. **Have a predetermined price in mind before you go**. Don't get caught up in a frenzy.

To buy a foreclosure takes time and effort ... and you can still get beaten out on the court house steps by competing buyers or even the foreclosed-upon owner. Finally, in a rising market, courts generally will side with the owner.

Do:

- Understand that all properties are sold 'as is, where is'.
- Research the area – what are regular properties seling for now and how do they compare to the foreclosed on you wish to buy?
- Do take the home inspector with you when you have access.

Don't:

- Assume, that a foreclosure is an automatic good buy.
- Think your accepted offer will be the final one...you may be outbid in court.
- Think Canada is like the U.S. U.S. foreclosures are much easier in execution, but there are more charlatans in the marketplace – selling programs for 'pre-foreclosures', selling foreclosures over the current market or offering 'short sales' that are not approved by a lender.

42

Ozzie Jurock

Deal making Tool Box II : Auctions

Best advice: *Sounds sexy too, but do your research.*

Real estate auctions are places where cash is really king. But to play this game, you need to have market knowledge, discipline, and patience if you want to avoid getting killed. If you lack even one of these qualities, they will hand you your head. You have to be able to go to an auction and sit there all night, bidding only up to your limit and no further. Often, you will go home empty handed time after time until you get what you want.

Although in Canada auctions are relatively new, they have been around for centuries elsewhere. Countries like Australia sell all their real estate via auctions. In the United States (in 2009) thousands of properties are sold via auctions. There are even bus tours in places like Phoenix where you get wheeled around to look at dozens and dozens of properties for sale at a time.

Generally, there are two kinds. One is driven by a developer who is trying to find a new way to market units. This kind you want to avoid, because the developer will not sell if he doesn't get his "reserved" price (thus there are few bargains to be had). The other auction is the type driven by financial institutions. (Or in the US – sheriff sales, court house step sales.) This is where you want to be. Here the institutions want to clear out foreclosed developments so they can get the most cash back as soon as possible. Usually, all of the units, or at least a good portion, have **no reserve** (i.e., any price will get the unit). You want to see the words **"unreserved auction"** in any auction advertising you attend.

The newest trend in auctions is the 'on line auction'. Half the audience could be sitting in a room somewhere, but on-line there are other registered bidders that participate as well. If you go to www.ritchiebros.com for instance you can see all the upcoming auctions – months ahead. And yes, all their real estate auctions are 'unreserved.' Good place to go thru the procedure a couple of times before actually buying … get comfortable on how it works.

Things to Remember about Auctions

1. **Auctions are never haphazard.** They are carefully coordinated and timed to create the maximum level of buying urgency. The idea isn't to give you a deal, but instead to get the maximum possible return for the vendor/developer/court sales.
2. **Watch out for shills.** While no reputable auction house would do such a thing, a disreputable one might employ a shill to bid against a legitimate bidder and boost the final price.
3. **Do your due diligence beforehand.** Look at all the properties on the auction block. Identify one or two you will bid on, and don't bid on anything else.
4. **Position yourself in the auctioneer's sightline.** If bids are made at the same time, tradition says the bidder closest to the auctioneer takes the deal.
5. **Auctions are a psychological game.** Do a head count when you arrive. If there are a lot of heads and not too much product, come in bold and strong right off the bat. If voice bids are allowed, jump right in instead of waiting for the auctioneer to prod the bids along. This will overawe the other bidders and allow you to scoop up a unit. A good auctioneer with a full room will actually encourage a "good buy" up front to get the crowd heated up. As the night goes on and the remaining bidders fight for dwindling product, people actually end up buying at more than market prices. If it is a cold and miserable night, however, and the auction room is half empty, you should consider the

opposite strategy. Rather than roaring in, wait for the true buy-ers to spend their budgets and then make your move.

6. **Never go in without your finances ready**. In most auctions in North America you will have to put up $5,000 to $10,000 and close very quickly. Be prepared with a large enough deposit to hold your suite and a pre approved mortgage (better yet – all cash) to allow for a fast close.

7. **Make your bid in small increments**. If an auctioneer has bounced along in $10,000 increments and the bidding has slowed, offer a much smaller increase. Let's say, for instance, that the bidding has slowed at around $120,000. When the auctioneer asks if someone will bid $130,000, offer $121,000. Often that will become the final bid.

Never forget that both types of auctions have only one objec-tive: sell the units. If the unit you pre inspected didn't sell or your bid wasn't accepted, consider going back to the auctioneer imme-diately after the auction and offering the same price again. The auctioneer, after all, eats only what he kills. He will go to the devel-oper to check, and it's possible that you will still get the unit at your price. I have seen this work very well if the auction was a disap-pointment. The frustrated developer might decide to wash his hands of the whole thing and let you have **your unit for cheap.**

Do:

- Get your financing ready – you will have to 'put up' quickly.
- Pre-register in an online auction.
- Go see, walk the property.
- Walk into a real estate office and see what a comparable prop-erty would sell for now.
- Bid only on what you had decided on ahead of time.

Don't:

- Get carried away.
- Get too excited – sit on your hands for a while.
- If you lose it – don't chase it up. There is always another opportunity.
- Learn to say: "So what? Next!"

43

Rick Ledding

Lawyer at Thompson & Elliott with input from a real estate investor and advisor (the "Investor")

BEST ADVICE: *You can make millions in real estate investing regardless of the state of the economy*

L et's face it, the typical property sale is a rather straight forward transaction that rarely requires a large degree of creativity: it's simple to draw up, review and advise on. However, during my 28 plus years in the real estate game, I have worked extensively in an area where investors can make deals with little or no money up front, minimize risk and experience huge returns.

Essentially, creative investors are those who aren't afraid to negotiate deals using mechanisms that veer from the status quo, be it drafting lease with options to purchase, flips, assignments, agreements for sale and/or vendor financing.

Among the creatively structured deals that stay with me was one that happened across my desk on or about 1998, a year that the real estate market in Vancouver was broadly depressed. The Investor entered into a lease with the option to purchase 24 townhouse units in Richmond, B.C. The Investor eventually secured a return of approximately $2 million on the units, while avoiding risking any assets of his own. The Investor provided a solution to the motivated seller while limiting its risk and avoiding upfront costs but getting full control of the operations of the properties. You may wonder why the units' owners would let their property be tied up by a $10.00 option fee and in this case, over a period of years.

When the owners put the units up for sale, the owner was losing thousands of dollars each month through negative cash flow and due to changes in the market, did not know how to recover its investment.

Once the Investor registered the lease with an option to purchase against each of the titles, the Investor went looking for rent to own tenant buyers. There is an abundance of keen buyers out there who are short on cash for a down payment or have poor credit and, as a result, are willing to enter into lease with option agreements.

The Investor negotiated each unit's lease for up to $400.00 more than he paid to the owners, creating considerable monthly cash flow on his investment. Think about it: $400.00 on 24 units works out to roughly $8,000.00 a month. And this with the Investor paying no money down.

The Investor gave each tenant buyer a few years of option to purchase, which usually culminated in a sale price that was say $50,000.00 to $100,000.00 higher than what he was paying to purchase the property at the end of the term.

He also asked each tenant buyer for an option fee of $5,000.00 to $30,000.00 which was credited to the buyer if and when he or she exercised their option. If they didn't, this amount was forfeited.

In other deals, he created an "equity build-up fund" in which some of the rent – typically $100.00 to $200.00 each month – was returned to the tenant when they exercised the option. To the tenant buyers, the fund acted like a savings plan. I structured the transaction in such a way that the Investor avoided the necessity of paying property transfer tax when the property was transferred to the end buyer on closing.

The Investor simply had to wait for the market to rebound which it did in 2001. While the purchase price of each unit was deflated in 1999, they eventually climbed to market value which exceeded the option price of the tenant/buyer. Some of the tenant/buyers were even able to flip their lease agreements with the Investor for returns of up to $50,000.00. So it was win-win-win.

That was the admirable part of these deals: at the end of the day, everyone was happy. In particular, my client, the Investor, the orchestrator of the deals, made a cool $2 million, all the while enjoying positive cash flow.

The Investor may seem like an opportunistic capitalist but in reality, as you can see, the Investor attempts to get win-win-win scenarios. As well, even though many realtors and/or mortgage brokers may perceive the Investor to be a competitor, the reality is that the Investor fills a niche that no one else can address and in the process creates buyers/owners out of people who would not otherwise be able to buy and creates jobs for people like realtors, mortgage brokers and property managers.

Do:

- Make a goal of executing on your strategy. Many investors understand the principles involved in lease-with-options, but very few act on them.
- Surround yourself with support people that share your philosophy: realtors, accountants, lawyers, mortgage brokers and mentors.
- Understand and look for value. The cheapest deal is not necessarily the most valuable one.
- Always register lease-with-option deals. You can hope for the best outcome, but it doesn't hurt to be prepared for calamities.
- Thoroughly plan and map out your investment strategy. It costs three times as much to fix something later than it does to plan for all eventualities at the start.

Don't:

- Wait for the perfect deal. The reasonable deal can be just as rewarding an experience.

• Be afraid to negotiate deals using instruments that veer from the status quo like it drafting lease options or affecting skip transfers.

• ... deals that leverage somebody else's misfortune. The best deals are those in which all parties walk away happy.

44

Richard Savage

Senior vice-president of Blackmont Capital Inc., member of CIPF and IIROC. During the past decade, he has studied Feng Shui under Grand Master Yap Cheng Hai in North America, Europe, and Asia.

BEST ADVICE: *In Feng Shui, the land doesn't define the house, it is the house that defines the land*

Originally known as "Kan Yu", Classical Feng Shui is the ancient Chinese art of placing things in harmony with their natural surroundings. Going back some 3,500 years, people have used this science in order to harness the forces of nature and improve their wealth, health and, ultimately, to move towards a harmonious life. It's serious stuff for Asian bank and casino owners who, at times, seek out multiple Feng Shui masters to maximize the potential of their real estate investments.

Whistler, B.C., a 90-minute drive into the mountains from Vancouver, is home to the most expensive real estate in Canada. It's also where some of Canada's best Feng Shui is. The region is filled with dragon's veins and channels of energy, or chi, that is carried by all the mountains and stops to "rest" in the region's lakes. Chi collects in the location of water. If you see water, you see chi.

Heaven, Man, and Earth

You can use Feng Shui to select or arrange your home, business, or real estate investment. More than location, location, location, Feng

Shui is Heaven, Man, and Earth. Heaven is a ship, your date of birth and family, things which cannot be changed. This represents one third of our luck in life. As Man, you are the captain, you can be a good person or not. You are essentially in control of this third of your life. The luck of the Earth is manifested in wind and water. Wind dispenses chi, while water collects it. So, the idea is to find wind-reducing real estate and introduce water. That's how we as humans can bring chi into our homes. As a result, you will be in control of two-thirds of your life, unlike the majority of people who are only in control of one-third of their life.

Medicine to one person can be poison to another

There are 216 types of homes and eight compass positions. For each individual, four compass directions are good and four are not. A colleague of mine once purchased a house with a beautiful view to the west. She was in love with the view, but west was her worst personal compass direction. Without spending one night in the home, she realized her mistake: buying out of desire instead of sense. It was a costly, $250,000 mistake. And she had difficulty selling the home even though it was an ideal location for the 50% of the population that have compass directions that oppose hers. It's difficult to translate into words why the location was wrong for her, but it's a lesson she hasn't forgotten. So, know your compass directions.

Feng Shui can be made

Feng Shui is about direction, location, and time. The direction a building faces is not necessarily determined by the location of the front door, but by activity in the area. For example, Feng Shui can be influenced by a nearby busy street. Location relates to the physical placement of a building. It must be a location that is compatible with your compass directions and that is supported by the landscape, or exterior Feng Shui. Time is the most important element of Feng Shui, and also the most complex. It relates to the date of your birth and when you move into any newly acquired real estate. For example, how do you define time when there a five people living in the same house? Understanding time can be the difference between positive and negative Feng Shui.

Feng Shui is like a human being. Look at a house, building, or business as if it is a person's face. Is it warm and welcoming, or is it triangular and unbalanced? Does the house sit on the landscape like a person sits on a chair? Is there support for the back of the home from another home, trees, or a mountain? Do the armrests exist as trees, facing outward from the house? In Feng Shui, these armrests are known as the green dragon on the left and the white tiger on the right. Is there an empty, bright hall in the front of the house, as if a person is stretching their legs out from a chair? What's not on your property can be created. You can plant trees outward from the front wings of the house. A two-foot-high rock on a property can fill-in for a mountain and a small pond can fill-in for a lake. Finding an auspicious location is your first step in Feng Shui. Wealthly people become so by living on the ground. Perhaps one in 10 wealthy people gained their wealth while living elevated in an apartment or condominium. Being close to the earth is important.

Interior Feng Shui – Three secret keys

In a home's interior, the locations and directions of the main door (the door you use most to enter and exit your home), kitchen stove, and bed, are essential to Feng Shui. These elements can be medicine or poison to your wellbeing. Chi enters the body through the mouth, and it enters a home through the main door. This "breath" affects the five elements: fire, wood, metal, earth, and water, which exist inside and outside every building. The stove, or fire mouth, cooks the food that feeds us, providing us with energy and chi. We spend approximately a third of our lives sleeping, so the location and direction (based on where your head points) of your bed is of great importance. In real estate, the main door, stove, and bed should all point to one of your four compass directions, but they don't all have to be in the same direction. If your compass directions are different than those of your spouse, pick the breadwinner to find the ideal positions of these key items in your home. If that person is happy and successful, the whole family will be. A new home is like a piece of uncut silk. In the hands of a Feng Shui master, it can be tailored into a masterpiece.

Do:

- Use Feng Shui to select or arrange your home, business, or real estate investment.
- Use Feng Shui to maximize the potential of your real estate investments.
- Understand that a home defines the land, the land does not define the home.
- Look for an auspicious setting for your home. Lay a waterway to the east, a street to the west, a mountain to the north, and empty land to the south.
- Look for dragons first, then build a home. Don't build a home and then look for dragons. This can be an expensive mistake.
- Understand that time can be the difference between positive and negative Feng Shui.

Don't:

- Never buy real estate at the top of a mountain. Nature is too powerful up there.
- Do not choose a cliff setting for your home. It may have a spectacular view, but may also cause your money to drift out to sea, leaving you bankrupt.
- Choose the wrong time. The best Feng Shui in the world at the wrong time is useless.

BEST ADVICE:
From real estate professionals

45

Rick Dubord

President, BC HomeLife Realty Services

BEST ADVICE: *The paperless real estate office is here to stay.*

In today's fast-paced world, technology is our reality. It is a fundamental component to the everyday person's life. It is inevitable, then, that technological innovations should become an essential component in businesses everywhere – or more specifically, in the real estate industry today.

When I entered real estate as a salesman in 1973, I possessed a natural interest in any and all technological advances going on in the industry. Looking back, it is possible to say I inherited this trait from my father, a flight sergeant in the Royal Canadian Air Force who was always fascinated with the newest technologies. He had that knack for fixing things. But my passion for technology really began with the original radiophone. I had programmed the phone so the horn of my 1976 Toronado would blast on an incoming call. I remember, during open houses, jogging out to the car to respond to callers. At the time, I never figured that my keenness towards the latest technology could benefit me throughout my career in real estate.

Working my way up from the role of entry-level salesman, I went on to manage an office in the small town of Aldergrove, B.C. By 1976, I was the general manager of Wolstencroft Real Estate

Ltd., and in 1983, Colin Dreyer and I started Benchmark Realty. Two years later, we bought the HomeLife master franchise, which went on to experience spectacular success as it grew to 35 offices in Western Canada.

It was in 1998 that my interest in technology would resurface – this time on the business front. I created WorldWideInfoSystems. com, the first national real estate website that operated in real time – meaning that listings could be entered and went live immediately. I subsequently went to work introducing others to the benefits of this new technology; I presented our system to Realty World America in Myrtle Beach, competing primarily against new innovations from American agencies. As a result, I was awarded a handsome $150,000 contract to do all of Realty World's web work. The reason was simple: unlike other entrants, my firm was actually in real estate – or more accurately, real estate marketing – and the industry itself was looking for new technologies that could improve the efficiency of real estate processes.

By 2000, the system had grown substantially and we had over 7,000 salespeople using our system. However, there were, of course, newer innovations on the horizon. While browsing the booths at the Connect Conference in San Francisco, I experienced my first virtual real estate tour. A San Francisco newspaper reported that "this technology will revolutionize the real estate industry." Realizing that this statement was absolutely true, I went to work, and introduced the "360 Virtual Tour" to our own company. As often happens, a new technology had come along promising to revolutionize the real estate business. But few salespeople believed in its benefits. We only produced thirty virtual tours in our first year, and only fifty in our second. Whether it was our perseverance or the fact that technology is now so much a part of our lives, the concept eventually gained popularity. Today, we have completed over 17,000 virtual tours.

Listing with the virtual tour on realtor.ca (mls.ca) draws substantially more traffic. Salespeople find that when client calls after viewing a virtual tour they are not calling just to see the property, but with an intent to buy it. Our virtual tour offering does not only draw interest from the real estate industry. We have completed projects for Science World, Boeing 747s, bed and breakfasts, hotels, resorts, theatres, and other businesses beyond the realm of real estate.

As a general manager of a number of real estate offices, I witnessed sales agents who were often reluctant to adopt new technologies, who did not understand how they would be helpful in managing such things as overhead – a task that, for me, was becoming increasingly overwhelming. In my view, real estate agents who embrace technology are able to communicate at a higher level. And today's public looks for that: consumers want more efficient service, better communications and mobility and, of course, reduced costs. With this in mind, I created the first paperless real estate office in 2007: REALTYNuance.

If you look at an average brokerage or realtor file, there is an exorbitant amount of paper wasted in order to manage the transaction from start to finish. There are so many ways to reduce paper-usage, save costs and save the environment at the same time. What started out five years ago as an interesting project to move files from the trunk of realtors' cars or homes to an Internet-based filing cabinet that is secure and accessible anytime, anywhere, has matured into a real estate transaction management platform used by some 4,000 realtors in 37 offices.

REALTYNuance is integrated into most of the real estate boards in B.C. and Alberta. It is a system for realtors, designed by realtors, and one in which the client is invited into the transaction. The salesperson does his or her work through a totally electronic deal sheet, improving the brokerage system and transaction processing time by up to 85%. The data from the deal sheet auto populates into the back-end accounting systems. Larger companies can provide centralized conveyancing services for multiple branch offices, allowing one conveyancer to handle up to two hundred agents. Using a Tablet, all papers can be signed in "real time" and the contract stands up in court. Real estate professionals note the security in knowing they have the option of leaving home for a few days while still staying connected to his or her client.

The companies and agents that are succeeding in real estate are those that are taking action to become more efficient, provide lower costs, and deliver more value to their clients. Ultimately, success in today's real estate industry is gained by those who take advantage of today's technology so they can reduce brokerage overhead, improve the quality and reliability of transaction information, enhance data security, and above all, provide "smarter" value-added services for the client.

Do:

- As a realtor, make technological innovations an essential component in your business.
- Always have an eye on making your services more efficient, more affordable, and more valuable to your clients.
- Provide "smarter" value-added services for the client.
- Be aware that there are always newer innovations on the horizon.
- Use technology to communicate on a higher level with clients.

46

Randy Forbes

General manager of Coast Realty Group (since 1993), leading the BC based firm from one to fourteen offices and more than 300 staff and sales representatives

BEST ADVICE: *Believe in your core values.*

What makes a good manager? That's easy: belief. I have an inherent belief that real estate is the greatest industry in the world. This fundamental principle has guided my business decisions during more than three decades in real estate sales and management. Furthermore and equally important, my values are aligned with those of the company I manage, Coast Realty Group. However, I did not arrive in real estate with a set of applicable skills. Rather, my skill-set developed according to the values and motivations I share with my company. My skills have become my core competencies; my primary responsibilities as a manager. And they focus on two separate points: the client and the company.

First, let's discuss the client. It is the real estate brokerage manager's responsibility to manage the needs of the client – the sales rep – in order that they are successful. I facilitate my clients' success through my core responsibilities: branding and brand maintenance, providing a venue for conducting business and business acumen – which includes fiduciary accountability and establishing company policy. The salesperson's client is the homeowner or buyer, and the salesperson's core competency is sales.

Undeniably, business know-how comes with experience. I knew

early in my real estate career that I wanted to manage, so I took every opportunity to learn about the industry. I volunteered on the real estate board, attended workshops and conventions, and trained other salespeople. Teaching others develops aptitude and provides opportunity to identify talent. I'm an insatiable consumer of articles, books and reports related to real estate and management. Real estate bodies are responsible for educating and licensing representatives, but additional education is necessary to gain a real understanding of the brand (and how to protect it), to adapt to changing technology, and to share sales techniques. My belief in the industry is manifested in my desire to build knowledge; its dynamic nature demands my willingness to learn.

In order to build and maintain the Coast Realty Group, every business decision I make corresponds with the company's values. This creates a foundational base for representatives to build their own brand, parallel to the company's. Brand protection is essential for business continuity, which is rooted in the success of salespeople and, initially, in public confidence.

I use time-tested maxims, or logical truths, that we at the office genially refer to as "Randyisms." Randyisms identify a lesson and offer a catchy phrase for easy memory. For instance, "The world is run by those who show up." Remember that governing bodies equalize the playing field. So what sets you apart? I urge my salespeople to volunteer on task forces, run for board elections, and serve their communities. After all, "Do something and something will happen … do nothing and nothing will happen, but you might not know the difference."

Next, let's discuss the manager's responsibility to the company. It's my job to ensure that my company's core competencies – real estate sales, insurance, and property management – are possible. Our company is unique in that it is independently owned and, therefore, can internalize cash flow and control image. Our precision focus is exemplified in our decision to limit geographic growth to fourteen offices on Vancouver Island and B.C.'s Sunshine Coast.

As real estate is a people-centric industry, a personal connection between management and salespeople is necessary. If Coast Realty Group expanded beyond its geographical capacity, management might lose touch with its sales force, or become ineffective due to a lack of regional knowledge. Either way, core competencies could be compromised and the brand diminished.

Any risk, however, *is* an opportunity. Despite market trends, my group risked opening subsidiary offices throughout the 1990s and 2000s. But bigger is not better – *better* is better. Each expansion considered whether the appropriate management was available to embody the company's values and competencies. When a salesperson first joins Coast Realty Group, I suggest to them to speak with people they know to see how our group is perceived in the community. This creates confidence for new employees and gives them a chance to evaluate whether their core values align with those of the company.

A real estate firm's greatest asset is its existing workforce. It would not be fair to give special consideration to new recruits, rather than rewarding those who already work hard under your banner. We offer salespeople and staff an opportunity to invest in our Mortgage Investment Corporation. Since its inception in 1996, this company-subsidized RRSP-investment fund has grown from less than $500,000 to more than $8 million with investors realizing an average of 10.24% in annual profits towards retirement.

As general manager, I am also responsible for operations and administrative staffing. Ideally, real estate groups should purchase their own buildings independently from the parent company, and initiate a lease-payment structure. Plan to gain clear title within a specific time period. Set a goal of ten to fifteen years.

Only hire administrative staff and salespeople that demonstrate the same values as your company. I have had top-producers express interest in joining my group. However, if they didn't share the company's values, they weren't brought on board. Risking the brand is not worth a short-term monetary payoff; always consider the bigger picture. That all said, my responsibility goes well beyond buying buildings and selecting talent. I am also in charge of changing light bulbs, unplugging toilets, and responding to late-night alarms.

To meet my responsibilities to client and company, I have developed a distinct style of management and have remained focused on my directives. As a result, I have gained experience, confidence, decisiveness, and accountability. Salespeople and staff gain confidence from a manager's decisive nature, and mirror that confidence in their own business practices. Confidence earns credibility. After all, "No decision *is* a decision." That is not to say that all decisions should be final: a favourable conclusion can be reached with thoughtful input from others. But it is important to be, as a manager, the expert authority. If you are not the final authority, then who is?

Managers must possess the proverbial people skills. I insist upon honest dialogue between colleagues, but am careful to avoid emotional responses, as they can skew perspectives. I draw on my professional experience to relay a lesson through a story, a joke, or a Randyism. I prefer to "check-in" rather than dictate orders. This allows individuals to develop at their own pace and to be accountable for their own actions. As a rule, I tend to answer requests with a "no" first, and then reconsider after further research. I can then make an informed decision. It's hard to take back a "yes." Additionally, I do not, as the saying goes, "Cater to the lowest common denominator." That is, I consider all angles and appropriate opinions before reaching a decision. Consider the majority, before the minority.

To conclude, I'll once again say that I believe real estate is the greatest industry. This belief has guided me to develop effective leadership skills, to identify my values and to realize my core competencies as a manager. Sharing values has facilitated the success of my clients, staff, and company. If you are willing to work, you have the ability to manage your own successes and rewards.

Do:

- Take every opportunity to learn about the real estate industry. Be an insatiable consumer of articles, books and reports related to real estate and management.
- Remember that governing bodies equalize the playing field. So you must set yourself apart from the pack.
- Speak with the community to understand how your company and brand are publicly perceived.
- Develop your own distinctive style of management.
- Remember that a real estate firm's greatest asset is its existing workforce. Reward firstly those who already work hard under your banner.

Don't:

- Hire those that don't share the company's values, even if they are top-producers.
- Cater to the lowest common denominator. Consider all angles and appropriate opinions before reaching a decision. Consider the majority, before the minority.
- Risk the brand for a short-term monetary payoff; always consider the bigger picture.
- Dictate orders. Allow individuals to develop at their own pace, but make them accountable for their own actions.
- Avoid emotional responses, as they can skew perspectives.

47

Sheila Francis

Full time licensed Realtor in the 'Tri-Cities' for 32 Years. She is a residential and relocation specialist with RE/MAX All Points

---

BEST ADVICE: *When buying for your own family to live in and call home, you must be excited and love it more on the second viewing. Compromise leads to regret.*

Television has a lot to answer for! Forty shows on making the best use of space, de-cluttering, renovating, decorating and generally creating a show piece. The viewing public is devouring the information, inundating Home Depot and Benjamin Moore and taking interior design courses.

Consequently – the #1 reason buyers have always purchased a home has changed. Location in most instances has taken second place to "bells and whistles". The buzz words – "hardwood – granite – limestone – stainless steel" bring in the buyers. The old buzz words "park like lot – established neighbourhood" are only effective when accompanied by those other glossy buzz words.

So ... there is a large price to be paid by sellers for original condition and bargains to be had for buyers prepared to have vision, buy homes with "good bones" and do the updating work themselves or hire someone to do it. This is definitely the market for handy people to build "sweat equity".

The price of brand new, beautifully finished homes in up and coming neighbourhoods is so low and so appealing (even if often on smaller lots – but not always) that it creates a real challenge for the re-sale owner. Location alone won't do it, therefore price reductions are now the order of the day until the seller finds that handyman. Therefore, it behooves sellers to insert some pizzaz wherever they can. Sometimes it's a matter of removing the old carpet and exposing the hardwood floors, exchanging the arborite for granite, and a pot of paint does wonders.

Thinking re-sale is critical when making a purchase

I have never forgotten Mr. Jurock's words from many years ago "you make your money in real estate the day you buy, not the day you sell." There are neighbourhoods where doing substantial renovations will pay off. I always tell buyers that it's my job to supply the sometimes uninvited real estate advice and it's their job to select the emotional fit. Hopefully, we can find the home that will be exciting to return to each day and will also hold excellent re-sale value. Cost out those necessary maintenance improvements, updates and renovations – if you couldn't re-sell it and cover the costs – don't buy it. The one thing I have learned over 32 years of selling real estate is that "there is always another home"! When buying for your own family to live in and call home, you must be excited and love it more on the second viewing. Compromise leads to regret.

When buying for investment, other factors kick in – like ensuring the rent covers the costs. The biggest mistake I made is common to many first time investors – I renovated the rental home to suit my own (expensive!) taste. Purchasing an investment property is when the big ticket items come into play – roof and furnace replacement may not be sufficiently sexy for the emotional buyer, but they are the "steak" for the investor. And – a busy location has value for a renter (and therefore an investor) while it is anathema to the emotional family buyer. Busy streets make for great deals!

Back to the bells and whistles and the sizzle that sells. **When doing renovations, while doing them for yourselves – still think re-sale.** I have been in many upper price range homes with beautiful kitchens with a 4 burner stove – not what the buyer sees in magazines and cooking shows. If you're going to the trouble of gutting and re-configuring a kitchen, maximize your re-sale value by adding those features (like a 6 burner stove and double ovens) desired by today's chefs and entertainers. In this tighter economy, people are "nesting", cooking at home and entertaining their friends, family and colleagues at home – and they want to impress. Buyers will compromise many other items in order to buy a fabulous kitchen.

Thanks to television interior design shows, many sellers are clever at giving a modern facelift to an old kitchen – up to the discerning buyer to realize what they are paying for (the sizzle not the steak).

Regardless of economy or whether the market prices are declining or on an upswing – there are spikes and valleys of activity. As sellers it's important to hit those times of increased activity – the (often narrow) windows of opportunity to achieve a faster sale and more money. In the Lower Mainland, the majority of our sales are made in the first 6 months of the year. If you want a "good deal", try buying in November and December. As buyers, good to avoid those times of low inventory and high activity – the traditional Spring market. Sadly, we truly are like sheep – as sellers in Vancouver, we like to wait until the flowers are in bloom, our gardens are at their best, and our power washing is completed before putting our homes on the market. This is exactly the same moment that the buyers have bought ready for a summer move and the market is winding down for school grads and vacation time! Yes – the homes still eventually sell, but mostly not with the same ease nor at the same price as earlier in the year. The early bird really does get the worm!

The 2 'P's are critical in any market – Price and Presentation.

The pricing part deserves as much thought and research as the presentation part. Your realtor has access to all the sales information – which often proves to be a total disconnect from the current active neighbourhood listings. Sellers are often hopeful of achieving previous higher prices while buyers are savvy and recognize the "right price" for today's market. So it is vital that each neighbourhood sale be reviewed for size, age and improvements (bells and whistles!) then compared dispassionately with your home. This is the toughest part – to divorce yourself from the blood, sweat and tears you've poured in and the happy memories of life enjoyed in your home. It's always valuable to put yourself in the buyers' shoes, these are the people setting today's market prices. You will often have a more intimate knowledge of your neighbours' homes than the realtor – this too is valuable in the pricing equation. It's a fine line to price so that you are sure that none of your money is left on the table – but you are equally sure it will sell.

What television has taught us is that "value" has a shifting definition and it's up to us as buyers and sellers to remain focused on the trends and use them to our advantage.

Do:

- Think always of re-sale when making a purchase even if it's your dream home.
- When doing renovations, while doing them for yourselves – still think re-sale.
- Sellers: insert some pizzaz wherever you can.
- When buying for investment ensure the rent covers the costs.
- Sellers: focus on price and presentation.

Don't:

- Renovate your rental home to suit your own (expensive!) taste.
- Forget to divorce yourself from the blood, sweat and tears you've poured in and the happy memories of life enjoyed in your home.
- Avoid those times of low inventory and high activity – the tradi-

tional Spring market.
- Buyers: don't be fooled by the cheap, trendy facelift!

48

Gerry Halstrom

Executive consultant to the land development industry. He brings over 30 years of land development, strategic sales, marketing and operations management expertise.

BEST ADVICE: *Ask the right questions & give back frank and honest advice.*

Early in my career, I worked for one of Canada's wealthiest men and was repeatedly scolded, "Stop selling me Halstrom – just give me the facts and tell me what the 'dickens' you think we should do!"

I was doing what so many salespeople tend to do: they talk too much, too much "gusto" mixing fact with emotions and hype. While this had served me well as a young salesman, this style was not working at the boardroom table. I changed my style and never looked back. **That change was to un-sell the salesperson in me.**

Since then, I have served at many of the posts in the Real Estate Industry. I had the privilege to sell a ton of Real Estate on behalf of developers and individual owners. I also – in my capacities as sales manager and advisor to developers, have hired, trained and mentored a lot of good as well as bad sales people.

I learned that, **many salespeople ask irrelevant, even silly questions.** For example, these questions were posed to me a few years ago: "Is the safety of your family important?" (Of course – what answer did you expect? No?)) and "Can you see the benefit of having a fire alarm in your home?" (Ditto) Or this one which was put to me just a few months ago by a well-meaning young man: "Can you see the benefit of having your product viewed by more qualified buyers through the internet?" (Ditto)

These are irrelevant - even aggravating questions that simply waste time and air. No top producing salesperson I have known uses this style of language. If you are using these, stop NOW!

Here is my best advice for effective client communications:

Let's say you have been chosen for an interview or, even better, hired! To make things easy, **ask, understand and advise:**

A) "Tell me how can I help you?" And then ... listen!
B) "These are the facts of my service/product and this is what it does."
C) "Here is what I think you should do." Be honest and frank.

Allow me to elaborate:

A) Can you help?

The most important aspect of a client relationship is assessing if you can help. If not, you are wasting your time. The best opening phrase I can give you is: "Let's get together so I can understand your situation and see if I can help. If I can't, I will tell you right away and try to send you in the right direction."

Boom – freedom to get all the details and professionally terminate the lead if it does not look like a winning situation. Sometimes you get better referrals from clients you did not do business with.

One of the signs of a great salesperson is someone who asks the right questions. Asking the right questions and understanding the situation instantly qualifies you as a pro.

B) Presenting the facts.

Words are your enemies. Too many of them will result in your client losing the point. Use the fewest words possible to outline the facts. As a professional speaker, I use power point to focus my audience on the key point I am speaking to. I use a heading to bring the attention to the point. Then, once I have the attention of the audience, I speak to the point. With each new point comes a new heading. Presenting facts is the same.

Remember the average human has an attention span of no more than 20 minutes. Thus, you should focus on the top facts that will help you solve your client's problem. I love to say, "I can give you over a hundred things I do that will get you your desired result but you are probably going to hire me for the top five things I do. Here they are..."

C) Being honest and frank. Tell the client what you think they should do.

Risky, yes. But this is why they are talking to you. Have the guts to stick to your guns, speak your mind and do not be afraid to change it if the facts change. The easy way out is usually the wrong way out, so remember: hard facts and hard work are almost always the right way. I can not stress this enough. If there is one thing my life has taught me – it is that the right way is usually the tough way. Tough – but who says life is fair? On the other hand, no one gets more praise and referrals than the professional who calls it like it is, in every situation.

Here is another example of how being honest and frank works.

I was leading a re-zoning and development process for a client. During a neighborhood meeting (part of the process), a lady stood up during the presentation and asked the architect, "How many units do you think you will build if the rezone is successful?" The architect stated, "We will address the question of how many units we will build after the re-zone is complete as the number of units at this point is not at issue." After a few seconds of uncomfortable silence from everyone, I stood up and honestly told the woman how many units we were contemplating. The architect was miffed, but the audience was won over because of the frank and honest discussion.

In summary:

In the end we are all human. Selling is not a game, nor blood sport; it is simply part of life. Treating your client interactions with both sincerity and frankness will leave you feeling good and your clients shall always be rewarded by your input and time.

Know yourself and love yourself – as to who you are. Present the truth to your clients and audiences so they can see the real you. Hiding the real you will only make the client nervous. Share what you are best at freely with the world. As well, be free with the truths of what you are not good at and how you compensate for that weakness.

We are all salespeople. From the 16-year-old trying to get a curfew extension, to the president of your favorite company, everyone sells. The key is doing it right. Un-selling the salesperson is the first step.

Do:

- Have the facts. Hard facts and hard work are almost always the right way.
- Treat your client interactions with both sincerity and frankness.
- Know who you are and share what you are best at freely with the world.
- Ask the right and the tough questions.

Don't:

- Ask irrelevant or silly questions.
- Be too wordy. Words are your enemies. Too many of them will result in your client losing the point.

49

Clara Hartree

Realtor that specializes in Vancouver's high end real estate – mainly in West Vancouver for over 23 years

BEST ADVICE: *As a buyer, don't chase the market. Markets are cyclical. If you miss it on the way up, chances are you'll catch it on the way down.*

In 1984 I landed in Vancouver for the first time. It was a corporate transfer for my husband. The company looked after everything including placing us in a serviced apartment until we found a house. We had moved here forever so we had our little daughter and a Brazilian nanny with us. Our realtor, also provided by the company, advised us that Vice Presidents of international corporations must live on Vancouver's West Side.

We were supposed to start looking the following day. In the rain? Yes, in Vancouver you don't wait for the rain to stop. So off we went in Ipanema clothes looking for houses in Shaughnessy. Wooden houses? Wooden steps and patios? Major adjustment.....

After days of looking at impossible houses we found our way to West Vancouver after a party at the house of another executive who had arrived before us. We liked just about every house here. Beautiful lots, winding roads, amazing ocean views, swimming pools and way better values. So we bought our first house in West Vancouver.

I often think how lucky we were. Our realtor was only familiar with Vancouver West Side and knew nothing about West Vancouver. (There is a harbour in between.) She didn't know where young families lived, best schools, sunny areas, areas that get more or less snow – nothing. We got the best house, in the best location for us, near the best school – by sheer luck.

Two years later, with my real estate license, I decided that relocation buyers would get a lot of my attention. It was 1986. Expo brought in a lot of visitors who turned into buyers. They couldn't believe how beautiful it is here! Many told me *"We just didn't want to leave"*. I think that's the reason we have so many people with small businesses. They moved here and then created their own jobs, doing what they were passionate about. It was a summer of beautiful sunny days. Some wonder whether the 2010 Olympics will bring a similar rush of new buyers ... I doubt it. Two weeks in the winter in the only Canadian city that has no winter...

Anyway, twenty-three years later, with thousands of stories attached to as many sales I would like to share a couple of random insights that I hope you will find useful:

- High end buyers don't dress up to look at houses
- They don't hire a limo (major red flag!)
- They buy on emotion. They walk into a house and know instantly that's the house they are going to buy. They are the easiest buyers and the deals are usually very easy to put together
- Canadians love waterfront – offshore buyers love views from the side of the mountain. They rarely care for our rugged Pacific Northwest waterfront, although there are exceptions. The **Prime Minister of an Asian country** owned waterfront in Whytecliff and the **Princess of Thailand** still does. **James Clavell** wrote one of his novels when living on the waterfront in Whytecliff. His widow once told me those were such happy times she wanted to try to buy the house back. She did buy another house on the waterfront in West Vancouver. On the other hand, **Oprah** never even looked at the Radcliffe house. It was a rumor spread by the real buyer who wanted to stay anonymous. The **Sultan of Brunei** was upset because West Van owners

didn't allow him to use a helicopter pad on the Seaside Place property – noise pollution – so he didn't buy.

Contrary to what happens in London and LA where tabloids employ annoying paparazzi, in West Vancouver celebrities shop and dine anywhere without being disturbed. We sat next to **Diana Krall** and **Elvis Costello** at dinner last week – nobody even looked! One recent buyer mentioned to me his concern about buying a house that didn't offer total privacy because he didn't want to be disturbed by paparazzi. He did buy the house and I heard that he is a bit disconcerted because – he hasn't seen any paparazzi!

High end buyers get their own financing if they want to. Beware of requests for vendor financing. What is acceptable when dealing with investors on low end properties is a red flag when selling high end. There is always some wannabe trying to fast track to the unaffordable. No *"lease to own."* Don't even rent your home unless you have excellent references. One of my best clients rented out a multi-million dollar waterfront penthouse to a man who tried to transfer the title to his name! Rare but it happens.

Vancouver West Side realtors continue to try to keep buyers on their side of the pond. One told me that showing houses in West Vancouver, for her, would be like showing houses on the moon! That may be the reason why West Vancouver offers incredible deals in high end real estate. Not just now. Always! And our property taxes are lower than anywhere else in the Lower Mainland. We have the lowest mill rate.

As a buyer, get a realtor who is familiar with the area; get an accountant and a lawyer who will explain the rules and implications of buying in Canada. As a seller, get a realtor who communicates with you, who uses the most effective marketing tools, has a network of friendly fellow realtors and has access to a good network of serious buyers.

West Vancouver prices vary from a low $800,000 to a rare, but once achieved, $28 million.

Most of my listings are in the $2 to $3 million range. For that price you get a good choice of beautiful new homes in great locations most of them with ocean views, ranging in square footage from 3000 to 5000 sq ft. I also have some bigger homes, around 8000 sq ft for higher prices.

And finally: it doesn't rain more in Vancouver than in most other cities. It just rains more than in the Prairies.

Do:

- Believe that there are no paparazzi in West Vancouver!
- Get a realtor that is familiar with the area.
- Use the services of a good mortgage broker.
- Remember, your friendly bank manager has less flexibility.

Don't:

- Rent out your high end home unless you have excellent (and checked) references.
- Ever, ever, buy without an inspection by a certified professional inspector.
- Chase the market. Markets are cyclical.
- Assume that the guy in shorts and flip flops is poor.
- Assume that the guy in the limo is wealthy.

238 ··· REAL ESTATE ACTION

50

Christina Hepburn

Realtor – Hepburn Real Estate
Re/Max Select Properties

BEST ADVICE: *Inspire Lasting & Meaningful Relationships.*

As a Realtor you can reap only what you sow. The work is to-tally commission-based, therefore the rewards come as a direct result of your personal efforts and motivation. I realized soon after becoming an agent in 1990 that the most important part of my business was to cultivate lasting relationships.

I learned quickly that the customer is always right – even when they are not. A client's culpability is an aside; the key thing is to professionally provide what is necessary to complete their purchase or sale. I have found that "going the extra mile" pays dividends, but only if it is a sincere gesture of service with no attachment to the outcome. The most important aspect of a transaction for me is the "win-win" and "highest-and-best-good-of-all" principle.

Before real estate, I spent ten years working for a seniority-structured telephone company. Becoming a Realtor – an independent contractor, essentially – was a drastic change from my previous vocation, but it turned out to be my greatest career move. I was instantly committed to creating a successful client-based business.

My husband Tony and I combined our real estate businesses in 1994, becoming a dynamic husband and wife team in the Westside of Vancouver, British Columbia. Fortunately, we share the same goals and an astute professional business ethic. We have built our business foundation on integrity, the "customer-is-always-right" and a "win-win-for-all" model.

An early mentor taught me that Realtors can earn each client's respect and trust in five minutes by treating them like they are the most important person in the world. Further guidance and inspiration came from Dale Carnegie's book *How to Win Friends and Influence People.* Stressing the importance of expressing genuine interest and truly listening to people, Carnegie's book, seemed to underline my values and speak directly to me as a Realtor

In the late spring of 2008, the Vancouver real estate market turned from a red-hot, any-price-goes seller's market to one of more balanced conditions overall. People ask whether my husband and I do things differently in an adjusting market. If anything, we boost our focus on customer service, treating each client all the more important and unique. This can mean spending additional money on marketing or simply staying in touch with clients to show our appreciation.

In recent years, Tony and I have expanded our personal real estate portfolio by buying & selling homes. I am also an art painter in essence and by combining my artistic abilities with 20 years of real estate experience, designing and renovating properties has become a gratifying creative outlet for me. There's nothing like hands-on experience to sharpen one's knowledge and expertise.

Of course, there are a slew of pitfalls for the investor to avoid. For example, there's the inaccurate rental income assessment or the runaway renovation budget. Often, investors simply pick the wrong property to renovate. Our investments give us better insight into what properties and locations suit particular buyers. We can also provide advice to sellers on how to enhance the value of their home— which inevitably, may bring them the highest sale price.

I make sure that every member of our team maintains my incredibly high standards. We like to think that we offer the same level of service to that of a high-end boutique hotel, rather than the impersonal service of the large, common hotel chain. And we've developed our brand to reflect just that. Our repeat clients – who, along with referrals make up roughly 80% of our annual business – have come to expect a marketing strategy that relies on high-quality advertising. With consistent color schemes and design, our market evaluations, buyer's packages, highlight sheets and correspondence all reflect the Hepburn brand.

Tony and I as well as every member of our team send a personal, handwritten note to at least one client each day. In a world that is increasingly driven by technology, a handwritten note is a great way to connect with clients on a more personal level to let them know that they're on your mind. After selling a property, we send our clients a gift to show our gratitude. Consumers have many choices today, and this offering expresses the sense of privilege we feel to have served a client.

It's the human condition to want to "sell for a million" and "buy for a dollar". There are many experts in the real estate field with undoubted credibility, and there are those who have lucked into the right situation at the right time and made millions. Then there are those who will be forever waiting for the right circumstance-- the perfect storm. This type will almost never buy a property at the right time. They are the ones who will float the same lines time and again, like "I should have got into the market ten years ago," or, "I just missed the market." By the time they gather up the nerve to buy a property, the market may have already doubled or tripled in value.

The good news is that it's never too late to dive into the real estate market. Ultimately, everything sells for market value; and market value is dictated by whatever price a buyer is willing to pay and a seller is willing to accept. And historically, in spite of the peaks and valleys, real estate will go UP in value.

In our fast-moving and ever changing business, the easiest thing to compromise is taking time to recharge and balance our lives. Whenever possible, Tony and I nurture ourselves with painting, photography, videography, yoga, a gym workout, skiing, snowboarding, travelling all over the planet and our ultimate pas-

REAL ESTATE ACTION ••• 241

sion – scuba diving.

It has always been my intention to enrich, inspire and contribute to other people's lives. Being a Realtor has given me that privilege. I define success not necessarily by numbers but by the quality of my life and the joy I feel from the wonderful relationships that I have.

Investors

Do:

- Buy in the best location your budget allows. Consider the neighbourhood and its demographics.
- Determine if the property is desirable to a future buyer. Consider the potential resale value of any property.
- Look for good bones – inspect the construction, design, layout, maintenance and renovation history of the property.
- Find out whether pending repairs are simple aesthetic improvements or costly structural defects to fix.
- If building or renovating, ensure your design and construction expenses are cost-effective for rental income and/or future resale.
- Thoroughly understand market conditions before getting into speculative buying or property "flipping".
- Have the option to rent or lease a property unless you intend to live in it for the long-term.
- Like your investment enough to be able to live in it.

Realtors

Do:

- Always act with integrity. Be clear and honest about market conditions and be conscious when negotiating a deal.

- Remember the basics of developing leads. Leads become listings, sales and repeat clients.
- Under promise and over deliver. Serve your clients well and develop long-term meaningful relationships.
- Dress professionally at all times. It sends the message that you care about your business and take it seriously.
- Return calls promptly.
- Attend a combination of at least four real estate conventions, personal development and/or educational seminars annually to stay up-to-date with market trends and technologies. This will improve your personal well-being, confidence and marketing strategy.
- Take the time to stay balanced in every aspect of your life – physically, mentally, emotionally and spiritually.
- Above all, practice the 3 "G's" – Generosity, Graciousness, and Gratitude.

51

Eugen Klein

Investor, writer, lecturer and consultant. He leads a commercial real estate team of highly specialized experts in international brokerage, investment, project marketing, and asset management.

BEST ADVICE: *Be Honest. Be Informed. Be Active.*

I learned probably one of the most important lessons in my first year as a commercial realtor.

I was referred to a very wealthy lady (let's call her Linda) who owned a few large investment assets. Linda was considering selling one and I wanted to earn her business. After a few meetings, although our conversations were cordial, I did not feel that I was building rapport.

Then one Saturday morning, something happened that changed the way I approach my business. I called Linda to speak about the assignment and some materials I had sent to her, but she was unable to hear me out. Speaking in a low voice she told me that she was experiencing a terrible migraine headache, that she suffered from them often, and that she could not continue the conversation. "Can I call you back tomorrow?" she said. "Of course," I replied, "I hope you feel better."

I hung up the phone and thought for a second. After reflecting for a few minutes on what had just happened, I picked up the phone and called a very good client of mine who was a top cardiologist at the local hospital. I spoke to him about Linda's ailment and asked if he knew of an expert I could refer her to. He was kind enough to give me the direct cell number of a doctor specializing in neurological ailments.

A quarter of an hour later, I was back on the phone to my client. *"Eugen,"* she answered, *"I'm sorry, but I thought we were going to speak about the assignment tomorrow?"* "Yes," I answered, *"We were, but that is not why I am calling. The reason for my call is that I have arranged for you two potential appointments with a top neurologist. I thought it would help you to get the opinion of an expert on the treatment of migraines."*

I then let her alone. Four days later, I received a call and she listed the property. Two days after that I had two referrals from her. Today, she is one of my best clients.

There are no limits when the people we serve genuinely matter to us.

When investing in commercial real estate, there are three key ideas to keep in mind:

First, profit is made on acquisition.

Most investors are aware that the simplest way to increase your return on investment is to pay less initially. When you prepare your offer, look for innovative ways to structure the transaction to obtain your investment at a desired price or terms: vendor financing, staggered payments, or balloon payments. The advantages of properly structuring your purchase are numerous: buy low, and you will make better returns on the given rents, or you can charge slightly lower rents while being more selective; better tenants and a complimentary tenant mix make your investment more secure and secure your returns long term.

Second, present offers often.

If you spend too much time waiting for the perfect investment to come along, you may wait yourself out of the game. There is a certain level of serendipity to the timing of offers; the more often you present, the more likely you will encounter a principal with strong personal motivation to sell that allows for above market returns at acquisition (see rule 1 above). Furthermore, if there is one thing that years of brokerage has taught me, is that it is much easier to establish the motivation of a vendor with a certified check and a written offer on the table. Somehow the real and imminent presence of money sharpens the focus and reduces any initial posturing.

Do not be afraid to revisit a situation a few times ... do not be put off by an initial refusal – situations can change quickly. Imagine being at the bar on Saturday night and meeting someone very attractive. Walking up to them and asking them out can almost guarantee that the first response will be no. Interest, orchestrated persistence and innovative thinking can lead to persuasion. No one wants to waste their emotions when interest is lukewarm or indifferent; likewise no buyer or seller will waste time with someone who does not demonstrate serious intent or divulge true motivations first time around. As people's situations can quickly change, so can their decision. A high priced, well located property today can be a motivated seller offering terms tomorrow.

Third, be informed.

You can never have too much information, and neglecting your due diligence may cost you dearly. For commercial transactions, the devil is in the details. Be willing to go over all documents in painstaking detail, and where you lack experience, enlist someone else's. It often amazes me that a smaller investor purchasing say a $5,000,000 building will balk at a $5,000 bill for a proper structural engineering report. Even if the building is sound, the peace of mind, and reduced contingency allotment alone will more than pay the cost. Review all tenancy agreements carefully and in particular ensure that there are no conflicting rights or costly clauses lying dormant. It is always pleasant to find out, a few years down the line, that the previous owner has accidentally granted a first right of refusal on a space that has just come vacant to two separate tenants.

Very often the true value of a property is buried deep:

- You review an offering and realize that the returns are below expected, so you pass on looking at the investment further. Little do you know that the income information was incorrectly stated because one-time capital expenses were included in the income information; thus the actual net income was actually much higher.
- While considering a sub-lease for your next location, you see a higher face rate and so you pass on reading the actual lease. Little did you realize that with this higher lease rate came an option to purchase the property at a price that was set five years ago.

If everyone has the same information, opportunity is gone. It is the unique information or insight that you possess that creates your key opportunities! Take the time to understand all the elements of the deal, how best to make it work, then act quickly and decisively to take advantage of an information deficit.

Do:

- **Always Keep Your Word**. My father taught me the importance of a man's word. In the capacity of trusted advisor, buyer or seller, transparency is of the utmost importance. Keep your promises, your appointments and exceed expectations. In a competitive industry like real estate, the temptation is always there to out-promise the competition. Committing yourself to something you can't do guarantees you will earn a bad reputation.
- **Passion**. It is best to find worth in something you enjoy doing. Complete tasks with a positive mind and intense passion. Enthusiasm is an underrated closing tool.

- **Innovation.** Today, innovation is sometimes made synonymous with technology, but true innovation is more than that. It is the use of knowledge, understanding, and creativity to experiment with greater possibilities for added value. If you achieve a reputation for adding value to transactions, investments or the lives of your clients, you and they will both enjoy above market returns.

- **Excellence**. My mother always spoke about taking your best work and finding ways to improve it; to never let pride prevent you from learning from the best practices of others. Excellence is striving to provide a level of service well beyond what is required.

- The evidence of success is not material wealth or possessions. It is the **sincere gratitude** of clients well served.

52

Brent Roberts

#1 Selling Realtor in the Surrey, North Delta and Langley area; the #2 Realtor in the BC Region of Royal LePage. Successfully negotiates one home every other day

---

BEST ADVICE: *Make Offers.*

When I was eighteen years old my girlfriend's father suggested I buy a house. I had only the princely savings of three thousand dollars, but I was in love with his daughter and thought it best to take his advice. A year later he told me: *"With your money, you should buy a fourplex."* Still in love, I once again obeyed. It was sound advice in both instances, but the old man had an ulterior motive – he was a real estate agent. Well, the girlfriend didn't last, but my love for real estate did. On top of my duties as a realtor, I have been a real estate investor for thirty years, owning single family homes, duplexes, fourplexes, half-duplexes and townhouse complexes that range from fourteen to one hundred eighty-three units. I once owned more than three hundred units simultaneously.

I recall being incredibly excited about my first real estate purchase. Anticipatory excitement is a fine sentiment if you're a prospective homeowner, but not recommended if you're a practical investor. Sometimes too much zeal during "the deal" finds buyers opening their wallets too widely. I have seen many foreclosure transaction in which the buyer, disarmed by the heady experience of making an offer, paid more than the property was worth. In the investment game, it's important to keep your emotions in check.

REAL ESTATE ACTION ••• 249

The same goes once you own a property. You may have the impulse to flip it and realize any gains you can. But it's wise to hold your investments for a time before you see any palpable returns on them. There is usually a direct correlation between the length of time a property is held and the return realized. The leverage gained by having tenants pay off your mortgage, in addition, to the capital gains, is what will build your nest egg.

I entered the real estate brokerage business in 1989 with Realty World Canada and have been with the firm ever since, although Royal LePage has since bought Realty World Canada. As an agent, I've had the pleasure of playing a part in building my clients' lives; guiding homeowners through the buying process and helping established investors strengthen their real estate portfolios.

I often offer this quote to my customers: *"The difference between successful and unsuccessful people is that successful people don't know they can't so they try. Unsuccessful people don't know they can, so they don't try."*

In the days before I bought my first home, my realtor told me: *"They will never accept an offer that low."* He was wrong. Sellers can't accept an offer if it isn't made. You won't be awarded every property you bid on, but being a prolific and disciplined offer-maker will see to it that you eventually find the right property at the right price.

Every seller has a unique history and is motivated by different circumstances. You don't know, for example, at what price the seller previously acquired the marketed property. Perhaps the seller is in a bind financially. The seller's realtor often doesn't know his or her client's predicament either. The only way to find if a property fits your price bracket is to make an offer.

And while there are always motivated sellers, you nonetheless have to do your homework before tendering a bid. People religiously keep track of their golf game or favourite hockey team. It shouldn't be any different in the real estate investment game. Understand your local market conditions: is it a buyer's or seller's market? What have similar properties in the area sold for? And what properties in the area failed to sell after a time on the market? Why?

It's a must to shape your investment strategy around a clear goal, even if that goal is to own only a single property in addition to your personal residence. Specialize: decide on a particular niche to play in. If you want to own a condo, target three prospective properties and become intimately familiar with them. The same thing goes for rental units. If it's a duplex you want, what do the duplex tenants in the area pay in rent? It's a matter of getting a handle on the property's prospective cash flow. Will tenant rental payments adequately offset monthly expenses? When it's shaped right, I don't know of a better investment out there than the rental unit. Where else can you put five or ten percent down and have someone else pay off your investment?

Read books about real estate; subscribe to real estate publications; take courses and whatever else it takes to learn as much as you can about the market. Education is a great motivational tool. It gives you the confidence to make the right moves. Understanding and learning about real estate investment is really about investing in yourself.

Then start making offers. Chances are, your most memorable experience in real estate will be your initial investment. So make it a good one. And that doesn't necessarily require diving headlong into the game. You don't necessarily have to begin with a ten-unit property.

And one last note: avoid negative news and negative people. I have seen hard times and happy times. Both tenants and owners experience them. But when the dust settles, it's always the owners that outperform the tenants.

Do:

- Have some money saved, even if it is only $5,000. If you have enough for the down payment, all you have to worry about is managing the property and having your tenants pay off the bank.

- Get a realtor that is investor oriented.
- Build a dependable team that can help strengthen your portfolio. Your team should include the right accountant, realtor, lawyer, and mortgage broker. Make sure they understand your objectives.
- Become well-acquainted with other investors. Find an investor that already owns a second property or two. Find out what they did right; what they did wrong. Buy them a lunch or two if necessary.
- Find a mentor that is always accessible.

Don't:

- Be impatient with real estate. After all, it's not – no matter how much we'd all like it to be – just another get-rich-quick scheme.
- Forget to educate yourself – take courses, read books.
- Be negligent in doing your homework before you make an offer
- Spend time listening to negative news and negative people.

BEST ADVICE:
Keeping what you have

53

David Benson

Chartered accountant with almost 30 years of public practice experience in Vancouver. He works solely with small businesses and entrepreneurs.

BEST ADVICE: *Build equity in your own home before building a real estate portfolio.*

So, you have decided to invest in real estate. You and your spouse have well-heeled jobs and the future looks bright. You own some stocks and bonds, but research tells you that the key to a long-term stable financial future lies in real estate. You've heard, however, that real estate investing is complicated, expensive, and only for those who can afford high-priced lawyers and tax accountants. This may well be the case in such matters as estate planning, trusts, property development syndications, joint ventures and partnerships. But for the majority of us who might aspire to own, at most, several Canadian rental properties to see us through retirement, the method does not have to be particularly maddening. Corporations can manage your real estate for you, but in the interest of simplicity, convenience and efficiency, manage your own properties.

After 30 years of public practice as a chartered accountant, I can attest that the equity in real estate can be a major tool on the path to financial independence. The key is in properly planning the purchase, maintenance and eventual sale of property; and under-standing the tax ramifications of each stage. Too often we buy impulsively without a long-term plan and without any forethought of tax implications. For most of us, real estate is a long-term in-vestment, so it requires a long-term plan.

Okay, where to start? Well, the first and most important place to begin your real estate adventure is right where you live. BUY YOUR HOME. Building a real estate portfolio without first build-ing equity in your own home is akin to erecting the walls of a house before laying the foundation. The appreciation of a principal resi-dence is the largest contributor to the wealth of many families, particularly in dense urban markets.

Building equity in your home in Canada is simple: it's tax free. No other investment offers this tax treatment. In many other coun-tries, including the United States, gains on principal residences are taxed.

Take advantage of your ability to transfer funds from an RRSP to purchase a home. Leverage the newly-created first-time homebuyer's credit or borrow from a willing relative. Cajole them into co-signing that first mortgage for you. Young clients too often come to me armed with literature from a real estate seminar and keen to purchase rental property to create some cash flow. But without some initial equity, it's difficult to borrow. Without equity, you have no safety net in the event the rental property doesn't per-form as planned.

Your first home is rarely your dream home, but buy carefully in the best area you can afford. Your principal residence can itself be a rental property of sorts. You can rent a small suite in the home, to help with the mortgage, without jeopardizing the tax-free status of your property at sale. You can even operate a business from home, claiming certain home expenses for business – as long as only a minority percentage of the home is allocated to business and rental activities. Be careful: the Canada Revenue Agency (CRA) is watch-ing for abuses of the principal residence rules. Many homeowners, eager to see their home pay for itself through business activities, claim such a high percentage of home expenses that the CRA comes calling for a piece of the gains at sale time.

People today are more mobile than ever. Changing residences can be an opportunity to crystallize your tax-free gain, arm yourself with liquidity, and explore a new investment. If you are buying and selling a number of homes over a relatively short period, it's wise to document the reasons for the moves. A better neighborhood, better school, larger home and closer proximity to family or work are all legitimate reasons to move. Moving to earn money from real estate could be viewed by the CRA as a business operation, even if the gains are derived from a principal residence. Avoid the wrath of CRA by documenting legitimate reasons for upgrading or downgrading.

Some of my wealthiest and most successful clients have built fortunes by astutely investing in principal residences. They buy carefully, often planting themselves in an inferior home in a superior neighborhood. They add marketable value often by making small cosmetic fixes, other times by making aggressive renovations. They never overbuild and, in a declining market, they are comfortable to hunker down and enjoy their homes.

It is a time-tested doctrine in Canada that a principal residence is a tax-free investment. Will this panacea ever change? Canada Pension Plan (CPP) benefits and old-age security benefits were thought to be universal entitlements. For now, home ownership – turbo charged by the fact that gains are tax-free – remains the best opportunity for wealth creation over the long run.

Now, it's a few years down the road and the economy has been kind. You have some equity in your home and some colleagues are talking about the success of their domestic rental properties. Unlike principal residences, rental property investments are subject to income tax. Both the annual net income they may generate, and the gains realized at sale time, are taxable.

Rental properties can simply be held personally – in your individual name – or in a corporation. Corporate income tax is incredibly complex. Different circumstances call for different vehicles of ownership, but the simplest approach is usually to hold rental properties personally. Under this structure, net rental gains or losses on a property each calendar year are part of your individual income and are taxed at your marginal tax rate, just as your employment or business income is taxed. And there is no two-stage taxation in individual ownership as there is in corporate ownership. The professional fees are also dramatically lower when rental properties are owned personally. Under corporate ownership, stringent accounting is required. I often tell clients that having a company is like having a child. It requires constant care and attention. If rental properties are held personally, revenues and expenses can be simply summarized once a year.

A general piece of advice to would-be real estate investors: SEEK SOUND PROFESSIONAL ADVICE. Ensure you fully understand the advice. And ensure that all ramifications are considered, not just the tax ramifications. Keep all the records of your purchases, financings, maintenance, ongoing operating expenses, capital improvements and selling costs. Maintain a ledger of the capital expenditures that add to the cost-base of your investment. It will be valuable at sale time, when it's time to determine your gain or loss.

Strongly consider having a qualified accountant prepare your annual tax return, even if you simply own investment real estate personally.

Claiming capital cost allowance (CCA) on the building portion of the property can have substantial tax implications. Recognizing deductible and non-deductible operating expenses and understanding capitalization policies and CCA limits is critical to producing a proper rental statement, which must be attached to your personal return. When it comes time to sell, ensure you obtain a pro-forma tax calculation prior to accepting an offer.

Although this all sounds daunting, real estate investing does not have to be. I have seen people set up multiple corporations, trusts and estate freezes all in the interest of saving taxes – only to later regret doing so. Complex tax strategies can occasionally result in a loss of control of your properties. I have seen families torn apart by estate freezes. I've seen siblings seize control of family property and sell it to fund a drug addiction. Often the best strategy is to simply pay your share of taxes and go home.

Your tax plan must be integrated into your life plan. Start by building solid equity in your own home. Over time, create a diversified portfolio of assets, using real estate as a cornerstone. Keep things simple. And at every step, seek the best advice you can afford. Good luck to you.

Do:

- Corporations can manage your real estate for you, but in the interest of simplicity, convenience and efficiency, manage your own properties.
- Be aware that the Canada Revenue Agency is watching for abuses of the principal residence rules.
- Different circumstances call for different vehicles of ownership, but the simplest approach is usually to hold rental properties personally.
- Seek sound professional advice and ensure you fully understand the advice.
- Keep well-documented records of purchases, operating expenses, capital improvements and other transactions and events.

Don't:

- Buy impulsively or without a long-term plan.
- Try to save money by using complex tax strategies.
- Over-build or over-renovate your home.
- Build your investment portfolio solely with real estate. Diversify.

54

Fion Yung

Bookkeeper and a real estate investor.

BEST ADVICE: *Get rid of the tax man in a couple of hours.*

I started investing in real estate about 6 years ago. I have bought and sold properties for profit and now I am still holding some for the longer term. Property appreciates through time. The longer you hold it, the wealthier you will be. While you are sleeping - properties are still working. Capital appreciation is fine, but if you want to sleep really well, you must also plan, prepare, and organize your tax information ahead of time.

Nobody likes the beginning of each year. Large credit card bills appear to pay for the Christmas presents you bought, RRSP contributions have to be made in February, Easter holidays need planning in March and income tax season comes in April. The first four months of the year are just not the best time to prepare your tax information for the previous year. I suggest you start planning early - a year in advance. No more last minute receipt hunting, missing paperwork, and ending up with an unhappy surprise - a huge tax bill.

Planning is important. I like to carry a small pouch to put away the receipt whenever I made a purchase and empty it to the appropriate files once a week. Here is the incentive to motivate you to start doing it today. Putting a receipt away is like putting money back in your pocket. The small pouch is like a portable savings account. At the end of the week spend 20 minutes or so to sort out your portable savings account and see how much you have saved.

Before putting away the receipt remember to write a brief note of what the expense was for and for which property. Three years later your note will act as a record reminding you of what you have spent on behalf of your investment property.

Why sort out receipts once a week? Small purchases or any minor events will only stay in our memory for a short time.

We tend to forget small expenses like parking ticket stubs from parking lot dispensers, meter parking, education, cellular phone usage, cleaning supplies, changing locks, key duplication fees, and especially receipts from dollar stores. There are other direct property expenses that can be written off like gifts for your tenants, bankers, lawyers, realtors and other advisors.

You can also write off minor repairs, cutting the lawn, as well as painting and cleaning done by your children.

Don't forget to claim your home office expenses. You can claim a small percentage of the internet connection, interest on your mortgage payment, stationery and so on if you have an office setup for real estate investing.

Write it down and put it in the pouch while you still remember it. I have seen people stare at a receipt for 15 minutes trying to figure out what it was for. After this long 15 minutes of thinking the receipt ended up often in a trash can and that means no tax savings. Learn from other people's mistake and organize your receipts once a week. Your efforts will pay off in the long run.

At the beginning of each month spend another 20 minutes to record all the expenses on a spread sheet for each property. This is also a good time to understand and review your savings and/or expenditures for each property on a monthly basis. Other transactions like cash deposits, rent deposits and transfers among accounts are easily forgotten. Photocopy the rent cheques before depositing it in the bank to avoid future arguments with your tenant or bank. Again make notes before it slips away from your mind. Now you have organized the paperwork for month end without pulling out your hair.

Bank reconciliation is next. Open a separate bank account for all your real estate transactions. It can get messy when you combine it with your personal banking activities.

Balancing a bank account sounds complicated, but you can manage it. The majority of people don't read their bank statement thoroughly. They just know roughly how much they have in the bank or they just view the balance online. What about fraud or bank errors? Are there any unknown charges on the bank account? Be aware of what is going on to your personal finances. I have seen people lose money from a fraudulent cheque without recourse. Banks are not responsible on fraudulent transactions. I highly recommend you reconcile your bank statement monthly.

Now the month end is finished. Use your month end data to create another spread sheet to track rental income and expenses for the year. This will help to forecast annual mortgage pay down, net income, cash flow situation, and mainly to plan your finances. All this valuable information should be organized in a binder with categories like rental revenue, bank statements, property tax statements, property assessments, and related expenses for each property. A nice and tidy real estate investment book is well organized. If the tax man wants to audit your taxes, your well recorded binder will get rid of him in a couple of hours.

With proper bookkeeping you will have a lot more fun and enjoyment in all your real estate investments. Always consult your professionals like your accountants and lawyers for advice specific to your situations.

Do:

- Write a brief note on each receipt for each property detailing expenses.
- Put all the receipt away immediately and organize them weekly.
- Reconcile bank statements monthly.
- Plan, prepare and organize ahead of time.

- Create a binder to put everything in one place.

Don't:

- Wait till the last minute to prepare your tax information for your accountant.
- Rely on your memory.
- Learn from your own mistakes, learn from other people's mistakes.
- Drag your feet, start with good habits today.

BEST ADVICE:
Buying and selling in the USA

55

Mark Dziedzic

Expert on how to buy property in the United States, as featured in several major publications and television networks in North America. He is a Financial Planner that tells it like it is.

BEST ADVICE: *Buy in neighbourhoods that have a good infrastructure in place.*

During chilly winters as a kid, my friend and I would dream of living in a warm sunny clime in the U.S. It was the joy of sifting your toes in the sand or building a sandcastle with your parents. Or what about hiking in the desert with perfect temperatures, followed by a dip in a pool? It's no surprise that so many Canadians are flocking to sunny spots in the U.S. in search of memories that last a lifetime.

I am one of them. I have used my experience, living part time in the U.S., to help other Canadians buy their dream home or investment property south of the border – the right way.

As a Financial Planner, my most successful clients always owned between two and four properties, in addition to their stock portfolio. They had their share of bonds and mostly held good companies that paid a dividend, like Canadian bank stocks or big oil. But in Real Estate, what made them so successful is that they bought homes that would cash flow or at least near cash flow. They were affordable houses in good neighbourhoods, or up and coming ones that had good infrastructure in place (roads, transportation and close to shopping). If you believe that wages will continue to increase over time then you should be buying houses, one to live in (it is your dividend) and one to three as an investment. Property provides the best opportunity for leverage: better because you can borrow from the bank to purchase the property, and earn an income to pay for that debt with tenants in place. In the US, Canadians can put 20 to 30% down to pick up their first property.

If you stick to affordable homes, the kind that the average person or family can afford, according to the affordable housing index, or better yet, buy them less than the index, then your element of risk goes down significantly. Now if you don't believe that wages will increase over time and in the future, don't buy investment property. Put your money in the bank in GICs and sleep at night. If you are fortunate enough to be wealthy, you probably already own property or are buying property in the U.S.

Many homes in the U.S. are selling for less than what it would cost to buy the dirt to build on. So you buy the home, and just pay for the soil. Still not convinced? Most homes are insured at $120 a square foot and are selling for less than half that cost. Buy a 2400 square foot home in Surprise, Arizona for $100,000 and rent it out for $995 a month. A similar story plays out across the U.S., especially in the Sunbelt states. In housing, this crisis started because of the 100% financing programs, causing the market to climb too far too fast. It was too good to be true. In stocks, look at Nortel and how high it climbed but then fell to nothing. Ultimately, it's a question of who has control. Unfortunately, as an investor in the markets, you have no control over the management of the company. With a home, you call the shots, and we all need a roof over our heads. The prospect of your home being worth nothing is not something that is in the cards, no matter how bad things get. If it's affordable, you will survive in any market.

Quite frankly with everything in life, the higher and faster they climb the harder they seem to fall. So keep things simple, if you get a quick double on an investment, it might be a good idea to sell. Same with stocks, unless you are still getting good cash flow and would, without a doubt, buy it at that price. When it comes to buying property in the US, don't complicate things and remember that buying there is not difficult, if you follow some simple steps. They actually do things a lot like we do, which is what makes it safe and easy.

First off, what are your objectives? Is this a second home or an investment property? A second home is simple. You obviously have the means to enjoy it and shut it down when you leave. Make sure it is looked after in your absence by a reliable neighbour or a good property manager. A gated community in that scenario is typically best, but don't rule out a good neighbourhood either. If you are looking to vacation, rent your property and earn some income, I have seen folks do it well in the outer areas where it is inexpensive, but also in the hotspots which are pricier. The key is to buy a home that has a "wow" factor to it, without paying too much. I bought a home for a client with a basketball (sports) court in the backyard in the mid $300s. He has so many requests for it as a vacation rental that he rarely gets to use it, and is not in the center of town either.

Lastly, be grateful. We live in the greatest country in the world. We can buy property in the U.S. at a fraction of the price because they didn't keep it simple. Will you?

Do:

- Buy in neighbourhoods that have a good a good infrastructure in place. In Phoenix, for example, during the 16 years that I have been visiting there, when the shopping centres go in the housing values go up.
- Be close to good public transportation if possible. Buy close to existing transit, or look to what plans your particular city of choice has for it in the future. You can get most of the informa-

tion online.

- When renting out property, make sure to rent to people with good credit. If they are repeat bad debtors, taking more will only get you less. While you can make an exception for someone that made a mistake, watch the repeat offenders. Be patient and get the right tenant. The potential extra money in the short term is not worth the aggravation.
- Stick to single-level and smaller homes, where possible. We are downsizing as a society and ageing. When purchasing a condo, a lower-level condo or one with easy access is a plus, but for those concerned about security an upper level is usually preferred.
- Buy where there is good job growth and stable government. Why would you want to put yourself through the misery of buying in countries with unstable governments that don't allow pure ownership.
- Use a realtor when buying, especially with builder deals. A good realtor will make sure you are finding the best deal possible at that given time. My team will always do their homework to ensure you are receiving the best price for the right property.

Don't:

- If you can, don't buy property or do business with friends and family. If you absolutely must, make sure you have a written agreement, or better yet , a partnership agreement in place. That will protect all parties and help resolve any issues that may arise.
- Buy investment property with high maintenance or condo fees. They are harder to sell later.
- Wait for the perfect time to buy. Trying to pick the bottom is near impossible, and when the herd moves in, your choices become limited. Some of the most successful investors I know are buying multiple properties in the US right now.
- When buying Limited Partnerships that invest in real estate,

LP's that take anything greater than a 20% share of profits is plain greedy. We structured our Limited Partnership with a minimum return to our investors before anyone gets paid on profits. This ensures that we put the interest of our investors first and not our own.

56

David Ingram

Gives expert income tax & immigration help to non-resident Americans & Canadians from New York to California as well as Mexico. He is a United States/Canada cross border tax, immigration and visa expert

BEST ADVICE: *File your taxes on time – late filed tax returns create cumulative penalties.*

I have been advising Americans and Canadians that work in each other's jurisdiction now for some 46 years. I have seen files that were absolute horror stories and I have seen files that would never see an audit. You want to be in the latter. One thing that is vital to realize is that the United States is a foreign country and every single state is another country to itself. For instance, not filing a California return can be worse than not filing a US Federal return. Florida property taxes are higher for non-residents than long term Floridians and so on.

Did you know? USA income taxation is based upon where you work – not always: "Just where you live." Canadians performing services in the United States, and in 43 of those United States in particular, are required to file the respective state return(s) and a US federal 1040NR or 1040 income tax return, even if their remuneration was paid from Canada. This applies, but is not limited to:

• Executives attending meetings in the US and, in particular, California, New York, Illinois

- Service technicians servicing Canadian products under warranty,
- Salespeople selling Canadian products in the US,
- Journalists (e.g. covering Canucks hockey games, INDY races or the OJ Simpson trial),
- Horse trainers, race car mechanics

The above are exempt from tax up to $10,000 of earned income but the taxpayer must file returns to prove his or her exemption per Article XV. If you earned over $10,000 in the US, US taxation depends on where the employer gets its ultimate tax deduction for the wages paid out. If you are in the US more than 183 days, you are usually taxable on your world income.

- Entertainers, actors, musicians, performers,
- Professional athletes, race car drivers, jockeys

The above are exempt from tax up to $15,000 in gross earned income (which includes travel expenses) but still have to file the return to prove their exemption under Article XVI. 15 to 23% non-resident withholding tax will apply.

- Transport Employees, Truckers, Flight Attendants, Pilots if over $15,000

Transportation employees are exempt from tax in most cases even if in the US for more than 183 days, if they are exercising their regular employment. They must, however, file the tax return to exempt the income and include form 8833.

- Canadian or French or any other country INVESTORS – If you have bought US investment real estate, you need to file a US 1040NR and State tax return for California, Arizona, Oregon, Utah, and another 39 states. There is a minimum penalty of $1,000 - plus 30% of the rent received for failure to file.

A Canadian working in the US while living in Canada will usually be filing a US 1040NR if working in the US for less than six months and a 1040 dual status or just a 1040 if there for more. If less than a year but more than six months, the Canadian would file a DUAL STATUS 1040. In either case, if in any of the 43 states with a tax return, it is also necessary to file the state return.

An American living in Canada is required to file a US tax return for as long as he or she remains a US citizen. No exceptions. And in fact, if there are children involved, the American living in Canada can receive a US Child benefit of up to $1,000 per child by filing their US tax return. If full tax has been paid to Canada on their income, it is rare that the American ever owes the US any extra income tax but they can easily end up with a $10,000 fine if they do not.

Why? Well, the US requires their citizens to report any signing authority a US citizen has over a foreign financial account. This includes, bank accounts, cash value life insurance policies, a HELOC, debit card accounts, a boy scout or girl guide account, the Xmas fund at work and the accounts that you may be a signing officer for at a job you work at even if you have no financial interest in the account. I have personally dealt with a $10,000 fine levied against a 105 year old resident of a Nursing Home in North Vancouver. Any US person including a Canadian working in the US with a TN, H1, L1 visa or a green card must also report any Canadian accounts they have left behind. They report the accounts on US form T D F 90-22.1 which is NOT filed with the tax return but is sent to the Department of Justice in Detroit

If you have an RRSP, the penalties get larger because the RRSP is considered a Foreign Trust and question 8 on the US schedule B to the 1040 return must be answered YES.

Failure to answer yes to questions 7 and 8 can result in penalties of $10,000 to $500,000 plus 5 years in jail plus 35% of the amount in the RRSP plus 5% for every year it remains unreported. As well as the TDF 90-22.1 above, form 8891 must be filed for each and every RRSP or RRIF account you hold.

Those are serious penalties and if you remember the 105 year old lady above, age or lack of knowledge is no excuse. Although I have no way to confirm the numbers I understand that 1072 clients of a Vancouver Financial Advisor, Jerome Schneider were all fined $10,000 or more and Jerome Schneider himself received 6 months in jail and a $100,000 fine for assisting his clients to avoid the reporting with offshore accounts. Jerome could have received 99 years in jail but plea bargained his way down by providing the details of his 1072 clients and the lawyers and accountants who had assisted him.

Do:

- File on time – late filed tax returns create cumulative penalties even if no tax is owing on the late return itself.
- Report all the income – Don't think income will not be found.
- File the long form – It has more deductions on it.
- Consult a competent US/Canada tax consultant.

Don't:

- Try and hide anything - Cross border computer system have become very sophisticated.
- Try and escape tax by joining a tax protestors group – mere membership is likely to trigger an audit on your finances.
- Use a consultant who suggests deductions that you did not pay. Although it is true that many things will squeak through, if suggested by an accountant, the chances are that he or she is doing it with everybody. When the CRA or IRS catches one person and they say that so and so accountant suggested it, all the clients of that accountant will be looked at.
- Offend your boyfriend, girlfriend, spouse, employee, fellow golfer or anyone else that knows of some tax you might have

avoided. Anyone can file US form 211 and receive an award of up to 30% of the tax recovered by the IRS. Canadians just get the pleasure of watching you squirm. Just a week ago, a Canadian lady told me about her ex-boyfriend's $320,000 tax bill after he jilted her.

57

Hubertus Liebrecht

Senior partner and founder of H. Liebrecht &
Associates, President of German Business Centre
North America Inc., President of German Canadian
Business Association

BEST ADVICE: *Always consult an experienced specialist for information about all issues of your investment.*

Today's Canada is the land of opportunity for international investors that it was for the explorers that first settled the New World. Political stability, safety, a stable financial system, a favourable currency exchange rate and low interest rates are among the country's immediate selling points. It's small wonder that Canada's population growth is fuelled by a continuous flow of new immigrants seeking a better life. Roughly 300,000 immigrants make Canada their new home each year. In other words, about 1% of the country's population is newly arrived immigrants. This fact alone leads to a steady demand for real estate.

About 75% of new immigrants settle in Canada's three largest cities: Vancouver, Toronto and Montreal. Business opportunities abound in not only these centres, but in the communities that immediately surround them.

The demand for commercial, residential and recreational properties in Canada has grown incredibly during the last eight years. That doesn't mean urban areas offer the best returns. There are many investment opportunities outside the major city centres that generate cash flow. It's in the 'burbs' that you can find real estate deals that offer a return – after costs – of 9% per year. That's at 0% financing. If you can negotiate 10% down and finance the other 90% with a 5% interest rate, you can realize returns of 45% on a property. The value of Canadian property has grown by about 250% in the last five years.

Canada's rental market is still strong and will likely get stronger. The chance of a sharp decline in the value of a cash-flow positive property is not impossible, but is probably minimal.

As a lawyer and real estate consultant for more than ten years, I have been personally involved in a number of international real estate deals. Investing into a foreign country can be lucrative, but some crucial questions need to be to be addressed. Here's the Canadian perspective:

1. **Can I freely transfer funds to and from Canada?**
   While other governments restrict the free transfer of funds into and out of their countries, the Canadian government does not. There also aren't any taxes tacked on to transfers. For international investors, it's important to check the investment regulations in their home country.

2. **Can I freely enter and stay in Canada?**
   Although citizens of some countries are exempt, most visitors need a visitor visa to enter Canada. If you want to live or work in Canada on a permanent basis, you have to apply to Citizenship and Immigration Canada. The immigration process is complex and intensely regulated, so retain the assistance of an experienced certified Canadian immigration consultant (CCIC).

3. **What are the tax implications of living and investing in Canada?**
   According to international tax law, tax rates depend not only on which country you invest in and the nature of the investment, but where you reside for more than 183 days of the year. Whether

you rent out or reside in your property is also a factor. You can buy and sell rental property without any problems but there will be a withholding tax for rent and capital gains of 25%. This is particularly important when you have your rental properties managed. Make sure that the tax is submitted.

Canada has signed tax treaties with several countries in order to reduce double taxation. But the treaties aren't perfect. Experienced tax specialists know the ins and outs of the various tax laws in each country.

4. **How do I finance part of my Canadian investment?**

International investors may not have a long-term relationship with a bank in Canada or be able to demonstrate an adequate credit history rating. As in the United States, credit ratings in Canada are determined by points. The points that a potential borrower accumulates affects the amount he or she can borrow and at what interest rate. If you do not have a positive credit history in Canada, look for financing outside of the country. Keep in mind the current and future exchange rate of the Canadian dollar.

5. **What are the legalities in Canada around making an investment and managing it?**

Many investors set up an incorporated company to buy and hold their Canadian investments in. The cost to set up such a company is roughly $1,000. Buy offers are presented to sellers in a complete contract that includes optional subjects. The closing and transfer of title ownership only takes a day. If you have a knowledgeable realtor and notary, you don't necessarily need to involve a lawyer on all the legal trivialities.

6. **How do I ensure that I am paying a fair market price for my investment?**

A good realtor can provide market research that includes data about the sale of comparable properties. Also, there are a variety of helpful databases available on the Internet, including www.landcor.com.

7. How do I investigate the condition of my potential investment?

Always make your offers subject to inspection. This way you can have the building inspected in detail before closing the deal.

8. How can I operate a property on a daily basis, addressing maintenance, leasing and rental issues?

Property managers are fairly common in Canada. Many of them offer a full service package that is ideal for many international investors. Managers are typically paid according to the revenue generated by the rental unit. Their fees can range from 5% to 15% of the collected monthly rent. Tying a manager's wage to the property's performance keeps the manager motivated to maintain the property's condition and to maximize its revenue potential.

9. How fast can I exit the Canadian market?

The answer depends on many factors. For example, what is the demand for your property? Is the market a buyer's or seller's market? A good realtor will create market exposure for you. Most listings are published at www.mls.ca.

As in any country, there are plenty of obstacles to making your Canadian investment a worthy venture. The issues may initially seem overwhelming, but being thorough and professional is an intrinsic part of maximizing your investment.

Bad: I have seen some investors who lost their entire investment by not doing the minimal due diligence and not consulting experts with proven experiences.

Good: On the other side we have consulted real estate investors who obtained the best advise they could get from different experts and got an annual positive cash flow of 7.5% after costs plus an increase of 250% over 4 years of the net value of their investment.

Do:

- Look outside the major city centres to find investments that generate positive cash flow.
- Always consult an experienced tax specialist for information about tax laws and how they vary from country to country.
- Keep in mind the current and future exchange rate of the Canadian dollar.
- Apply for a visa in Canada to be able to get to your property. Only that way you can make sure to have access all the time.
- Always make your offers subject to inspection. This way you can have building inspected in detail before closing the deal.
- Tie your property manager's wage to the property's performance. That way, the manager is motivated to maintain the property's condition and to maximize its revenue potential.

BIOGRAPHIES

Benson, David

Is a Chartered Accountant and partner at Benson + Company, Chartered Accountants, a small boutique firm of chartered accountants practicing with small entrepreneurial businesses and individuals.

Born and raised in Vancouver. Attended UBC (Bachelor of Commerce 1977, Licentiate in Accounting 1978). Articled with Touche Ross in Vancouver and obtained CA in 1980.

Benson and Company provides accounting and tax services to small to medium private corporations and to individuals. Many of their clients have real estate investments.

Benson + Company, Chartered Accountants
Website: bensoncompany.ca
Telephone: 604-689-1019
Fax: 604-689-1029
E-mail: david@bensoncompany.ca

Berg, Scott

Started in the Barter business in February, 1995. After 9 years as a life insurance agent with Sunlife, he decided he wanted a greater challenge and found a start-up Barter company called Mutual Exchange Canada in Vancouver. When the head office of this company moved to Toronto, the service to the clients dropped off. In April, 2002, Scott and his partner Wayne Edgar decided to start their own Exchange to provide the service they knew their clients deserved. Trade Exchange Canada is now Western Canada's largest commercial trading company with over 1200 business clients trading over $20,000,000 per year in goods and services without cash.

Trade Exchange Canada
Telephone: 604-294-5881
E-mail: scott@tradeexchangecanada.com
Twitter: twitter.com/tradeexchangeca

Berkeley, Jennifer

Is a Principal Residential Stylist for Urban Presentations, a Vancouver, BC based home staging company with an extensive portfolio of staged properties throughout the Greater Vancouver area. Her philosophy is that home staging services should be flexible and able to adapt to each client's individual needs. Urban Presentations creates contemporary, clean-lined interiors that sell; using design principles that appeal to the broadest number of prospective buyers.

Jennifer is an active member of Ozzie Jurock's Real Estate Action Group, makes presentations to homeowners and investors, and loves to share her knowledge as an adult educator and mentor. Jennifer has a master's degree from the University of California and is a certified member of Professional Real Estate Stagers.

Urban Presentations
Website: www.urbanpresentations.com
E-mail: Jennifer@urbanpresentations.com
Telephone: 604-518-9570
Twitter: www.twitter.com/up_staging

Betteridge, Mark

Is currently the President and CEO, Mark Betteridge & Associates (MBA) Inc. (angel investing in technology companies and agricultural land).

Executive Director & CEO, Discovery Parks Trust, Vancouver

Past Chair of the Board, Covenant House Vancouver

Chair, BC Agri-Food and Bio-Products Advisory Committee, BCIC

Director, BC Technology Industry Association

Member, Lambda Alpha

Previously

President, University of British Columbia Real Estate Corporation (now UBC Properties)

Assistant to City Manager, City of Surrey

Held positions in real estate development and municipal government across Canada

Education
The Royal Grammar School, Guildford, Surrey, England
High School in New York and New Jersey
BSc.Hons – Geography and Economics, Trent University
M.A. - Regional Planning, University of Waterloo
MBA Inc. specializes in the development and management of complex real estate assets in both the private and public sectors, including public/private arrangements and the application of new technologies.
Mark Betteridge & Associates (MBA) Inc
E-mail: markbetteridge@discoveryparks.com

Blanes, Gary

Is the founder and owner of an award-winning renovation and custom home building company, G.W. Blanes Construction. He graduated from the structural engineering technology program at the Southern Alberta Institute of Technology in 1979, became a journeyman carpenter in 1982, then traveled the world. Upon his return to Canada in 1984 he began selling real estate, while working on a degree in industrial education and business. Following graduation, he managed the special projects division of PCL Constructors Northern Inc. in Yellowknife. He moved to Vancouver in 1991 and has been growing G.W. Blanes Construction ever since.
G.W. Blanes Construction
E-mail: gblanes@shaw.ca

Brisebois, Gary

President, AmeriSpec Inspection Services, Vancouver
Registered Home Inspector (RHI), Canadian Association of Home and Property Inspectors (BC License #47524)
Gary operates a successful multi-inspector company specializing in residential and property inspections throughout the Vancouver Lower Mainland, as well as home energy efficiency evaluations on behalf of Natural Resources Canada
A well-rounded business and inspection professional, Gary graduated from Wilfred Laurier University, with an Honours Bachelor,

Business Administration and then spent 12 years with IBM in the corporate business sector

Since 1994, Gary and his team of professionals have completed ongoing training and education in commercial and residential property inspection, building envelope analysis, interior air quality, and home energy assessment

AmeriSpec Inspection Services
Website: www.amerispec.ca/vancouver
E-mail: amerispec@telus.net
Telephone: 604-430-0343

Busey, Shell

Shell's 45-year career started at the age of 18 in Ontario, at a local Beaver Lumber store, eventually taking him across Canada. CJOR, approached Windsor Plywood to have a home improvement expert make guest appearances on their station – Shell was that guest. Moving to television as host and co-producer of Home Check, and helping launch BC Hydro's Power Smart, Shell now hosts the Home Discovery Radio Show. Shell leads the most recognized home services referral network in Canada – the HouseSmart Referral Network.

HouseSmart Referral Network
Website: www.TheHouseSmart.com
Telephone: 1-888-266-8806

Case, Ralph

Is President of the Real Estate Action Group(TM), an organization with monthly membership designed to help members take action in Real Estate investing. Ralph doesn't just talk the talk, he practises what he teaches! From 2004 to 2008 he bought and sold over 1400 residential units either individually or with his joint venture partners. That represents about one every day over four years! Clearly he is a man of ACTION!

An investor since 1981, one of the key things he teaches is life balance. Work smart, not necessarily hard. Become financially free as fast as possible and use that freedom to enjoy life and make the world a better place. He has been married for 24 years and has 3 children who are budding Real Estate investors.

Real Estate Action Group (TM)
Address: 253 – 970 Burrard Street, Vancouver, B.C. V6Z 2R4
Website: www.reag.ca
Telephone: 604-683-1111
Fax: 604-683-1707
E-mail: Ralph@reag.ca

Campbell, Michael

Is British Columbia's most respected business analyst. He is best known as the host of Canada's top rated business show – Money Talks – heard across the country on the Corus Radio Network. Each week Campbell and his guests track financial trends, to help listeners find ways to maximize their investments. Campbell is also Senior Business Analyst for Global News and a frequent contributor to the national Canada Tonight broadcast. Campbell is author of the national bestseller titled *Cooking the Books with Mike: Michael Campbell's Favourite 50 Recipes for Instant Financial Success*. He also hosts the most successful MoneyTalks radio show on CKNW 980 every Saturday.

Trained in New York, Campbell worked in the investment business for 10 years and currently is a successful business owner. He says that making far too many amateurish investing mistakes and enduring the ups and downs of operating a business gives him an important perspective on the real world of business and economics.

Money Talks Radio
Website: www.moneytalks.net

Chapman, Bert

Celebrating 40 years as a licenced Realtor. 28 years in Vancouver and the Fraser Valley, 3 years in Palm Springs, California, then 13 years and counting as Managing Broker/Owner of Premier Canadian Properties in Kelowna, BC, a company that has a better idea! It has located its Real Estate information centers where clients spend their leisure time on the golf course at Quail Ridge, home of the world class "Bear" and "Quail" golf courses in the Okanagan golf community and on the lakeshore between the Delta Okanagan Grand Hotel and the Sunset Waterfront Resort.

Premier Canadian Properties
Address: 102 – 1180 Sunset Drive, Kelowna, BC V1Y 9W6
Telephone: Toll Free (877) 717-1886 or (250) 717-1886
Website: www.pcrealty.ca
E-mail: bert@pcrealty.ca

Cowling, Randy

Is the owner of Mortgage Alliance – Meridian Mortgage Services Inc. established 1995 – a top five Mortgage Alliance mortgage brokerage franchise in Canada. Mortgage Alliance is the top brokerage in Canada with over $8 billion in mortgages funded in 2008.

President of Frontera Financial Services Canada Corporation – the National Insurance Network for mortgage brokerage companies across Canada – which offers home, life and personal insurance products to clients of mortgage brokers.

Member Canadian Association of Accredited Mortgage Brokers as well as a member of the Mortgage Brokers Association of British Columbia.

Mortgage Alliance – Meridian Mortgage Services Inc
Telephone: Office: 604.949.1070 ext 6 Fax: 604.949.1040
E-mail: rcowling@mortgagealliance.com

DePrato, Ed

Is a long time real estate investor. He provides other investors a completely problem free opportunity to invest in real estate and his Rent-To-Own program through a generous profit sharing arrangement. He is a consistent top producing Re/Max Realtor in Edmonton specializing in working with investors and property sellers. Ed has achieved Top 100 Re/Max agents in Canada status in addition to numerous other plateaus. In addition to his work, Ed maintains a balanced and philanthropic lifestyle. He's an active volunteer with 'World Vision' and has participated in a humanitarian project in

282 ... REAL ESTATE ACTION

Jakarta, Indonesia. When he's not in his office, you might run into him while fly-fishing or skiing in the Canadian Rockies.

H.O.P.E. Canada
Website: www.endrenting.ca or www.edeprato.com
Telephone: 780-499-2851
E-mail ed@edeprato.com
Facebook: 'Ed DePrato'

Donohoe, Ryan

Is a graduate of the Landscape Horticulture program at Capilano College in North Vancouver. Ryan was the recipient of the Capilano College Entrance scholarship and the C.D. Yeomans Scholarship from the Vancouver Rose Society. After working in the landscape industry for 10 years, Ryan started his own company: Nor-Wes Landscape and Design Ltd. operating in the greater Vancouver area. Ryan is an active member with the British Columbia Landscape and Nursery Association and the Canadian Home Builders Association.

Nor-Wes Landscape and Design Ltd.
E-mail: norwesld@telus.net

Dubord, Rick

Is one of three founders of NUANCE System Ltd., the real estate transaction management software company who developed REALTYNuance. He co-founded Benchmark Realty in 1983, founded Worldwide Info Systems Corp. in 1998 and SeeVirtual360.com in 2000. Rick also sits on the broker council of the Fraser Valley Real Estate Board and is a director of REBA; the Real Estate Brokers Association of British Columbia. For seven years running, he has been the chairman of the HomeLife Variety Annual Golf Tournament, which raised $45,000 last year and a total of $220,000 to date.

NUANCE System Ltd.
Website: www.homelifebc.com
Telephone: 604-575-3130 or Cell 604-644-4491
Fax Number: 1-866-444-0433

E-mail: rick@rickdubord.com
Twitter: www.twitter.com/rdubord

Dziedzic, Mark

Has specialized in the Canadian investment industry for over seventeen years. He has made Phoenix his frequent destination for over fifteen years, and has spent the last three years helping Canadians with their second home or investment property purchase.

He started his successful career at one of Canada's top-rated banks offering full-service financial planning, including mortgage consultations. He then went on to own a thriving financial management business where long-term customer relationships became the key to his success. Mark is excited about bringing his extensive financial planning experience and superior customer service skills from the Phoenix and Las Vegas areas.

His full-service approach includes helping Canadians with purchasing real estate, property management, loan options, cross-border financial/tax planning, and bulk purchases.

Crossborder Realty
Website: www.crossborderrealty.com
E-mail: mark@crossborderrealty.com
Telephone: 602-882-5702
Twitter: twitter.com/CrossBorderRE

Edgar, Wayne

Graduated with a Bachelor of Commerce from the University of British Columbia in 1990 and set out to find something interesting to do for a career. After a few years in the investment industry that did not provide the excitement he was looking for he set off on a safari to Africa for 3 months to clear his head and decide the next step in life. In 1995 he came across a new company that was starting in Vancouver in the barter industry and he decided to see if it would provide the excitement he was looking for. 14 years later he and his business partner Scott Berg own the largest and most successful barter company in Western Canada helping clients do $20,000,000 a year in barter and trade. Trade Exchange Canada is an industry leader in the world of trade and barter. Wayne's passion for the business is only surpassed by his passion for his lovely wife Fiona and his two brilliant children, Aidan and Lauren that are due to take over the company in 2040.

Trade Exchange Canada
Website: tradeexchangecanada.com
E-mail: w.edgar@tradeexchangecanada.com
Telephone: 604-294-5881

Eisenhauer, Dan

Has had a 30 plus year career in the real estate industry. Graduating from university with a B.Comm., he wasn't sure initially about his career path. Since then, Dan has worked as a residential sales agent, and apprentice real estate appraiser as well as Certified Property Manager in the process.

Dan specialized in commercial leasing and sales before joining the family business developing multi-use industrial buildings, an industrial park, office buildings, and a regional shopping center.

Together with joint venture partners, he now owns several residential buildings in Edmonton, Alberta. He has created a website for those who are interested in renting a home to own. And together with several partners is buying small to medium sized office buildings.

RentToOwnItNow
Address: 207 - 150 E 15th St.. North Vancouver, BC, V7L 4N9
Website: www.RentToOwnItNow.com
E-mail: danfromvan@shaw.ca
Telephone: 604-982-9151
Fax: 604-982-9161

Eppich, Lis

Is a real estate investor, project manager for Eppich International Group Holdings, and director of EBCO Industries Ltd. She is a member of Ozzie Jurock's Real Estate Action Group, which awarded her the Gold Investor Status for excellence in real estate investing 2006.

Eppich International Group Holdings
Email: lgeppich@shaw.ca
Telephone: 778-998-0248

Fawcett, Jeff

Went to Windsor Secondary High School, Capilano University 2 year Marketing Certificate Program and a Professional seminar junkie. He started licking postage stamps for mailouts & cleaning Fawcett Insurance offiice at age of 8. He also was one of the youngest ICBC licensed broker in the province at age 16.

Founding Member Tuesday Morning Breakfast Networking Group 1989

Founding Member West Coast Whiskey Society
Past Chair North Shore Chamber of Commerce
Past Chair Sales & Marketing Vancouver
Past Chair Seycove Families of School Auction
Past Chair Change The World Foundation
Awards:
NVCC Nominated for Employer of the Year 1989
Winner of North Vancouver Chamber of Commerce Business Person of the Year 2000
Best Insurance Broker, North Vancouver *North Shore News*
Fawcett Insurance
Address: Seymour Mountian. #106-1169 Mt. Seymour Road, North Vancouver, BC, V7H 2Y4
Telephone: 604-929-3494
Fax: 604-929-3174
Website: fawcettinsurance.com
E-mail: jafawcett@fawcettinsurance.com

Ferguson, Doug

During 23 years as a Canadian journalist at newspapers in Saskatchewan, Ontario and Alberta, Doug Ferguson has done everything from covering murder trials to interviewing bluesman B.B. King – along the way earning awards for both reporting and editing that include a citation of merit for layout and design at the

National Newspaper Awards, and a North American Award for page design from Thomson Newspapers. He currently works at The Calgary Herald, where his duties include copy editing and laying out the paper's Saturday recreation and investment properties section. He draws on his background as a Calgarian who grew up in what was formerly a much smaller city, living long enough to see his family's once remote, favourite camping spot in the nearby Kananaskis Lakes become a location for cheesy Hollywood movies like X2, the second X-Men film.

The Calgary Herald
E-mail: dferguson@theherald.canwest.com

Fisher, Willie

Has over 8 years of real estate transaction experience with extensive knowledge in residential, multi-family and commercial projects. He has successfully completed 17 real estate deals with a $75-million total value to date of property acquired and sold. He has done land deals on over 337 acres and purchased over 363 multi-family doors. Willie also has over 13 years of entrepreneurial and management experience and has established, managed and successfully sold various restaurants and retail enterprises across British Columbia. In addition, Willie established a successful import/export organization and is currently a director in multiple international business operations.

Bluecreek Properties
Address: 210-15272 Croydon Drive, Surrey B.C, V3S 0Z5
Website: www.bluecreekproperties.com
E-mail: willie@bluecreekproperties.com
Telephone: 604-536-6770 Office, 778-889-3474 Cell
Fax: 604-536-6771

Forbes, Randy

Became a licensed Realtor in 1976 for NRS Block Bros Realty (Nanaimo). He earned his Agent's license in 1979 and moved into management before the age of twenty-five. Randy has spent more than a decade serving as an elected Director on the Vancouver Island Real Estate Board and was appointed Director to the Real Estate Errors and Omissions Insurance Corporation of British Columbia in 2008. He is also the President of CRG Mortgage Investment Corporation and has been the General Manager of Coast Realty Group since 1993, leading the company from a single office to fourteen offices with more than 300 staff and sales representatives.

Coast Realty Group
Website: www.coastrealty.com
E-mail: forbes@shaw.ca
Telephone: 250-758-7653

Francis, Sheila

Immigrated to Canada from England as a newspaper reporter in 1967 and became a licensed realtor in the Tri-Cities in 1976. Every aspect of real estate sales became a passion and Sheila still loves the business of negotiating, marketing and building lifetime relationships. She now works with her husband, Terry Willies, and partner, Michelle Hawthorne as one of the top selling teams both locally and nationally. Sheila has attained her Lifetime Achievement Award, and Circle of Legends with RE/MAX. Family, church, friends, and community make for a busy, fulfilling life in a wonderful place to call home.

Team Sheila Francis
Address: 2346 Clarke St. Port Moody, BC, V3H 1Y8
Website: www.sheilafrancis.com
E-mail: sheila@sheilafrancis.com
Telephone: 604-936-7653 or toll free 1-888-938-6838
Fax: 604-936-7654

Halstrom, Gerry

Brings over 30 years of land development, strategic sales, marketing and operations management expertise gained from his years in Land Development, Corporate Franchising and Real Estate, serving at one time as Senior Vice-President of one of Canada's largest real estate companies.

Leveraging his expertise in leadership, management and finance, Gerry has a proven track record for success. In addition to his real estate ventures, Gerry is as well an author & speaker, engaging management and sales audiences throughout North America on topics such as personal performance/motivation, sales and sales management.

Today, Gerry serves as an executive consultant to companies in the land development and franchising industries. Gerry resides in Vancouver BC.

Address: 1005-1328 West Pender Street, Vancouver BC, V6E 4T1

E-mail: gerryha@shaw.ca

Telephone: 604-657-8041

Hartree, Clara

Is the President of Re/Max Clara Hartree in West Vancouver. She has achieved the highest rewards bestowed by the Vancouver Real Estate Board and Re/Max International. She is a Life Member Medallion Club (Real Estate Board of Greater Vancouver), a member of the Re/Max Diamond Club, the Hall of Fame as well as the Circle of Legends. She is also the exclusive Vancouver representative in Associated Realty of the Americas (areamericas.com). A member of the Vancouver Board of Trade, her real estate advice has been successfully followed by many since 1986.

Re/Max Clara Hartree

Address: #200 - 1455 Bellevue, West Vancouver, BC, Canada V7T 1C3

Web sites: clarahartree.com, clarasluxuryhomes.com

E-mail: clara@clarahartree.com

Telephone: Cell: 604-889-9977, Office: 604-926-6233

Fax: 604 9221228

Hepburn, Christina

Realtor since September 1990, MLS Master Medallion Club Member

Partner – Hepburn Real Estate d.b.a. Tony and Christina Hepburn, Re/Max Select Properties

Certified Luxury Homes Marketing Specialist

Creative Director – Hepburn Productions Inc.

Artist – Watercolour, Oil, and Acrylic Paintings

Interior Designer & Decorator

Published Writer – Real Estate, Scuba Diving & Travel related articles

World Traveler & Travel Professional – Dive Travel Luxury & Deluxe

Underwater Videographer and Travel Documentary Specialist

Certified PADI Open Water Scuba Instructor

Yoga Practitioner, Snowboarder & Gym Enthusiast

Ultimate Over-Achiever

Re/Max Select Properties

Address: #250 – 4255 Arbutus St. Vancouver, BC, Canada, V6J 4R1

Websites: HepburnRealEstate.com, HepburnProductions.com, ChristinaHepburn.com

Email: Christina@HepburnRealEstate.com

Phone: 604-737-8865

Fax: 604-737-8512

Twitter: twitter.com/cchepburn

Iles, Bill

Came to BC from Ontario as an 18 year old with 1 year of university. Worked as a logger, tree planter, construction labourer. Present owner of a construction and real estate co. with real estate holdings in BC, Alberta and Arizona. Responsible for the formwork and concrete for over 30 hi-rise buildings in the Greater Vancouver area.

Ingram, David

Was born in Vernon, BC in 1942. Raised in White Rock, Winnipeg and Regina, he wanted to be a veterinarian but after a year in Veterinary College, fell into the coffee house business with part ownership of the Forth Dimension in Winnipeg and the Louis Riel where Neil Young, Joni Mitchell, Burton Cummings, The What Four, Judy Orban, Karen James, Sonny Terry and Brownie McGee, Lenny Breau and even the great George Carlin performed at the start of their careers. That was the fun. Then he got serious and went into money and finance and ended up with tax and real estate offices in 30 states and four provinces and 46 years later, this is what came out.

CEN-TA
Website: www.david-ingram.com, www.centa.com
E-mail: taxman@centa.com
Telephone: 604-980-0321

Ilkay, Ender

Has been involved in the real estate industry since 1985 including several years as one of Canada's top selling real estate agents and six years as a business coach to high performing realtors from across North America. Since 2001, he has been purchasing and developing waterfront subdivisions in scenic locations across BC. His current projects encompass more than 6,000 acres and eight kilometres of lake and ocean frontage. He loves the process of working with local residents, government staff and industry professionals to create highly desirable communities.

Ender has been married for 15 years and has a young family. He enjoys hiking, camping and participating in a number of sports, with a particular passion for ball hockey and mountain biking.

Cedar Coast Properties
Website: www.cedarcoastproperties.com
Telephone: 1-877-879-8137
Email: ender@cedarcoastproperties.com

Johnston, Doug

Has been an electrician for 30 years, beginning his career in Alberta as a residential electrician. Today, his company, Surrey-based Mustang Contracting Electrical Installations, along with business partner Brett Welsh, specializes in servicing large and small commercial and industrial projects as well as design/build projects. The company has been involved in developing and servicing many local projects including Vancouver's Convention and Exhibition Centre, the Holiday Inn Express Squamish, Vancouver's RAV line SkyTrain transit system, Richmond's River Rock Casino Hotel and Parkade, Coquitlam's Boulevard Casino Parkade, along with several commercial warehouse complexes in the Lower Mainland.

Mustang Contracting
Doug or Brett can be reached through their website at
Website: mustangcontracting.ca
Telephone: 604-551-9431

Jurock, Ozzie

Is a Fellow of the Real Estate Institute of Canada (F.R.I.), the author of Forget About Location, Location, Location and What, When, Where, and How to Buy Real Estate in Canada and publishes The Real Estate Insider monthly and weekly. He is the only Canadian real estate advisor featured in Donald Trump's real estate book. Peter C. Newman in his book *Titans* called him a Real Estate Guru.

Ozzie Jurock served as the past president of Royal LePage (Res.) in charge of over 7000 salespeople as well as the chairman of NRS Block Bros. He managed real estate companies in Taiwan, Hongkong and Tokyo.

Ozzie Jurock is known as one of Canada's leading business motivators and his investor outlook conferences attract audiences of over 700 attendees every time. He loves boating, skiing and golf. Golf does not love him back.

Jurock Publishing Ltd.

Website: www.ozziejurock.com
E-mail: oz@jurock.com
Telephone: 604-683-3222
Fax: 604-683-1707
Twitter: www.twitter.com/77ozzie
Facebook: www.facebook.com

Keenan, Lawrence

Was born in New Zealand and has been a Canadian for 20 years.

Co-owner of C.S.L.I. (Canadian as a Second Language Institute)

'Uniting the World with English' since 1992

2008 Consumers Choice Award

Co-founder of Rose Charities Micro Credit, supporting over1000 tsunami-affected families in eastern Sri Lanka

An ultra-marathon runner, Keenan is planning to complete the entire TransCanada Trail in 2010 coast-to-coast.

C.S.L.I. (Canadian as a Second Language Institute)

Address: 188 Nelson Street Vancouver, B.C. Canada V6B 6J8

Websites: csli.com, rosecharities.org, rosemicrocredit.org, unitingtheworld.org

E-mail: lawrence@csli.com

Telephone: 604-683-2754

Facebook: 'RoseCharities'

Klein, Eugen

Is a B.Comm(UREC), CRES, ARM®, RI, FRI, CCIM, CLO, CIPS

Commercial Real Estate Investment and Advisory

He served as:

BCREA - Director Region IV (2008 - 2010)

Director At Large - Real Estate Board of Greater Vancouver (2007 - 2011)

Chairman - BC Commercial Council (2006 - 2008)

Past President - Real Estate Board of Greater Vancouver Commercial Division (2006 - 2008)

Klein Group

Address: Royal LePage City Centre | Suite 204 345 Robson St. Library Square | Vancouver BC Canada | V6B 6B3

Website: www.kleingroup.com

E-mail: eklein@kleingroup.com

Telephone: 604-684-8844, Toll Free 1-877-877-0417

Fax: 604-818-5888

Ledding, Rick

Graduated with his law degree from the University of Victoria in 1981 and was called to the bar in British Columbia in 1982. He has a varied solicitor's practice focusing on real estate, corporate and commercial transactions, trust and estate law.

Rick acts for a large number of "creative" real estate investors as well as traditional real estate purchasers, investors, syndicators and developers and frequently speaks at various real estate investment presentations, including Ozzie Jurock's seminars for real estate action groups.

Rick is also the corporate solicitor for many corporations throughout British Columbia and has been serving various sectors of the business community in Vancouver and throughout British Columbia for over twenty years.

Thomson & Elliott

Address: Barristers and Solicitors, 800 – 1285 West Broadway, Vancouver, B.C., V6H 3X8

Telephone: 604-742-2288 (direct)

Fax: 604-731-6527

Email: rickl@te-law.com

Liebrecht, Hubertus

Is a German lawyer educated and admitted to the bar in Germany and registered with several provincial law societies in Canada. He founded the first German law firm in Canada. H. Liebrecht & Associates with offices in Vancouver, Toronto and Calgary and Munich.

He also initiated the German Business Centre North America attracting a wide range of European trade initiatives and international real estate investors.

As a Certified Canadian Immigration Consultant specialized in business immigration Hubertus Liebrecht also leads the immigration firm ProCanada Consulting and offers his expertise to international investors and entrepreneurs.

He holds several honorary positions in the German-Canadian business community like the presidency of the German Canadian Business Association and has received the medal of honour of the French Senate for his achievements in the European-Canadian relations.

H. Liebrecht & Associates
Address: Suite 1504, 1166 Alberni Street, Vancouver, B.C. Canada   V6E 3Z3
Website: www.liebrecht.com
E-mail: office@liebrecht.com
Telephone: 1-604-605-3000
Fax: 1-604-605-3011

McCallum, Harvey

Was born in Wetaskwin, Alberta, raised in New Westminster/ Coquitlam. He has been licensed since 1981 as a realtor. In the last 6 years he has worked as a mortgage broker with his company CENTUM Creative Mortgage Broker Services. He enjoys helping people and loves to find creative solutions for his clients. Harvey: "I am like the 'Mike Holmes the builder' for mortgage solutions."

CENTUM Creative Mortgage Broker Services
Website: canadamortgagecenter.com
E-mail: harveymccallum@shaw.ca
Telephone: 604-484-7040
Fax: 604-628-3813

McNeill, Cameron

Is the co-founder of MAC Marketing Solutions. In 2007, MAC Marketing Solutions sold some 1.2 billion dollars worth of real estate. Since the year 2000 MAC has marketed over 10,000 properties valued over 4 billion dollars.

MAC has earned over one hundred industry awards including:

Top Sales Team by Canadian Home Builders Association (Gold Georgie award 2001, 2002, 2004, 2005, 2007)

Top overall Marketing Campaign by Canadian Home Builders Association (Gold Georgie award 2001, 2002, 2005)

Top 40 under 40 in 2006 (Business in Vancouver)

Top 20 Most Influential People in Real Estate in 2008 - 2009 (Canadian Homer Builders Asc. and BC New Homes Magazine)

Marketer of the Year - 2008 (Canadian Homer Builders Asc. and BC New Homes Magazine)

Member of the prestigious Young President Organization (YPO) and is a regular speaker to real estate development industry events.

Founder of TAC Real Estate Corp.(Trusted and Committed) - a traditional realty company that maintains a boutique and elite group of agents focused primarily on multifamily residential real estate.

Co-founder MPC Intelligence and The TRAC - Western Canadas leading provider of market intelligence and consulting in the field of multi-family development.

Cameron is married to another successful business owner Sarah and has two children. He lives in Vancouver and enjoys reading and is an avid skier.

MAC Marketing Solutions

Website: www.macmarketingsolutions.com, www.tacrealestate.ca, www.thetrac.ca

E-mail: cameron@macrealestate.ca

Meribian, Peter and Gottfried, Astrid

With 17 years of experience in real estate investing, Peter Merabian and Astrid Gottfried's complementary skills fuel their remarkable success. Astrid's expertise includes negotiation, planning, marketing, and acquisition development. Peter's diverse entrepreneurial experience provides economic and market analysis and investment management skills. Their company Turning Point Investments now offers partnerships to people who want great returns in real estate without having to invest their own time, energy, or expertise.

Turning Point Investments
Website: www.turningpointinvestments.ca
E-mail: info@turningpointinvestments.ca
Telephone: 778-231-4654

Miller, Steve

While attending Vancouver College in the early 1990s, Steve Miller spent two semesters working with the British Columbia Assessment Authority, a government run program responsible for the valuation of all real property in BC for the purposes of property taxation. After graduating from college he began in the private sector doing fee appraisal work for lending institutions throughout the province. In 1997 he branched off and formed Bakerview Realty Appraisals Inc. and now specializes in a broad array of real estate valuations and consulting services. He has been a member in good standing with the Appraisal Institute of Canada for nearly 20 years and often appears in various radio and tv programs providing updates on the market and educating the public about the profession.

Bakerview Realty Appraisals Inc.
Website: www.bakerviewappraisals.com.
E-mail: sdmiller@bakerviewappraisals.com

Murphy, John

Is the Chairman & CEO of 20/20 properties. He is a past international board member of the Young Entrepreneurs' Organization (EO) and provides the overall vision and leadership for the 20|20 Group. He has an exemplary track record of success in both entrepreneurial ventures and real estate investments. His passion for developing real estate programs and strategies has helped investor clients purchase almost a billion dollars in well selected investment real estate, locally and internationally.

20/20 Group Inc.
Website: www.2020groupinc.com
E-mail: John.Murphy@2020groupinc.com

O'Brien, Frank

Is the Vancouver-based editor of a number of leading real estate publications, including the *Real Estate Weekly* and *Western Investor*, as well as specific trade magazines related to the real estate and construction field. He co-founded the successful Home Makeover magazine with the BIV Media Group in 2004. A writer and editor specializing in real estate topics, O'Brien has been published nationally and internationally, and was named among B.C.'s top business writers in the Jack Webster Journalism Awards, 2006. O'Brien is a graduate of Algonquin College, Ottawa, in 1969, and makes his home on the Sunshine Coast of B.C.

Western Investor
E-mail: franko@dccnet.com

Osmond, Robert

Is a singer-songwriter and founding member of the musical group, 'Pennan Brae'. His 2009 debut release, 'Shaded Joy', has received airplay in North America, Europe, Australia, New Zealand and Japan. The album has garnered exposure on the North American College Radio Circuit, receiving airplay on over 70 stations. His lead single, 'Anyways' entered the Top 10 of FMQB's Top 40 AC Chart and has achieved over 900 spins of U.S. Radio airplay. His second release, 'Amber Glow' is scheduled for release in 09-09. He currently resides in Vancouver.

Pennan Brae
E-mail: rosmond71@yahoo.ca

Peerless, David

Is the president of Dexter Associates Realty. He is a B.Comm, RI(BC), Chartered Arbitrator and the past chair of the Real Estate Errors and Omissions Insurance Corporation of B.C. He is also a director of the Real Estate Board of Greater Vancouver.

Dexter Associates Realty
Website: dexterrealty.com
E-mail: peerless@dexterrealty.com
Telephone: 604-263-1144

Roberts, Brent

Has been recognized as the #2 Realtor with Royal Lepage Canada out of over 12,000 Realtors. He has been the #1 Realtor in Western Canada with Royal Lepage. He has been the #1 Realtor for all companies in his local market year after year for almost 20 years. He has been the #1 Realtor recognized throughout North America with the Floyd Wickman courses.

Royal LePage Brent Roberts Realty
Address: #6 - 9965 152 Street, Surrey, BC V3R 4G5
Website: www.brentroberts.com
E-mail: brent@brentroberts.com
Telephone: 604-585-7653 or 1-800-220-0202
Fax: 604-581-4745

Ryznar, Pete

Education – University of British Columbia – BA – International Relations

Profession – Real Estate Advertising Sales Manager at Pacific Newspaper Group, publishers of the Vancouver Sun, the Province and West Coast Homes & Design Magazine

Past Business Experience – Advertising Account Executive for Pacific Newspaper Group – Automotive, Retail, Entertainment

Pacific Newspaper Group
Address: Suite 1, 200 Granville St Vancouver B.C. Canada

V6C3N3, A division of Canwest Publishing Inc.

Website: www.vancouversun.com. www.theprovince.com www.homesanddesign.ca

E-mail: pryznar@png.canwest.com

Telephone: 604-605-2373 Cell 604-329-2755

Twitter: twitter.com/pryznar

Savage, Richard

Is the Senior Vice President, Blackmont Capital Inc., member of CIPF and IIROC, Richard graduated from Flagler College, Florida, with a Bachelor of Business Administration. He has been an investment advisor with Blackmont Capital Inc., formerly Yorkton Securities Inc., for 21 years.

Richard's community involvement includes his position on the board of the Artists for Kids Trust, which was established in 1989 by some of Canada's finest artists and North Vancouver School District.

Passionate about finding the best in their field, he has Harry Dent as his teacher for economic forecasting. His other teacher is Grand Master Yap Cheng Hai, widely regarded by many as the top Feng Shui exponents in the world today.

Blackmont Capital Inc.

Website: www.blackmont.com

E-mail: rsavage@blackmont.com

Telephone: 640-640-0553

Fax: 604-640-0234

Staley, Liesl and Kevin

Are 30-somethings who've been together since first year university. They both work in post-secondary institutions helping students. With an M.Ed in Math Education, Kevin teaches math at Douglas College. With an M.Ed in Educational Leadership, Liesl works in Student Affairs at Simon Fraser University. Liesl writes personal essays related to juggling motherhood and career aspirations at

mammalogs.blogspot.com
>   **Website:** mammalogs.blogspot.com
>   **E-mail:** babykandl@gmail.com

Stark, Randy

Has 25 years experience in various aspects of real estate including building, developing and investing. He truly believes that not only can real estate developing be very profitable, it is a necessary and important cornerstone to any culture.
>   **E-mail:** randystark@shaw.ca
>   **Telephone:** 604-536-6770

Marv Steier

Is the president of TVS Tenant Verification Service Inc. Marv, a retired police officer and former fraud investigator had an idea that evolved into a successful business serving the Residential Rental Industry across North America
>   **TVS Tenant Verification Service Inc.**
>   **Websites:** Screen Tenants: www.tenantverification.com, Tenant forms and info: www.tenantsinfo.com, Province and State laws: www.tenantverification.com/tvs-links.php
>   **E-mail:** tenantverification@shaw.ca
>   **Telephone:** 1-877-974-9328

Scott Ullrich

Is the president and CEO of Gateway Property Management. Prior to joining Gateway Property Management as Controller in 1983, Scott Ullrich was a Chartered Accountant with Deloitte & Touche, where he specialized in auditing, taxation and consulting for a variety of real estate management and development companies. A graduate of Simon Fraser University with a Bachelor of Arts (Major in Business), Scott also has a diploma in Urban Land Economics from the University of British Columbia, is a Fellow of the Real Estate Institute of Canada, and a Certified Property Manager through the Institute of Real Estate Management. Scott participates on several industry and non-industry association boards in the capacities of Director, Treasurer, Governor and President. He also serves on a number of committees focused on advancing industry education and improving government policy affecting the rental industry across Canada.

Largest Reward: Working with my family to grow our real estate investment company, Park Place Investments Inc.

Gateway Property Management
Address: 11950 - 80th Avenue, Suite 400, Delta, British Columbia, V4C 1Y2
Website: www.gatewaypm.com
E-mail: parkplace.investments@telus.net, sullrich@gatewaypm.com
Telephone: 604-635-5000
Fax: 604-635-5003

Fred van Hunenstijn

Founded 177398 Canada Inc, dba Advantage 24 Hr Emergency Services in 1972. He holds a Red Seal Plumbing License, Gas Fitting License, Dipl'T in Electrical - Electronics, and is a Licensed Residential Builder in BC. Together with his wife Anne, (Dipl'T Business Administration), his son Bruce, (Dipl'T Building Technology), and his son Tom, (B.Sc, B.Ed) they provide Plumbing, Drainage, Heating, Septic and Flood Restoration Services throughout the Lower Mainland.

Advantage 24 Hr Emergency Services
Website: www.advantage24hrservices.com
E-mail: fred@advantage24hrservices.com
Telephone: 604-521-4900
Fax: 604-521-4940
Twitter: advantage24

Vernon, George

Education: Business Management & Marketing, B.C. I. T., Agriculture, UBC

Experience: Real Estate sales, management and development; Marketing/Advertising for B.C. Dairy Industry; Owner of trucking/road construction company

Awarded: B.C. Marketer of the Year

Speaking Engagements: Addressed B.C. Credit Unions, national investment firms, charity lotteries, U.S. Dairy Industry regarding innovative marketing, advertising concepts and increasing market share.

Park Place Investments Inc.
E-mail: gvernon@telus.net
Telephone: 604-531-1262

Westlund, Andrew

Is the founder and president of Apex Wireless Inc., one of the top five Telus Mobility resellers in Canada. Founded in 1989, the company has 10 stores in Metro Vancouver and employs 100 people. Westlund also recently founded Sky Helicopters Inc. Andrew Westlund's greatest aspiration is to make a meaningful, positive impact on the lives of everyone who works at Apex. He encourages and inspires all staff to dream big, and set plans in motion to live the fullest life they can. He is tremendously thankful to have employees who motivate and inspire him in kind. In recent years he has worked with orphans in Uganda and helped raise funds for water wells in Honduras.

Apex Wireless Inc.
National Headquarters: 13734 104th Ave., Surrey, BC V3T 1W5
Website: www.apexwireless.ca
Telephone: 1-888-776-3339

Mike Wintemute

Has been licensed in the real estate profession since 1986. He sold real estate in North Vancouver for eight years before his appointment as Manager, Royal LePage, Kitsilano branch. In 1995 Mike moved to Whistler in the capacity of Manager at the Whistler Real Estate Company. In 1992 he moved to RE/MAX Sea to Sky Real Estate, Whistler as General Manager of the company. During his time in Whistler he developed the Whistler Listing System, the first internet based property listing system for the real estate companies in Whistler. Mike has also been involved in Whistler Minor Hockey, Whistler Soft Ball, the Whistler Chamber of Commerce and currently a member of the Whistler Healthy Community Committee. He is also a member of the Professional Conduct committee of the Real Estate Board of Greater Vancouver.

When not working Mike spends his spare time skiing, hiking and biking in the Whistler community.

Whistler Real Estate Company
Website: www.myseatosky.com
E-mail: micwin@telus.net
Telephone: 604-938-4134

Woolley, Bryan

Graduated from the UBC Urban Land Program and from BCIT with a diploma in Business Management. He is the president of Maverick Real Estate Corporation, a specialist project sales and marketing firm operating in Western Canada and the United States. Partner in Finger Print Strategies Inc. in Canada and the United States, offering a unique strategy for real estate developers to sell and market their projects to premium purchasers.

Past Vice President and General Manager of Bentall Property Management

A well rounded real estate entrepreneur with experience in development, sales, marketing, management and leasing of commercial and retail properties, equity lending and joint ventures.

Maverick Real Estate Corporation
Websites: www.maverickrealestate.com

www.fingerprintstrategies.com
E-mail: bryan@maverickrealestate.com
Telephone: 604 661-1868
Fax: 604-689-8024
Twitter: www.twitter.com/bryanwoolley

Yee, Freeman

Has a Bachelor of Commerce degree from UBC, majoring in Urban Land Economics. He has been involved in financing real estate for 18 years. For four years, he worked for the largest land investment company in Alberta, working extensively with investors and financial planners. His company, HighPath Capital Corporation, independently offers alternative investments and real estate financing.

> **HighPath Capital Corporation**
> **Website:** highpathcapital.com
> **E-mail:** fy@highpathcapital.com

Yung, Fion

Is a bookkeeper and a real estate investor. She started her freelance bookkeeping career more than 10 years ago and serves clients from the restaurant and catering industries, furniture manufacturers to law firms and production companies. Currently she is concentrating in her work mainly on budgeting, cost accounting and production accounting for the commercial and TV series industry. As her real estate investing grows she reduced her workload from what seemed to be 8 days a week to 5 days a week. Now her investment is working harder than her.

> **E-mail:** fionyyung@gmail.com

About the Author

Ozzie Jurock is a Fellow of the Real Estate Institute of Canada. He is the president of Jurock Publishing Ltd.

Vancouver Magazine ranked him among the 45 brightest people in Vancouver; he appears every 2nd Wednesday on Global TV Noon Newshour.

He has written hundreds of published real estate articles in *The Vancouver Sun, Business in Vancouver, The Calgary Herald, The Edmonton Journal, The Globe and Mail, The Western Investor* and dozens of magazines. He has been on the cover of some leading business publications such as the *Western Investor, Business in Vancouver* and *The Courier*. Several thousand people have subscribed to his monthly and weekly newsletters *Jurock Real Estate Insider* and *Jurock's Facts by Email*.

But he is not just talking about real estate. He is living it. He has sold, bought, owned and managed it. Today he is also teaching how to invest in it. Ozzie Jurock served as the past president of Royal LePage (Res.) in charge of over 7000 salespeople, the past chairman of NRS Block Bros., as well as managed real estate companies in Taiwan, Hong Kong, Tokyo and the USA. He has served on the advisory boards of some of Canada's largest corporations. He has served on the boards of the BC Real Estate Council, the Vancouver Real Estate Board, the UBC Real Estate Research Bureau and the Quality Council of BC among others.

His busy life found him elected president of the Canada Taiwan Trade Association, serving as a judge for the Ernst & Young Entrepreneur of the year award and he still finds time to hold over 80 speeches a year.

Ozzie Jurock is known as one of Canada's leading business motivators and his annual Land Rush and Outlook investor conferences attract audiences of over 700 attendees every time. Thousands of students have attended his secrets of real estate investment action courses. There is only one reason: Ozzie Jurock delivers more than he promises.

You can also follow him on YouTube (youtube.com/jurockvideo), twitter (www.twitter.com/77ozzie) or Facebook, as well as on linkedin.com, goodreads.com.

He and his wife, Jo currently live in Vancouver, Canada.

Other Books By Ozzie Jurock

Forget About Location, Location, Location
What, When, Where, and How to Buy Real Estate in Canada

Products and Services

The **Jurock Group of Companies** offer a number of products and services. For corporations and executives, Jurock offers:

- Real Estate Conferences ... 700 plus attendees - with opportunities for booth display and sponsorships
- Keynote business motivational speeches
- Keynote economic and real estate forecast presentations
- Real Estate Action Group Investor training
- Real estate sales and motivational training, management training and business consulting
- Executive planning and strategy sessions
- Quantity discounts on books, tapes, business plans, and other materials

Go to: www.OzzieJurock.com

For Investors and Individuals:

- Jurock's Weekly Facts by E-mail
- Jurock's weekly Hotline
- Real Estate books, motivational tapes

Go to: www.Jurock.com/products

For Real Estate Investment Study:

- Real Estate Action Express Days
- Real Estate Action Weekends
- Home study real estate courses

Go to: www.Reag.ca

Advertise on the Jurock Websites
The Western Canadian Real Estate Marketplace:
www.Jurock.com
Jurock Products and Services: www.e-moneywheel.com
Canada's Largest Real Estate Bulletin Board:
www.RealEstateTalks.com
Jurock "Media Kit" for advertising: www.Jurock.com/advertising
Real Estate Action Group: www.REAG.ca
Become an expert: www.Askanexpert.ca
Buy Ozzie's latest books: www.forgetlocation.com
Motivational reminder cards: www.CommitPerformMeasure.com
Ozzie on YouTube: youtube.com/jurockvideo
Ozzie on Twitter: www.twitter.com/77ozzie

In Canada call toll-free **1-800-691-1183**
Or call **604-683-1111**; Fax **604-683-1707**
Email **info@jurock.com**